nai010 publishers intend the Reflect series to focus attention on socially relevant themes for architecture, urban planning, fine art and design.

D0770489

reflect
#12

Ending the Anthropocene

Essays on Activism in the Age of Collapse

Lieven De Cauter

nai010 publishers

Reflect #12

Ending the Anthropocene

Contents

Overview

If we want to avoid collapse, we should end the Anthropocene. This sounds like an impossible idea, but it is the crux of this book. The Anthropocene, literally the geological era of (Wo)Man, was invented because of the gigantic, devastating impact of our species on planet Earth. It might well be that the collapse of our world system with its mantras of growth and acceleration, based on extraction and overconsumption, is the only hope for the biosphere. 'Ending the Anthropocene' therefore means several things: deconstructing the term, shrinking our footprint, or even embracing collapse. With this book I try once more to look our epoch in the eye, to be at the level of the present, which is really not an easy task today. Key to understanding the method of this work: reading the future in the present, the art of overstatement in translating the signs of the time, time diagnosis by injecting contrast medium into the fabric of our world.   *predicting*

'Boarding the Anthropocene' is an overture which tries to give a synthesis of all the themes and melodies, the mode, the mood of this book. The first part of this collection of essays is devoted to philosophical soul-searching of our epoch. It meditates on the deep, unspeakable sadness in the time spirit caused by the certainty of major climate disaster, to then unearth the term Anthropocene.

From these dark insights, in a second part the book moves towards one of the most hopeful events of our times: the resurgence of the commons. This rediscovery of the forgotten and excluded third, besides public and private, contains the seeds of another worldview, another conception of human nature, and another politics. From this new perspective of the commons, identity and heterotopia too can be read in a new light. Beyond identity is the way to go. And other spaces for the Anthropocene are what we need. That makes for part three. The commons forms one of the kernels of this book and the horizon for the extensive part four on activism. In a world craving change, activism is worth reflecting upon.

The final part is on the corona crisis. Biopolitics, the infamous term of the 'late' Foucault, the care for the life of the population by the state, has gained an unexpected new topicality with the age of pandemics. Gear up for some jargon juggling (besides biopolitics, zoöpolitics, thanatopolitics and cosmopolitics). But no worries, the mix of philosophical, theoretical texts and more concrete newspaper articles make for a broadly accessible, exciting book of 'activist essays'. A sort of cyberpunk philosophy for the twenty-first century. Even if geologists are not quite sure when the Anthropocene has begun, it is high time to end it.

Boarding the Anthropocene (Overture)

Humans are part and parcel of the great global common, which is the biosphere, the ecosystem of planet Earth. We have become the predominant species, insofar as an entirely new geological epoch has been named after 'Man': the Anthropocene. Our predominance, our footprint as a species, puts the ecosystem in danger. Some call it 'Gaia', as it is not a mechanistic, inert system but a complex, self-regulating, self-sustaining synergy of organisms (James Lovelock's Gaia-hypothesis), and at the same time a 'ticklish assemblage' with which we have to settle a deal (Isabelle Stengers), the backdrop that becomes actor (Bruno Latour). The prophecies of *Limits to Growth*, the famous report to the Club of Rome of 1972, come true: We are in a logic of 'overshoot and collapse', with clustering consequences such as climate change and loss of biodiversity, sea level rise, refugee crises, new conflicts, pandemics, starvation, and so on. But the term 'Anthropocene' also suggests 'Man' on his triumphant march through history as his-story, as Isabelle Stengers squarely puts it, even if it proves disastrous. Maybe we need another history: 'her-story'. *Exit Anthropos.*

Capitalism should be blamed and shamed for this destructive growth, many claim, not the human species as such, as a large part of the world population is almost entirely innocent of these changes and their logic. We should, T J Demos writes in a book of that title, be 'Against the Anthropocene'. Blaming the species is diffusing the guilt. *Exit the Anthropocene. Enter Capitalocene* (Jason Moore). And other terms. Unspeakable ones like 'Chthulucene' (Donna Haraway), Plantationocene (Anna Tsing)... Fair enough: eco-feminism and decolonization theories deconstruct the dominant tale and self-image of the West... But our footprint is also a mere result of our demographic explosion, which cannot be attributed to capitalism or colonialism, but rather to progress in medicine, for instance. We know that the ongoing demographic explosion is due to a lack of education of women, but can you blame capitalism for it? Eight billion of any species of mammals would be a major problem for the equilibrium of the biosphere, especially with the sort of footprint many of us have. Add to that the mammals we use for meat and dairy production and you have a disastrous situation. Together we make for some 95 percent of the total biomass on the planet. Timothy Morton blames it on 'agrilogistics', the worldview that came into being with the agricultural revolution—some 12,000 years ago, so quite a while before capitalism. It was the beginning of the fatal split between nature and culture. We are a vector of destruction from the beginning. *Dark ecology.*

The tragic world-historical irony, which is unfolding before our very eyes is that the demographic explosion and climate change are largely playing out in the global south, mostly Africa, parts of South East Asia and to a lesser extent Latin America. The migration crisis, which has just begun, is the coming together of climate change caused by the North, the neocolonial extractivism by capitalism, also largely northern, on the one hand and on the other failing states and the demographic explosion, largely taking place in the South, region of the ex-colonized. Globalization and the interdependency that comes with it, and the one ecology of the biosphere, therefore called Gaia or not. This makes a nice opposition between the good and the bad side untenable, unfortunately. That is the ugly truth of complexity theory.

Let's not beat around the bush, the fact is that today we humans are a plague to Gaia, a scourge to planet Earth. For indeed even in its geology it is scarred by the human footprint, in its bones, so to speak. Under the conditions of relentless 'creative destruction' and the 'extractivism' of carbon-based capitalism, humans have become a plague to all other species and the ecosystem itself. As we are hitting the limits of the ecosystem, we are also rats on a sinking ship. The planet of the naked apes is in overshoot, meaning ecological disaster, and a infectious relationship between animals and humans, called 'zoonosis', with the corona pandemic as *memento mori*, as sign of the times: the Age of Collapse, as 'collapsologists' have it.

The dream of exodus has begun. Elon Musk, Richard Branson, and Bill Gates are working on it—the captains of industry and the world elites will try to have an escape ready, just in case. This is the age of realized science fiction, a bit more day by day. Against this macho transhumanism we posit our resistance: from 'Other-Globalism' over 'Occupy Wall Street' to the 'commons movement' and the anti-Anthropocene discourse. Against the conspiracy between state and market called neoliberalism. So far, this new phase of techno-capitalism has proved deadly for the biosphere on a global scale.

On a more local social scale, the economic crisis has brought scarcity to the doors of Southern Europe (Greece, Spain, and Portugal). Both these phenomena have fuelled what has been termed 'the rediscovery of the commons'. As the commons are under threat, we become aware of the commons. The unholy trinity of neoliberalism: liberalization, deregulation, and privatization has unchained a new wave of enclosures (from land grab to gentrification, from gating to patenting). The new wave of enclosures and the rediscovery of the commons form a crucial constellation of our time.

Against the backdrop of the new wave of enclosures that threaten the global commons, this book is devoted to activism in the age of collapse, to the disclosures of the (un)common(s). *Dis-*

closing the *un*common might be the only way to unravel the riddle of what we have in *common, beyond identity.* What can local, 'particular commons' mean for a transition to a circular, not-carbon-based economy? How to preserve this 'universal common', the biosphere, for humans and nonhumans alike? The attempt to extend the concept of law to nonhumans is a noble goal (animal rights and all that), but it seems futile compared to the business as usual of extraction and growth.

The challenge of this book is thinking about the biosphere, and other universal commons, like language and knowledge, from the perspective of the local commons. The local commons, the commons in the proper sense, are 1) self-organized communities, that 2) govern via rules 3) a so-called 'common-pool resource'. Besides the perennial examples of Nobel Prize winner Elinor Ostrom—alpine meadows, fishing grounds and irrigation systems, Wikipedia is a textbook example of a commons in the digital age: a self-organizing community with rules resourcing and disclosing all the knowledge of mankind as a common, for free, that is beyond, besides, without state or market. Hence the great hope for the commons not as something from the past but as a model for the future, a future beyond state and market.

Bye-bye to the Anthropocene—of the geo-engineers, who want to control the climate by large scale intervention like aerosols to block the sunlight—and also bye-bye to utopian 'posthistory' of anarcho-communism, the dream of a self-organizing multitude of creative producers of immaterial labour that does away with capitalism and the state. What we need is a philosophy of history for the present day. Presence of Mind. Exercises in speechlessness, yes, but also lessons in urgency. A true hope resides in the new cross-cultural communities, be it my local neighbourhood or my international student groups. I therefore dedicate this book to you, my students. Let us morph, hybridize, mix and enrich our identities. Exercises in globalization we will need badly. In a world of mobility and migration, future shock is culture shock. Fasten seatbelts.

must acknowledge past and forsee future symbiotically

I Spleen of the Anthro-pocene

A Small Anatomy of Political Melancholy

'Horrified the melancholic sees the Earth relapsed into a mere State of Nature. No shimmer of former history surrounds it. No aura.'

(Walter Benjamin)

Psychopolitics

The term 'psychopolitics', coined by Peter Sloterdijk, draws attention to the role of psychological disorders, emotions, and affects in politics. It forms an important, probably underestimated perspective on 'the political'. An entire cartography is to be made of political affects: rage, naivety, cynicism, honour, pride, cowardice, courage, firmness, perseverance, indignation... These are all political emotions that in the political transcend the individual and can become mass phenomena that direct the masses (as shown by Sloterdijk in *Zorn und Zeit*[1]). In this text we want to reflect on melancholy as a political sentiment.

Of course this theme of politics and melancholy hasn't been plucked out of the air. After the euphoria of the Arab Spring, there was a deep sadness and a state of confusion. After the revolutionary excitement of Tahrir Square, the Indignados movement, and Occupy Wall Street, disillusionment came (the intervention in Libya, the civil war in Syria, the reign of terror of el-Sisi in Egypt, the horror of ISIS, and so on). The manic condition was followed by depression, the enthusiasm by dejection. This much is clear: The theme of 'political melancholy' is highly topical. One could, in the light of the climate catastrophe, even speak of a new 'posthistoric melancholy'. But first, what is melancholy?

[handwritten margin note: new the engine, then it dies out]

A Bipolar Syndrome

Melancholy is not only a morbid gloom of the contemplative mind. It also contains visions, manic enthusiasm, and ecstasy. The opening lines of Robert Burton's *The Anatomy of Melancholy* [1621]—this interminably long work (three parts, 1382 pages in total[2])—contains a clear view of what the author means by the anatomy of melancholy. The expression harks back to a legend in which Democritus supposedly cut open dead animals in search of the location of downheartedness. *The author's abstract of Melancholy* is a poem which, as the title says, should somewhat summarize the argument. Of course it's not just a scholastic summary, let alone an 'executive summary', rather an evocation in verse, therefore an overture which, like in an opera, represents the main topics of the piece, or even better, is a baroque prologue:[3]

THE AUTHOR'S ABSTRACT OF MELANCHOLY

When I go musing all alone,
Thinking of divers things fore-known.
When I build castles in the air,
Void of sorrow and void of fear,
Pleasing myself with phantasms sweet,
Methinks the time runs very fleet.
All my joys to this are folly,
Naught so sweet as melancholy.
When I lie waking all alone,
Recounting what I have ill done,
My thoughts on me then tyrannise,
Fear and sorrow me surprise,
Whether I tarry still or go,
Methinks the time moves very slow.
All my griefs to this are jolly,
Naught so sad as melancholy.
...
I'll not change life with any king,
I ravisht am: can the world bring
More joy, than still to laugh and smile,
In pleasant toys time to beguile?
Do not, O do not trouble me,
So sweet content I feel and see.
All my joys to this are folly,
None so divine as melancholy.
I'll change my state with any wretch,
Thou canst from gaol or dunghill fetch;
My pain's past cure, another hell,
I may not in this torment dwell!
Now desperate I hate my life,
Lend me a halter or a knife;
All my griefs to this are jolly,
Naught so damn'd as melancholy.

The entire antithetical structure of the poem reminds us of the Shakespearian chiaroscuro, albeit a little less brilliant and poetic. The baroque changes in mood are rather didactic panels. It is more a didactic poem than a lyrical text. If the author is right and this is the summary of the argument concerning 'the anatomy of melancholy', then the diagnosis is clear: melancholy is a syndrome, and what is more, it is a syndrome we know well. Until recently it was called 'manic-depressive', at present it is being called 'bipolar' (since the term manic-depressive sounded too stigmatizing). Or more carefully: although melancholy maybe doesn't coincide with the above-mentioned syndrome, it is in any case bipolar.

Indeed, we find this bipolarity in about all diagnoses of melancholy, from Aristotle until now: States of ecstasy and genius alternate with periods of enormous disconsolateness. Melancholy is a disorder of extremes: overestimation of oneself and despair, enthusiasm and existential or even metaphysical disillusionment.

In Benjamin's famous book about the baroque tragedy, *Ursprung des deutschen Trauerspiels*[4], this bipolarity of melancholy is extensively addressed. In the tradition on this theme contemplation and melancholy are, according to him, rightly and deeply connected. Of all contemplative intentions it is the most suitable for mortal creatures, because, according to the theory of temperaments, it goes back to the *humores*, the life blood, and ascends this way 'from the depths of the domain of the created'. Here he touches the motif of connecting the highest, the divine, with the lowest, the natural. This connection is somewhat the alchemy of the melancholy person. For example: the melancholic is looking for the synthesis or short circuit between mysticism and eroticism. Therefore, Benjamin chooses a conception of melancholy which he explicitly calls dialectical. According to him, it's more particularly in Aristotle—more than in the medieval theory of temperaments—that the concepts of melancholy, genius, and madness are connected. What interests Benjamin in melancholy is the 'contrast between the most intensive activity of the mind and its deepest decay'. On the one hand the melancholic is, according to the ancient thinkers, gifted with visionary powers. On the other hand he is resentful, vengeful, and suffers from fits of rage.

Through the connection of melancholy with Saturn in astrology, this characterization in extremes becomes strengthened, according to Benjamin: melancholy refers to slowness and obtuseness, as well as to intelligence and concentration. It unites the highest with the lowest, the divine with the beastly (since Chronos/Saturn is the god of extremes, according to Panofsky: the god of the Golden Age as well as the besmeared and dethroned god). In the Middle Ages melancholy was promoted to be one of the seven cardinal sins: the slowness of the heart, the *acedia* that plagues the monastery cells as a *démon du midi*. The *vita contemplativa* is constantly threatened by it: The devil finds work for idle hands. During the Renaissance the melancholic type became topical again, however without the medieval possession by evil spirits. The depraved was toned down by the theory of genius. Through a spiritual diet, the depraved were conquered and the melancholy person became 'jovial' (being under the influence of Ioves, Jupiter). But older characterizations of the melancholy person also still have an effect in modern times. Until Kant's thinking, Benjamin indicates with some satisfaction, this person is characterized by vengefulness, impulses, appearances, temptations, meaningful dreams, conjectures, and miraculous signs. So far for Benjamin.

[handwritten marginalia: how do we stay hopeful?]

[handwritten marginalia: must go low before going high]

[handwritten marginalia: capitalism]

two-faced

weight of the world

This bipolarity is also the cause of some sort of vicious circle that characterizes melancholy: the *acedia* of the monks, for instance, is caused by reading, but also makes reading impossible (as Agamben indicates briefly in his book *De la très haute pauvreté*[5]). It remains ambiguous, also in pathology: a 'manic' episode doesn't mean that the patient is cheerful all the time. In fact, it happens more often that someone in a manic episode is sensitive and easily irritated. However, the manic phase can be really euphoric too. Of course, this big intensity of thought processes can also lead to vehemence, and as a consequence, to outbursts of anger. For 'The songs of the Dawn Man' mentions 'the braking distance is squared with the thinking speed'.[6]

The Romantic melancholy differs possibly from the baroque melancholy as a result of the fact that the euphoric state seems to be forgotten, or at least because it was separated from melancholy defined as sadness. This way one retains depressive melancholy as the real melancholy. By separating manic melancholy, or better, by separating melancholic mania and presenting it as being alien to melancholy, and as its opposite, melancholy becomes depressive. And with it the manic becomes contradictory, as one feels in the expression 'manic melancholy'. That is strange actually, for the Romantic exaltation is the necessary, almost natural antipode of the Romantic *Weltschmerz*. A *topos*, a trope in itself.

In the poetry by Baudelaire—the pre-eminent (late) Romantic poet that became at the same time one of the founders of Modernism—bipolarity, however, was also one of the central ideas: visions full of flushes of happiness and timeless beauty to then wake up as a slave of time and in the hands of boredom. One finds this chiaroscuro in *'La chambre double'*, a prose poem from *Le spleen de Paris*, but also in countless poems from *Les Fleurs du mal*, particularly in the cycle 'Spleen et idéal'. In *Les Paradis artificiels. Opium et haschisch*, the unrivalled phenomenology of the flush of happiness, this dialectic of elevation and regression, of ecstasy and disgust is described at length.[7] Baudelaire is without a doubt one of the great masters of Romantic melancholy in its full ambivalence of ecstasy and abysmal downheartedness.

In Freud's *Trauer und Melancholie* the separating of the depressive from the manic in melancholy is completed: in Freud's text melancholy is only sorrow, without ecstasy, mania, or vision. It yields, however, an immortal definition of melancholy. Whereas sorrow or grief have a specific object—it is grief over the loss of something or someone—melancholy doesn't have a specific object: it is grief without object.[8] This absence of an object is well expressed in the German word *Weltschmerz*: suffering from the world. However, Freud focuses particularly on the pathology of depression and, by his own account, doesn't know what to do with the euphoric, manic moments.[9]

Bipolarity and Politics

*[handwritten margin notes: initiate bipolarity; foresight**; I need someone like Trump to initiate...; today, destruction of man – tmrw, restoration of earth]*

After this short, all too short, outline of the cultural history of melancholy, the question regarding melancholy and politics can be modernized—'bipolarity and politics'. Hypothesis: politics is structured in a bipolar way. Today victory—tomorrow defeat. Today revolution—tomorrow restoration. Etcetera. Which doesn't mean that bipolar personalities are pre-eminent politicians, maybe quite on the contrary. To sail the turbulent waves of politics, you'd better be equipped with equanimity and imperturbability, and therefore you'd better be, in terms of the theory of temperaments, phlegmatic.

Probably—that is our hypothesis—politics will become more bipolar by the day. The more extreme the situation becomes, the more melancholy there will be: moments of hope and inconsolableness seem to succeed one another at an ever-faster pace. And more and more they collide. There is confusion everywhere. It is no longer possible to draw a clear picture of Syria and Iraq, let alone to form an idea of a 'solution' for global warming, overpopulation, or the refugee problem. What are experiencing an unprecedented intensification of the political melancholy syndrome, which is, as such, at least as old as modernity and 'historical consciousness' itself.

Those who reflect on politics and on the battlefield of politics, which is called history, cannot but become despondent. Why does history not only make us nostalgic, but deeply melancholic too? Because history is a history of wars, the history of technology is a history of armaments, the history of religions is a history of oppression rather than one of enlightenment. Because history is a history of exploitation, slavery, a history of cruelties, of abuse of power, an orgy of greed.

In the wake of Walter Benjamin one could situate the starting point of *political* melancholy in the Baroque period: history ceases to be a history of salvation, without God the world is empty, and what happens is purposeless. History becomes a natural history and the condition of the world a state of nature: the eternal recurrence of exploitation, injustice, suffering. The world and politics are dominated by the everlasting law of the jungle, the incessant civil war, the war of all against all. Shakespeare's political tragedies are from this perspective anticipating the political theory of Hobbes. This baroque (proto)modern melancholy transformed itself over time, after a long euphoria over 'progress' in modernity, to postmodern political melancholy, *'une sorte de chagrin dans le Zeitgeist'*, some sort of grief in the spirit of the age, which was brought to the fore by Jean-François Lyotard as a mourning over the lost modernity: the end of 'grand narratives' about progress and emancipation.[10]

Almost without exception, scientific reports tell us the same thing and they have been doing so for half a century, starting with *The Limits to Growth*, the famous report to the Club of Rome[11]: Progress has become unsustainable, the logic of growth, mobility and consumption, linked to the ongoing demographic explosion, is now colliding with the limits of the planetary ecosystem.

This collision is depicted quite literally in Lars von Trier's film *Melancholia*: the planet Saturn approaches as a threatening, gigantic ball above the horizon and will inevitably crush Earth... In another depiction the radical ecologists of 'The Dark Mountain Project' started from the awareness that it is too late to avoid catastrophe and it is time to learn to mourn and deal with this awareness.[12] The psychopolitics of ecological depression. We seem to relapse into a new 'state of nature'. Besides the neoliberal competition as the war of all against all and in addition to the rising number of civil wars and failing states, there is global warming as a limit, downfall, turning point, catastrophe.

Excursus on Revolutionary Nostalgia

The relapse of history into the state of nature is not, or not only, something awaiting us, something that may happen and is even imminent at this moment in history, but a different view of that same history, a disenchanted view, the view of disenchantment. Benjamin expresses it, with a clear reference to his baroque book, in the essay about Baudelaire, using a mesmerizing formula (which has been accompanying me for years and which also serves as a motto for this essay): 'Horrified the melancholic sees the earth relapsed into a mere state of Nature. No shimmer of previous history surrounds it. No aura.'[13] This is an exalted, poetic quote, but also an overwhelming awareness. However, this quotation contains a dialectical spark too: a craving for previous history. This nostalgia for *Vorgeschichte*, previous history, is the material for a 're-auratization': the magic of the primitive, the childhood of the author, or of history, even the prehistory of humankind. Behind the sadness about the disenchantment lies a longing for a re-enchantment. We could call this dream the dream of a re-enchantment of the world. According to Michael Löwy, who devoted a whole oeuvre to it, this longing is active in revolutionary Romanticism. One could call it 'melancholy politics' (as opposed to 'political melancholy'). In it, nostalgia becomes fertile.

In a collection of essays on the re-enchantment of the world[14] Michael Löwy argues that a critique of Modernity is implied in Romanticism and that this Romantic critique still affects many leftist thinkers today. He demonstrates that idealizing the past not only can be regressive or reactionary, as in 'reactionary Romanticism', but becomes an opposite of the disenchanted present, and

longing for "before"

he shows how in what he calls 'revolutionary Romanticism'—this becomes a foreshadowing of a different society. Here his almost hymnic definition: 'With Romanticism I don't mean, or at least not exclusively, a literary school from the 19th century, but something much wider and deeper: the big protest movement against the modern capitalist, industrial civilization, in the name of values from the past, a protest which started in the middle of the 18th century with Jean-Jacques Rousseau and which, throughout German Early Romanticism and after that throughout Symbolism and Surrealism continues until today. This deals with, as Marx had already pointed out himself, a criticism that accompanies capitalism like a shadow, ever since the day it was born and until the (blessed) day of its death. As a structure of sensitivity, as a way of thinking, as a worldview, Romanticism covers all terrains of culture—literature, poetry, art, philosophy, historiography, theology, politics. Torn between nostalgia for the past and the dream of the future it denounces the devastating effects of the bourgeois modernity: the disenchantment of the world, the mechanization, the objectification, the fact that everything is to be expressed in figures, the disintegration of the human community. Despite a continuous reference to a lost Golden Age, Romanticism is not necessarily oriented towards a recovery of the past: in the course of its long history Romanticism has known reactionary as much as revolutionary forms.'[15]

Löwy's attempt to put Romantic melancholy and nostalgia in a positive light provides an interesting perspective since we are not used to seeing Romanticism as revolutionary and we are even less used to seeing leftist thinkers as Romantics. We tend to forget it readily. Nevertheless, many leftist thinkers have Romantic roots. Löwy demonstrates how this is the case for many, very different, authors: Marx, Lukács, Kafka, Luxemburg, Péguy, Buber, Landauer, Mariategui, Benjamin, Adorno and Bloch, Breton, and Surrealism, up until Guy Debord. Revolutionary Romanticism takes history as a model, an inspiration, as a foreshadowing, as an anticipation of a future, different world. The really existing past, whether idealized or not, becomes the proof that a not yet existing different social order is possible and desirable.

Against the alienation, the chilling atmosphere, the objectification, the automation, the infernal era of industry and machines, the individualization of modern society, a peaceful archaic community is placed as a counter-image. The antithesis between community and society, between *Gemeinschaft* and *Gesellschaft*, coined by the sociologist Ferdinand Tönnies, is the leitmotiv in Löwy's texts. In Marx and Engels he stresses their quest for models in the past, the old German *Mark* or village community, or even the prehistoric clan structure of *gens* (they learned about it through the work of Morgan). Marx and Engels were also inspired by the old Russian *religion as a commons*

village communities. In Rosa Luxemburg's writings, the agrarian, primitive communism functions as the opposite of the catastrophes of industrialization and colonialism, and also as an opposite of linear progress. In Benjamin's work it is the matriarchate of Bachofen. In Mariategui it's the Inca communities; he even speaks of 'Inca communism'. In the light of these primitive communities (whether medieval or prehistoric) modern society based on private property appears as a transition period, i.e., between the old communist, agrarian communities, and the future communism. All these historic configurations are used as prefigurations of a coming history, of a better society. Often it's also religion that serves as a model for an alternative. In Péguy's thinking the example is medieval Christianity; in Bloch it is mainly the reformation, more particularly Anabaptism and Thomas Münzer. In a similar vein Buber, Bloch, and Benjamin are deeply inspired by Jewish Messianism. Opposed to the 'transcendental homelessness of modern man' (as Lukács put it in *The Theory of the Novel*[16]), one warms oneself by the egalitarian communities or the religiosity of olden times. Notably the concept of redemption exerted its revolutionary powers in the past. As opposed to the disenchantment of the modern, to put it briefly, the past provides the material for a 're-enchantment of the world'. The past history, the previous history of childhood, of the matriarchate, of primitive people, of old religion, of rural communities, of the Incas, etcetera, is not only a sheer regressive nostalgia, but according to Löwy has become a source of inspiration in the work of the above-mentioned authors, a foreshadowing of a possible different history. In short: it contains elements of utopia.

How do nostalgia and melancholy relate? Homesickness is not wistfulness or melancholy. Melancholy doesn't have an object. There is no consolation because there is no lost object. Homesickness does have an object: One longs for the sense of wellbeing of a home. Therefore, nostalgia has a consoling aspect. Consequently, in nostalgia, melancholy finds an object. One can, possibly (with Löwy's work in the back of our minds[17]), as a psychological exercise, distinguish three kinds of nostalgia: a regressive nostalgia, which only wants to quench its thirst with an idealized past. In political terms this kind of nostalgia can rapidly become reactionary. Then there is the critical nostalgia, which uses the past as the opposite of the present, as an operating base for exerting criticism. It can often be anti-utopian, because it doesn't believe in the future or in a better world, and instead is disillusioned about the present, or critical of it, and in any case alienated from it. One could also call this reaction conservative, or moderate, also sceptical, sometimes even cynical. Finally, there is what one could call 'utopian nostalgia'. This oxymoron properly reflects the tension between past and future. Utopian nostalgia is not nostalgia in the sense of a reactionary regression, but a search for anticipations of a different, better world, a more social, common, deeper, richer, more just, more egalitarian social structure. Thus we have the three time dimensions together: reactionary nostalgia is oriented to the past, critical nostalgia to the present and utopian nostalgia to the future.

The latter nostalgia is possibly the euphoric, manic side of political melancholy. I think we see this utopian nostalgia also at work today and I even dare to claim that we sorely need it. I will return to this matter at the end of the text. But before we look ahead to the future of nostalgia in our psycho-political explorations, we need to dig deeper into melancholy.

Modern melancholy, and perhaps even all melancholy, stems from overconfidence, the manic phase in which everything is possible, including the most reckless behaviour. This *overdrive*, this 'hyper' condition, is followed by depression and *burnout*. In the past *hubris* was overconfidence of the tragic individual human being, now there is a new *hubris*, the *hubris* of the species: the combination of an ongoing demographic explosion, technological expansion, economic growth based on planned obsolescence, and the mobility society based on fossil fuels has positioned us on a collision course with the cosmos.

[handwritten margin note: over exertion / over estimation of capability]

Posthistoric Melancholy

The Anthropocene is by now the official name of the geological age in which humankind has become overpowering. This awareness of the all-decisive impact of our species makes us susceptible to an immense political melancholy. The unsustainability of our world system has become, perhaps for the first time in history, a scientific fact: the survival of humankind (and many other species) is at stake. In her book *Au temps de catastrophes. Resister à la Barbarie qui vient*, philosopher of science Isabelle Stengers calls it somewhat stubbornly and polemically 'the intrusion of Gaia':[18] An entity that is at the same time irritable and completely indifferent. She calls Gaia a 'ticklish assemblage'. Of course the planet itself will survive everything, it will shake us off as it did the dinosaurs. The intrusion of Gaia together with Saturn looming on the horizon— von Trier's image—is the disrupting, almost unthinkable, unprecedented situation of our era. It will be extremely difficult to stay below a global warming of 2°C—in itself already problematic enough. With a global increase in temperature of 6°C (which will be inevitable if we don't intervene urgently and radically) nothing is sure anymore, according to scientists. The melancholy this brings about could be called postmodern, even posthistorical: postmodernity was the end of the idea of progress and emancipation, posthistory then is a history after history as progress, or even more: progress leading to the real end of history, of mankind, and of

OG, capitalist bastard

many species with it. This yields a completely new constellation of political melancholy, an enlargement without equal, a *novum* in human history: the catastrophe is the result of progress itself, of our world system, our worldview and our vision of human nature, and especially also of our life pattern.

'Extraction', exploitation through digging in the subsoil, together with progress and growth, is the basic gesture of modernity. It is literally and figuratively the engine of that growth and progress. The windmills of Don Quixote had to give way to mine shafts and slag heaps. First there was mining for metals and later also for the exploitation of fossil fuels. No modernity without mining and oil drilling. Naomi Klein calls this syndrome 'extractivism'.[19] She points at Francis Bacon as the 'patron saint' of this conception of the planet as machinery at our disposal, as an object, as a 'resource'. In Bacon own words: 'For you have to follow and as it were hound nature in her wandering and you will be able, when you like, to lead and drive her afterwards to the same place again. ... Neither ought a man to make scruple of entering or penetrating into these holes and corners, when the inquisition of truth is his sole object.'[20] Whether one is merely looking for truth with this penetration of Mother Earth remains, in the light of colonialism and rising capitalism, highly questionable. The macho sexist tone in the metaphor, of course pointed out by Klein, does not really hint at a disinterested search.

In the sixteenth century there was still a debate about whether one was allowed to drill the soil on ethical-theological grounds. In the first classic work about mining, *De Re Metallica* from 1557, Georgius Agricola (aka Georg Bauer) brushes aside all possible counter-arguments. The following is a synopsis of his reasoning in Book 1 of his twelve books about mining: 'The arguments range from philosophical objections to gold and silver as being intrinsically worthless, to the danger of mining to its workers and its destruction of the areas in which it is carried out. He argues that without metals, no other activities such as architecture or agriculture are possible. The dangers to miners are dismissed, noting that most deaths and injuries are caused by carelessness, and other occupations are hazardous too. Clearing woods for fuel is advantageous as the land can be farmed. Mines tend to be in mountains and gloomy valleys with little economic value. The loss of food from the forests destroyed can be replaced by purchase from profits, and metals have been placed underground by God and man is right to extract and use them. Finally, Agricola argues that mining is an honourable and profitable occupation.'[21]

One could call this book, which is nearly a century older than *New Atlantis* and other writings by Bacon, the birthplace of a new concept of man: the engineer-entrepreneur, the capitalist subject par excellence. In the meantime, five centuries later, this concept has been exalted to the educational ideal: If everything is business, and can and has to be conceived of in such a way, the consequence is that each child has to be brought up to be an entrepreneur.[22] The book can also be considered the birthplace of a new worldview: the world as an object, as a machine, as a body that is to be exploited and drilled. Many contemporary ecological problems are a direct consequence of Agricola's reasonings. One can even recognize many contemporary landscapes in it. We need only look at the Borinage or the Limburg mining area, regions that are marked forever and are still struggling to recover from the raping of man and nature. The pernicious implications of this modern worldview are only now becoming clear. The Platonic-Christian-Cartesian worldview—the dualism between body and soul, Man as the king of creation and self-contained solipsistic mastermind, as subject in and against the world of objects—has given modern Man a license to not see the big coherent unity of life in the lap of Mother Earth as sacred—this was, totally in line with the colonial mind, dismissed as primitive and animistic—but as rough, inert, available, profitable raw material. *capitalists afraid of "primitivism"*

Robert Burton, who was born a year after the publication of this work (and therefore makes the bridge between Agricola and Bacon, so to speak), of course mentions this constellation in his book about everything, his *Anatomy of Melancholy*, with which we started this meditation. In part II he wants to explore the air, but also 'the bowels of the earth', 'the intestines of the earth' (the macho metaphor is firmly-rooted in this worldview). And in this exploration he devotes himself sometimes, as he should, to manic visions:

'The whole world belike should be new moulded, when it seemed good to those all-commanding Powers, and turned inside out … top to bottom, or bottom to top: or as we turn apples to the fire, move the world upon his centre; that which is under the poles now, should be translated to the equinoctial, and that which is under the torrid zone to the circle arctic and antarctic another while, and so be reciprocally warmed by the sun: or if the worlds be infinite, and every fixed star a sun, with his compassing planets (as Brunus and Campanella conclude) cast three or four worlds into one; or else of one world make three or four new, as it shall seem to them best.'[23]

In short: everything is possible, we can heat up entire parts of the Earth by turning it inside out or upside down and we can even make several worlds. It reminds us of Jules Verne, or the drawings by Granville. In the light of our constellation, this quotation sounds prophetic and highly ominous. That we will need several planets if our ecological footprint keeps on growing as it is doing now, has become a commonplace warning in the meantime. But what this visionary, manic quotation also makes clear is that from the beginning disaster was ingrained in this new worldview. That is perhaps the deepest, metaphysical layer of our 'postmodern' political melancholy: There is something fundamentally wrong with our modern attitude towards the world and our behaviour towards 'nature'. If one defines Romanticism, from a political angle, as the protest against this modern, objectifying, industrial attitude towards nature, as Löwy does, we can now say Romanticism has proved to be right. But it goes beyond Romanticism. This grief stretches back to the Baroque and Renaissance. Even in the famous picture by Dürer, Dame Melancholy is surrounded by instruments that symbolize mathematics and industry. The depressing alienation is inherent in the objectifying approach of reality: the grief about the absent object (Freud) is the sadness about the disenchanted, devitalized world. A straight line runs from Agricola's mining industry via the vision of Burton and Bacon to the insanity of *geo-engineering*: the tinkering with the climate, for instance by inserting particles in the stratosphere in order to dim the sunlight.[24] Modernity: five centuries of 'being creative' with the planet.

The capitalist system cannot and does not want to step out of 'extractivism' and the logic of economic growth, which will prove fatal to us and to many co-inhabitants of the biosphere. Even worse: the solution is always more of the same. At the very same time when we needed a radical change to limit the CO_2 emissions, we started to exploit even more polluting and dangerous fossil fuels: shale gas, tar sand oil, deep-water drilling, brown coal. What should have become the age of 'transition', turns out to be 'the age of extreme energy.'[25]

While we should turn to the 'soft technology' of solar and wind energy, and to ecological, local farming, we are switching to extremer forms of extraction. The extractivism of modernity is getting into its highest and most dangerous gear. A wholly new capitalism even emerged. This kind of capitalism brings about catastrophe, but at the same time it cashes in on it as military-industrial complex: 'disaster capitalism'.[26] The whole planet, so to speak, is now becoming an extraction zone, from the North Pole to Antarctica.[27]

Our collective powerlessness is stunning and the time window to prevent the very worst is closing. A collective consciousness and a sense of responsibility are gradually starting to grow, but those in charge are behaving totally irresponsibly, as they are stuck in the logic of accumulation, extraction, and growth. All this leads to a psychopolitical identity crisis and an unparalleled political down-heartedness.

The new melancholy that takes possession of us can definitely be called postmodern: '*post modernitatem, animal triste*'. After the ruthless rape of Mother Earth, all animals, including humankind, are in a sad condition. But the new melancholy is more than post-modern, it is to be called posthistoric: the history of man itself, that Big Entrepreneur, is coming to an end as a history of conquest, as a colonization of the planet, and this may lead to an exodus, a colonization of space, perhaps through technology rather than through humanity.[28] Hence all visionary, manic *captains of industry* who see the storm coming, Bill Gates, Elon Musk and Richard Branson, are preparing themselves with might and main for a space exodus.[29] Depressiveness is for the stragglers, the *losers*. The exodus is also the horizon in several pieces of Lyotard, in particular the above-mentioned *Postmodern Fables* and *L'inhumain*, but he conceived of that exodus in the light (or rather the darkness) of the death of the sun. It is a horizon that we, unfortunately, must take seriously. The happy few will skedaddle and the rest of humanity can drop dead on an overheated, polluted planet. It is the continuation of the logic of colonization of the world. The dualization of the world (between poor and rich people, between *haves* and *have-nots*) will, if it comes to that, have become absolute. I am convinced that this 'exodus-project' should be considered not only as mad, but also as criminal.

But one thing is sure, from now on a *different* history starts, *la seconde histoire*, as Stengers calls it: as opposed to the first history of progress.[30] However, it is far from certain that this other history will come about, it could also be utter barbarism, the barbarism that is coming (with reference to Stengers), or a relapse into the state of nature (as we called it previously with reference to Benjamin and elsewhere to Hobbes), or even, the end of mammals and higher plant species. Whether what comes will be comparable to the collapse of the Roman Empire—the migration of peoples and the raid of the barbarians on an unprecedented scale—or with the disappearance of the dinosaurs, remains to be seen.

Or on the other hand, alas, it does not remain to be seen. The degree of our extreme addiction to fossil fuels, to extractivism, accumulation and growth, will decide it. Posthistoric melancholy is none other than the disconsolateness, the sorrow over the inevitability of this terrible catastrophe.

Optimistic Postscript

For the record, the planet will survive everything. Except for the death of the sun. The intrusion of Gaia and Saturn looming ahead should persuade us to stand up against our unsustainable and therefore criminal world system. But between dream and act, laws and practical objections stand in the way, but also a melancholy,[31] which we have tried to explain here. In that sense, one could say that reconciling ourselves to our melancholy, giving in to our powerlessness, is the worst we could do. But then, what will be the solution?

Stopping to think in terms of solutions is a start, since problem-solving behaviour is the essence of the conception of man, in which the entrepreneur is the highest ideal of subjectivity: the pre-eminent capitalist subject. I believe in the usefulness of 'exercises in speechlessness'.[32]

However, this does not mean that we have to throw in the towel. Perhaps our cursed bipolarity is here as a last dialectical rescue board. For the occasion we could translate my personal mantra 'Pessimism in theory, optimism in practice'[33] into the following formula: 'Melancholy in contemplation doesn't necessarily rule out enthusiasm for activist practices.' *Psychopolitics of urgency*: it is my deep conviction that we will only stand up once we truly realize and recognize that our world system is unsustainable. Only when we know and are fully aware that our ship will sink, shall we leave it. Unfortunately, it will possibly be too late, as it goes with most ships or shipwrecked persons. 'Now or never' has never sounded as fatal and topical as Now.

We should not be regressively nostalgic, but we urgently need to learn from the ancestors, the first earth dwellers, the animists. Maybe we should even bet on a new revolutionary nostalgia: neo(eco)animism as an alternative to our extractivism? We live in such a way that we need several planets; they lived in symbiosis with the universe. In an almost fairy-like report on the victory of the natives over a bauxite mine in India, which was about to destroy their natural habitat, the Niyamgiri mountains, which is at the same time their sanctuary, one of the first inhabitants says (in a video): 'We need the mountain and the mountain needs us.'[34]

To me this is not Romantic mysticism, but (albeit vague and illegible) a signpost, a pointer to the future. If there still is a future, then it lies there, in this kind of treatment of our habitat. If we can truly recognize this and act accordingly, we will already be halfway: 'We need Mother Earth and Mother Earth needs us.' Although the latter is doubtful: Mother Earth needs us to save the biosphere, however, the planet itself survives even the most dramatic transformation of the biosphere. If we learned only a little bit from animism, from the idea that nature itself is sacred and that we're entirely part of it, that we're not the master of creation but children of nature, we would be on the right track. And this can become very practical. In *This Changes Everything* Naomi Klein documents in many pages how indigenous people, with their old rights to intangibility of their *commons*, their ground, form one of the spearheads in the coalitions against extreme energy and the frenetic extractivism of shale gas, tar sand oil, deep-water drilling, and so on.[35]

Stengers, in her attempt to formulate a resistance to the coming barbarism in times of catastrophe, also bets on this kind of coalitions where local knowledge is shared and new roads in our thinking are collectively taken. The 'GMO-event' is for her, as it is for the author of this article, of crucial importance in this context.[36] The protestors against genetically modified organisms, are coalitions of citizens, organic farmers, anarchists, scientists, whistle-blowers, activists, who try to stop the conquest of food monopolies based on patents on GMOs of transnational corporations such as Monsanto, rather successfully for the time being: The public opinion is alerted. If we think seriously about the *commons* and participate in 'practices of commoning', we dig up an ancient knowledge, an ancient treatment of our environment.[37] But this is not regressive or nostalgic: this rediscovery of the commons clearly forms a configuration of emergence with the open source movement (with Linux, GNU, Wikipedia, as most famous examples, but all networked global activists also furnish evidence of this).[38] Consequently, this rediscovery of the theory and practice of the *commons* is futurist rather than neo-medieval.

In the light of this worldwide rediscovery of the *commons*, there may still be hope. From, but far beyond posthistoric melancholy, utopian nostalgia can become the postmodern, yes even 'metamodern' (melancholic) politics of the future. With the famous words of Hölderlin, perhaps one of the most melancholic minds of modernity (he ended up in madness): *'Wo aber Gefahr ist, wächst das Rettende auch'* (where danger is, the redeeming grows too).[39] Dialectical bipolarity: only when we have sunk deepest, shall we be saved. We don't really need to believe in this Messianism, in this Kabbalah[40], as we don't need to convert to animism, but we need to learn from it. And fast.

(*envoi*) May this substandard exercise in speechlessness, this sublunary meditation about posthistorical melancholy, be a lesson in urgency.

Notes

1   Peter Sloterdijk, *Zorn und Zeit, Politisch-Psychologischer Versuch*, Frankfurt am Main, Suhrkamp, 2006 (Published in English as *Rage and Time*, 2010). Sloterdijk starts from the concept of '*Thymos*' (sense of honour, pride, dignity, indignation, rage), which also plays an important role in Fukuyama's famous book on the end of history (Francis Fukuyama, *The End of History and the Last Man*, Penguin Books, London/New York, 1992). The concept goes back to Plato. In Fukuyama, the argument goes that dignity is an underestimated political factor, and that the soft revolutions in the Eastern Bloc were founded on it. Václav Havel's citizen movement being the major example of this. Thus, Man is more than just economy and Fukuyama's conclusion is of course that this dignity leads to the liberal democracy as the final stage of history. In Sloterdijk's work, rage is, in fact, resentment that is brought into action by 'resentment

Communism is futuristic

banks' (rather than rage banks). He uses the Christian religious apocalyptic resentment and the violent excesses of communism as major case studies. ISIS too could serve as an example of this ruthless wrath, this resentment that becomes political. (On the role of anger in politics, see my text 'The Days of Anger: Humiliation, Fear and Dignity in the Middle East', in chapter ten 'Everywhere Tahrir Square! Reflections on the Revolution in Egypt' (in my book *Entropic Empire. On the City of Man in the Age of Disaster*, nai010 publishers, Rotterdam, 2012). We are fully aware that Byung-Chul Han subsequently used the term psychopolitics, even as the title of his excellent and concise book on the psychological politics of neo-liberalism, but for this text we stick to the meaning of Sloterdijk.

2   Robert Burton, *The Anatomy of Melancholy*, New York: Review Books, 2001 (1621). Like a Renaissance/Baroque *Wunderkammer* wanting to represent the entire world, Burton's *anatomy of melancholy* is a book about literally everything, but as a consequence of this enumeration spree and 'name and quotation fetishism' also slightly about nothing. It is a game of questions and petty facts without taking positions. Like a 'wonder chamber': a highly amazing jam-full 'curiosity cabinet'. At the same time an inexhaustible source, a crazy encyclopaedia of the world, especially digitally accessible (https://www.gutenberg.org/ebooks/10800).

3   I quote the first and the last two stanza to give an idea, but it would be advisable to read the whole, rather long poem online (see previous footnote), to make the heaving rhythm of heights and depressions fully sink in.

4   Walter Benjamin, 'Ursprung des deutschen Trauerspiels', in *Gesammelte Schriften*, Frankfurt am Main: Suhrkamp, Tiedemann and Schweppenhäuser (eds), 317-334.1975, p. 318-334 (the so- called baroque book was originally published in 1925); my discussion here goes back to my book *The Dwarf in the Chess Machine. Benjamin's Hidden Doctrine*, (Translated by Bram Mertens), nai010 Publishers, Rotterdam, 2019, pp. 180-183.

5   Giorgio Agamben, *De la très haute pauvreté. Règle et forme de vie (Homo Sacer, IV, 1)*, Paris: Bibliothèque Rivage. 2011.

6   Lieven De Cauter, *The Dwarf in the Chess Machine*, p. 53.

7   Charles Baudelaire, *Les Paradis artificiels. Opium et Haschisch*, Paris: 10/18 UGE, 1962; Charles Baudelaire, *Le Spleen de Paris. Petits poèmes en prose*, Paris: Le Livre de Poche,1972. Pocket editions can easily be found at the antiquarian. However, one can also find the text in Baudelaire's complete works or online, see for instance 'La chambre double': http://www.poetica.fr/poeme-1446/charles-baudelaire-la-chambre-double/. Here I provide the beginning and the ending of the widely known prose poem 'Enivrez-vous': «Il faut toujours être ivre. Tout est là: c'est l'unique question. (…) pour ne pas être les esclaves martyrisés du Temps, enivrez-vous; enivrez-vous sans cesse! De vin, de poésie, ou de vertu, à votre guise.» (Baudelaire,

1972, p. 1354) (online available at: http://www.poesie.net/baudel1. htm).

8   Freud, 1998. Sigmund Freud, 'Trauer und Melancholie', in Sigmund Freud, *Gesammelte Werke, Zehnter Band, Werke aus den Jahren 1913-1917*, Fischer, Taschenbuch Verlag, Frankfurt am Main, 1998, pp. 428-446.

9   Ibid., p. 440.

10   Lyotard discusses this grief *Le Postmoderne expliqués aux enfants: Correspondance 1982-1985*, Paris, Galilée, 1986. p. 123 (see also p. 50). The end of 'grand narratives' is construed in: Jean-François Lyotard, *La Condition Postmoderne: Rapports sur le Savoir*, Éditions de Minuit, 1979.

11   Donatella Meadows; Dennis Meadows; Jørgen Randers; William W. Behrens III, *Limits to Growth. A Report for the Club of Rome's Project on the Predicament of Mankind*, New York, Universe Books, 1972.

12   The Dark Mountain Project is described as follows: 'The Dark Mountain Project is a network of writers, artists and thinkers who have stopped believing the stories our civilization tells itself. We see that the world is entering an age of ecological collapse, material contraction and social and political unravelling, and we want our cultural responses to reflect this reality rather than deriving it.' (see: http://dark-mountain.net/about/the-dark-mountain-project/). Their manifesto is a terrific read.

13   'Mit Schrecken sieht der Schwermütige die Erde in einen Bloßen Naturzustand zurückgefallen. Kein Hauch vor Vorgeschichte umwittert sie. Keine Aura.' Walter Benjamin, 'Über einige Motive bei Baudelaire' (1938), in Walter Benjamin, *Gesammelte Schriften*, I, 2, Frankfurt am Main, 1975, p. 643 (my translation).

14   Michael Löwy, *Herbetovering van de wereld. Romantische wortels van linkse denkers* (edited and translated by Johnny Lenaerts), Leuven: Socialisme 21—Grenzeloos—Uitgave Fonds Ernest Mandel, 2013, This collection is for the greater part made up of essays by Michael Löwy, *Révolte et mélancolie. Le romantisme à contre-courant de la modernité*, Paris: Payot, 1992 and Michael Löwy & Sayre *L'esprit du feu. Figures du romantisme anticapitaliste*, Paris: Editions du Sandre,2010.

15   Michael Löwy, op. cit., p. 173, my translation.

16   Georg Lukács, *Theorie van de roman*, Amsterdam, Van Gennep, 1980, p. 37. By 'homelessness' Lukács means that in the novel meaningful transcendence disappears and that man, who dissociates himself from the group and his traditions, is in the hands of an empty immanence, an empty world, the novel gives shape to this desperation. Equally strong is the metaphor of the transcendental homeland, modern man appears in the novel as 'transcendentally homeless' (op. cit., p. 131).

17   Löwy distinguishes between reconstructive, reactionary, fascist, resigning, reforming, and finally utopian or revolutionary Roman-

ticism (Löwy, op. cit., pp. 27-28).

18   Isabelle Stengers, *Au temps de catastrophes. Résister à la barbarie qui vient*, Paris, La Découverte, 2013, pp. 33 and following. Also available in English as *In Catastrophic Times. Resisting the Coming Barbarism*, available online: http://openhumanitiespress.org/books/download/Stengers_2015_In-Catastrophic-Times.pdf .

19   Naomi Klein, *This Changes Everything: Capitalism vs. The Climate*, London/New York: Allen Lane Penguin Group 2014, p. 161 and following.

20   Francis Bacon, *De Augmentis Scientiarum*, 1623, cited in Klein, op. cit., p. 170. Of course Klein points to the particular choice of the metaphors. More extensive and even more impressive is Sylvia Federici's chapter on the mechanistic worldview in her masterpiece on the witch hunt: Sylva Federici, *Caliban and the Witch*, Autonomedia, New York, 2004.

21   Wikipedia, 2015. The first book by Agricola is definitely worth reading, available online: http://www.gutenberg.org/ebooks/38015?msg=welcome_stranger. The work by Agricola has already figured in my very first essay, in which I tried to show how the machine as a metaphor enables early modernity (Da Vinci etc.) to reify, to manipulate and to colonize the world (Lieven De Cauter, 'De Machinale Metafoor', *'Fase 2'*, *Tijdschrift voor beeldvervalsing*, 1986, 9, p. 17-86). In the light of extractivism and the age of extreme energy, extreme extraction, the book by Agricola and the essay have become topical again.

22   This educational ideal is officially embedded in the 2015 Flemish coalition agreement. Meanwhile the 'entrepreneurship learning pathway' has been introduced at the Department of Architecture at the KU Leuven, where I work. It is, according to our politicians to become, the backbone and ultimate aim of education, from Kindergarten to university.

23   Robert Burton, *The Anatomy of Melancholy*, New York: Review Books, 2001, p. 40. It is also freely available online at Project Gutenberg: https://www.gutenberg.org/ebooks/10800,

24   For more about this, see the chapter 'Dimming the sun: the solution to pollution...is pollution' in Klein, *This Changes Everything*, op. cit., p. 256-290.

25   Klein, op. cit., p. 314.

26   Naomi Klein, *The Shock Doctrine. The Rise of Disaster Capitalism*, London/New York: Allen Lane Penguin Group, 2007. Klein writes the history of this disaster capitalism starting in Chili in the 1970s (Pinochet was assisted by the neoliberal economist Milton Friedman!) up till hurricane Katrina in New Orleans and the Green Zone in Baghdad. The shock doctrine is simple, it's about three shocks: 1) a natural disaster, a coup d'état or war, 2) the implementation of a radical neoliberal shock therapy (privatization, liberalization and deregulation) and 3) repression for those who protest

(electroshocks, from Pinochet to Abu Ghraib). In *This Changes Everything* (2014) we see an extractivist industry at work as part of this disaster capitalism.

27   This is extensively described in *This Changes Everything* (particularly in the chapter 'Beyond extractivism', see also p. 284, p. 310 and the paragraph 'All in the sacrifice zone'). A territory that is branded for exploitation and is ecologically destroyed by it, is called a *sacrifice zone* by Klein, a zone given up for exploitation, and her point is that by means of new techniques they can now be found everywhere. At the same time, Naomi Klein also sees a sign of hope in it: because, like in her own country Canada, also more affluent citizens are now confronted with it, the protest is getting stronger. She mainly thinks of the tar sand oil wells that threaten to turn big parts of the Alberta province into an apocalyptic moonscape. One can no longer downplay the problem as being far away. The perils of gas extraction in the Netherlands, causing earthquakes around the city of Groningen, are comparable.

28   Jean-François Lyotard, *Moralités postmodernes*, Paris: Galilée, 1993 (translated as *Postmodern Fables*, University of Minnesota Press, 1999). He also speaks about this hypothesis for the exodus of the techno science that took over from man. I discuss this hypothesis in 'Postscript to the future' (in my Book *Entropic Empire*, 2012).

29   Naomi Klein devotes a whole chapter to Richard Branson, who in his 2006 pledge promised he would do something about climate change, but in the meantime has tripled his fleet of Virgin planes and as a result has also tripled the Virgin CO_2 emissions. The entrepreneurs will not save the world. Klein also speaks about the exodus plans of these visionaries (see the chapter 'No messiah' in *This Changes Everything*, pp. 230-255).

30   Isabelle Stengers, *Au temps des catastrophes*, op. cit., pp. 11-13.

31   Reference to the in Flanders world-famous poem 'The marriage' by Willem Elsschot, written in 1910.

32   Lieven De Cauter, *The Capsular Civilization. On the City in the Age of Fear*, Rotterdam: nai010 publishers. 2004. As I have already written in my first text about the theme of climate disaster in my book *The Capsular Civilization*. Stengers speaks about an '*expérience de perplexité*' (*Au temps des catastrophes*, p. 25).

33   In almost all my recent books the expression appears, starting with *The Capsular Civilization* (2004), also in *De alledaagse apocalyps* (2011) and *Entropic Empire* (2012). It is often ascribed to Antonio Gramsci (but might in fact be originally by Romain Rolland). He uses the expression: 'pessimism of the intellect, optimism of the will' - Antonio Gramsci, *Selections from the prison notebooks*, New York: International Publishers. 1975, p. 175 (note 75)

34   An illustration that I found on the internet and that I posted with the publication on my blog 'Lessons in Urgency', of a piece of the Master's thesis of an Indian student of mine (Ranjani Balasubramanian,

Indian Avatar, the victory of the first dwellers, see: http://community. dewereldmorgen.be/blog/lievendecauter/2015/02/21/indian-avatar-the-victory-of-the-first-dwellers, also available in Dutch. Both the text and the illustration are dear to me because they carry hope and are food for thought at the same time.

35   Klein, *This Changes Everything*, pp. 294-419.

36   Stengers, op. cit., p. 25 and following.

37   See the text 'Common places: considerations on the spatial commons', elsewhere in this book.

38   David Bollier, *Think like a Commoner. A Short Introduction to the Life of the Commons*, Gabriola Island, Canada: New Society publishers, 2014. David Bollier pays a lot of attention to the discovery of the digital commons. Stengers too paid attention to the configuration of the open-source movement in informatics. The rediscovery of the commons did not escape her notice either (*Au temps de catastrophes*, p. 71 and further) and she has recently published some texts on it in collaboration with Serge Gutwirth.

39   Famous poem by Friedrich Hölderlin, 'Patmos', online accessible in English: https://www.poemhunter.com/poem/patmos/

40   In the Kabbalah the term '*Tikkun*' refers to the turning point when decay is worst and redemption is near. For more about this, see the work of Gershom Scholem. This image is also present in Benjamin's thinking (a lot has been written about this - see also my book *The Dwarf in the Chess Machine*).

End of the Anthropocene

The Beginnings of the Anthropocene

We don't know yet when the Anthropocene began, but we might be living its end. The beginning of the Anthropocene, the new geological epoch indicating the significant human impact on the Earth's geology and ecosystems, is the moment when 'Man'—we will come back to this—became the predominant species on the planet, determining it into its depths, into its geology. The term Anthropocene, originally coined by the Russian geologist Alexei Pavlov, was proposed by Paul Crutzen and Eugene Stoermer in 2000[1], but only in May 2019 the Anthropocene Working Group of the International Commission on Stratigraphy officially accepted the term. They are however still debating when to set the beginning of this geological era.[2] That is not easy to determine, and the discussion about this so-called 'golden spike' is not yet over (almost, but not quite yet). It might be the Agricultural Revolution, the Discovery of the Americas, the Industrial Revolution, or the Atomic bomb.

These possibilities are interesting and telling. Should it be the rise of agriculture, of 'agrilogistics', as Timothy Morton calls it?[3] It made the split between nature and culture that according to him (and many others—think of ecofeminism)[4] marks the beginning of the alienation from the conception of the environment as a 'web of life' of which humans are an integral part. It also paved the way for the exploitation of animals, as tools and livestock. Furthermore, it marked the beginning of monocultures, of domesticated vegetation (basically wheat crops). This nature-culture split exploded in modernity and is now hitting us in the face. However fundamental and somehow fatal, the odds of the Agricultural Revolution being chosen as the golden spike were low from the start. For the Anthropocene would then just be a new name blotting out the Holocene, the era that was supplying the climatological stability that opened up the possibility of the Agricultural Revolution in the fertile crescent and subsequently elsewhere, which we are now jeopardizing through anthropogenic ecological disasters. That doesn't make sense, not even if the Holocene contained anthropocentric and anthropogenic intervention in our habitat in an embryonic and paradigmatic form, since the 'agrilogistics' contain the blueprint for the agro-industry which is, up to the present day, one of the basic drivers of both global warming and loss of biodiversity. On the contrary, the beginning of the Anthropocene will mark *the end* of the Holocene. The Holocene indicated climatological stability; the Anthropocene will be an epoch of utter instability. On all levels,

earth became a resource in a agricultural revolution

one can predict that blindly.

Equally telling is the discovery of the Americas and the almost genocidal effects thereof on the indigenous peoples, whose numbers went from 56 million to 6 million during a short span in the seventeenth century. This caused a massive reforestation, visible in the geological layers because of increased carbon dioxide absorption by trees.[5] It is a painful, unknown, untold world-historical event. This so-called 'Orbis Spike'—for the discovery of the Americas united the globe and the two histories of the hemispheres became intermingled for the first time[6]—with the proposed date of 1610, will most probably not make it either, but it deserves to be remembered.

Especially in the light of the Anthropocene, it also becomes an allegorical moment where the sharp decrease in population by criminal exploitation, extermination, and epidemic decimation—in short by colonization—becomes visible in the recovery of nature, in the form of reforestation. The decrease of the world population from 2050 onwards, foretold in the first Report to the Club of Rome *Limits to Growth* of 1972, will maybe have a similar effect. The reduction of pollution due to the 2008 economic crisis and the corona crisis supplied miniature versions of this. The Orbis Spike, marking the rise of colonialism as a first wave of unequal globalization, also coincides with the beginning of capitalism. Colonialism and 'the enclosures of the commons'[7] are fundamental and foundational to capitalism: primitive accumulation, as Marx called it in the monumental last chapter of the first volume of *Capital,* the appropriation, dispossession of the commoners, and straightforward theft of resources, combined with slavery and forced labour, starts the cycle of capitalism.[8] Hence a postcolonial gaze on the Anthropocene will be needed.[9] In the global South this plunder of resources has destroyed landscapes and ecosystems. And original accumulation, the plunder of resources, is still ongoing in a major way. In a sense it is even intensifying as resources are becoming scarce and demand is sky-high.

The Industrial Revolution, of course, might be the most self-evident date to mark the beginning of the Anthropocene. The smoking chimneys of the factories in Northern England and Southern Belgium are iconic, engraved in our collective memory. It is a strong marker because it forms a historical constellation with the American and French Revolutions, with the Enlightenment, the invention of the idea of Progress and the breakthrough of modernity. The Industrial Revolution, with coal and soon petrol as fuels, the infamous 'fossil fuels' as its motor, marked the beginning of the 'thermo-industrial civilization' we are still living in. It ignited our addiction to oil. In seconds we consume sedimentations that took ages, millions of years to form. It also shows the breakthrough of 'extractivism', which profoundly marks our way of life.

The term 'extractivism' refers to the extraction of resources through mining, but it also points to the social injustice of this extraction, the exploitation of humans and the ecological destruction that comes with it. In that respect, we have to become aware that mining is a fundamental base or infrastructure of the modern world, which is often hidden or forgotten when we discuss modernity. The term extractivism underscores this.

Surprisingly enough, the atomic bomb, more precisely the Trinity Test of 1945, might win it as a golden spike that marks the beginning of the Anthropocene. This last date has been officially proposed by the Anthropocene Working Group in May 2019.[10] This date might gain consensus because it coincides with the beginning of what has been called 'the Great Acceleration': the exponential growth of all imaginable parameters since the end of the Second World War, with the typical and ominous steep graphs on all sorts of topics: production, population, pollution, tourism, resource depletion, extinction of species, temperature rise, CO_2 emissions, ocean acidification, and so on. This acceleration is spinning out of control. These opposed graphs of growth and depletion showing the same steep slope indicate that we are on the way to collapse.[11] The collapse of the ecosystem is not ahead of us; it is happening now. The sixth mass extinction, also called Holocene or Anthropocene extinction, is the dying out of all sorts of species. It is one of the most significant extinction events in the history of the Earth. With the sharp decline in insect and bird populations in our regions since 2000, the sixth mass extinction is coming very close to home indeed. The Anthropocene is Here and Now.

On the other hand, one could go so far as to date the beginning of the Anthropocene with... Mowgli. Yes, one could propose to locate the golden spike in the taming of fire: it was perhaps our first technology and it somehow seems to be our last as well, as fossil fuels are a form of fossilized woods. Almost all our technology is based on burning, our weapons are spears of fire. 'Fire power' says it all. But also, our cars are fire on wheels, and our planes are fire on wings. Our transport, our machines, even our digital technologies—they all burn vast quantities of fossil fuels and keep needing more, as we are all always online and on the move. Ever since the Mowgli moment, despite all our phenomenal technological progress, we basically obtain all our energy from burning wood, albeit in the fossilized form of coal, petrol, or gas. For the technological optimists among us this is a very sobering realization.

The fact that this burning logic, despite all high-tech innovations, has brought us and our environment to the brink of destruction, could be called 'the Mowgli complex'. Of course, this is not acceptable as a golden spike, as it would erase or overwrite quite a bit of geological eras and in a sense is older than Anthropos: the Neanderthals were the first to master fire, paleo-anthropol-

always altering climate conditions (handwritten margin note)

ogists claim. We/they started burning some million years ago and it might, as said, be our first technology, almost even before language. We started talking because of these long nights around the fire. Could well be. In any case, as the Neanderthals already had fire, it is not a good start for the Anthropocene. The fact that the Mowgli complex is so persistent—and crucial to understand agrilogistics: no bread without baking, no agriculture without cooking—shows how far back the technological vector in humanoid species goes, and how deep anthropogenic climate control goes. For the record: this is not a fifth proposal for the Anthropocene's golden spike, it is just a mind-blowing philosophical bug.[12]

Critiques of the Anthropocene

Even if we don't know yet when the Anthropocene has begun, we may be living its end: the moment when the logic of growth and acceleration is destroying the biosphere beyond repair. Capitalism with its technological vector has revealed itself as a self-destroying process. Hence Jason More and Donna Haraway have proposed the term 'Capitalocene' for naming the force that has brought us into this situation, without blaming all humanity as the term Anthropocene does.[13] They argue that many people are innocent of global warming, as their ecological footprint is low. The term Anthropocene would obscure this unequal responsibility, exactly by referring to Humankind as a species. According to T J Demos, we should be 'against the Anthropocene', as it is a specific rhetoric. In his analysis this discourse, embedded in a highly mediated, representational computer aesthetic, is close to the spirit of geo-engineering, so on the Dark Side.[14]

women's rights are eco rights (handwritten margin note)

We should go beyond the Anthropocene. Ending the Anthropocene begins with ending anthropocentrism. The term Anthropocene forces us to discuss anthropocentrism. We must end the Anthropocene by opening a posthuman ecology, as claimed by ecofeminists such as Rosi Braidotti and Donna Haraway.[15] Haraway rejects the term Anthropocene because of its male anthropocentrism and proposes the term Chthulucene, a convoluted neologism based on chthonic (earth force) and some cosmic tentacular beings. She is part of the ecofeminist tradition that goes back to the sixties[16], starting from the basic assumption that the exploitation and oppression of nature and the exploitation and oppression of women are linked. We can learn from the ecofeminist critique of Western civilization, as it points to several major factors: the patriarchal, monotheistic split between male spirit/god/man/ culture and female nature/matter/mater/matrix/mother; the mechanistic world view; the critique of Enlightenment that was defending colonialism and even slavery; and, finally, the war against women that was the witch hunt. All these are fundamental factors in our world view and our practices: The theological and mechanistic reduction of 'mother nature' to a collection of soulless objects has opened up the industrial abuse of animals and the ruthless exploitation of all nature as 'resource'.

What is impressive about ecofeminism is that it is not only a theory but also a practice.[17] It is the attempt to do politics in a completely different way, from the occupations and protest camps of the eighties onwards, full of playful pagan rituals, empathy, remembering and reclaiming the witches, reinventing animisms.[18] Donna Haraway tries to open up new ways of thinking and doing by stressing how we are part of the web of life, and are linked to other species; she even speaks about 'multispecies love'. According to Anna Tsing, in her mesmerizing book *The Mushroom at the End of the World*—an anthropological account of the harvesting of the *matsutake*, a rare mushroom and an expensive delicacy in Japan— we have to go beyond apocalyptic thinking and learn to live with 'contaminated diversity', in degraded landscapes with displaced populations. The matsutake only grows in degraded landscapes and it is harvested by displaced communities... In short, ecofeminists are theorizing and practicing 'other ways of world making'.

Isabelle Stengers calls the Anthropocene a first history: '*his*-story', the second history she calls '*her*-story'. And she evokes Anthropos as a macho marching in big boots through History, through His-Story. She too squarely opposes the term Anthropocene: 'Many peoples have nothing to do with the global destruction of what was called the Holocene, and which refers to an era with a quasi-stable climate. I have yet to meet this *anthropos* who claims to take the Earth in charge. I have only ever met people who take themselves for *anthropos*. *Anthropos* is a western creation. Anthropocene is a name for history as *his* story.'[19]

However true it is that modern history and capitalism are driven and dominated by males up to the present day, the ecofeminist critique of the word Anthropocene is linguistically somewhat unjust. I retain the critique on anthropocentrism, and on the machismo and patriarchalism in most cultures, but the term itself cannot be blamed for this—it is neutral, and I think we should embrace this neutrality and reclaim the gender-neutral Anthropos: '(s)he who looks up'. *Anthropos* (human) is not *Aner* (ùan) in ancient Greek. A neutral word is needed, so we have one: *Anthropos*. For it is an unforgivable lack of English and French (and all Latin languages, which have forgotten the difference between *homo* and *vir*) that these languages have no neutral word for the human species (and *human* itself will never really do, for it is not properly speaking a noun: 'a human' will always sound more awkward than 'a human being'). Which in Dutch is the simplest, the first of words: *de mens*, in German *Mensch*. Philosophically speaking, the word *Mensch* or *Anthropos* should be (re)introduced

theology is origin of destruction

as this neutral term to make it possible to speak of our species as a whole. In English, '(Wo)Man' could do—not likely to be a success, but it is at least a playful suggestion, as it point to a lack. The history of (Wo)Man could never be *his*-story.

On a deeper, serious level, the ecofeminist critique of patriarchal Western civilization and religion makes it very clear that the term Capitalocene will not do. The theological anthropocentrism of man as 'the king of creation' is one of the fundamentals of our abusive attitude towards most creatures; it goes much deeper and is a lot older than capitalism. Capitalism is a dark force and an irresponsible system, but the ills of our thermo-industrial civilization go deeper and further. Like patriarchy and the theological anthropocentrism, the technological vector is not to be reduced to capitalism, as the ancient Chinese, the Babylonians, the Egyptians, the Greeks, and most of all the Romans, prove: all of them were, for their time, very technological. And communist Russia was a non-capitalist thermo-industrial society. Capitalism, with its logic of growth, is of course a phenomenal force driving us off limits, towards the abyss, but as said, when one looks for the deeper causes of our predicament, capitalism is not the only factor, even if it is the main culprit today.

Finally, colonialism has known its apogee or full blooming under capitalism, or vice versa, capitalism bloomed due to colonialism, but colonialism is much older, as again the Greek and Roman civilizations prove. So, placing all the blame on capitalism, to avoid placing it on all humanity, will not do. For similar reasons, other terms that have been suggested, such as 'Plantationocene' and 'Chthulucene', may be inspiring as they point to interesting constellations but they will not make it as alternatives to the controversial term Anthropocene. Even if indeed the colonial plantation was an important paradigm for the rise of the standardized exploitation of both plants and humans, in a sort of factory-like manner, by bringing alien crops and alien individuals, slaves, in an ordered, but artificial monocultural environment, and even if it contained the embryo of ecological disaster as it killed both biodiversity and anthropological cultures[20]—the word is simply not suitable. Furthermore, the confusion between Latin and Greek makes most of the alternatives lexically and aesthetically unbearable. The same goes for Haraway's Chthulucene. She tries to point towards a sort of post-Anthropocene attitude, but by using such farfetched idiosyncratic terminology she risks ending up in theoretical rococo.

A Philosophy of History for the Anthropocene

The term Anthropocene contains a strange constellation that might make it somehow survive all criticism: It is at the same time very big—the scale of millennia—and at the same time it is the name for what is happening now. It is here—the anthropogenic climate change, the anthropogenic destruction of the biosphere. This makes the concept mind-blowing. What I am actually trying to say is: We need to embrace and hate the Anthropocene, debate, ponder over the term, for it confronts us, in a totally freaking new way, with all the big questions afresh: Where do we come from? Where are we? What are we? Where do we go to? Or, more sophisticated: Does history have a *telos*, a goal, a direction? And what is history then, only human? Or should we start to include nonhumans in our history? How to make sense of the Anthropocene, how to mould this into a big new story, a new grand narrative? Or is that exactly what we should not do?

We need to try to face the challenge of the present and formulate a philosophy of history beyond modernity. How to think about history after progress, how to think history without the idea of progress? Walter Benjamin was perhaps the first to point to progress as catastrophic.[21] For him the idea of progress had to be seen as a catastrophe of exploitation. Lyotard's famous postmodern condition was anchored in the end of this grand narrative of progress and emancipation.[22] He wrote beautiful pages on the necessity of thinking in terms of cosmological time and our incapability to do so.[23] This challenge has been taken up recently: We have to think in cosmological, geological, ecological time, the time of Gaia, facing Gaia, facing and 'composing' with her intrusion—to speak in the terms of Stengers and Latour.[24] We have, claims Dipesh Chakrabarthy in a similar vein (and in chorus with Latour), long split history and nature, as the latter was the inert backdrop of human history, yet now we discover that nature and history are inextricably linked—nature is entering history with a vengeance.[25]

Fukuyama had a point after all: We are living the end of history. But it is not the triumph of liberal democracy and the free market but a chaotic posthistory, the end of linearity, the end of progress as the arrow of time, the beginning of a nonlinear time, a very slippery path, chaos theory in action. To think this new situation is one of the ultimate challenges of philosophy today: a new philosophy of history in a world where globalization and climate change are colliding. What is humanity as a geological force? Can we think this? How to think of this new subject of history?[26]

All myths and religions contain a big story in which all other stories fit. One can call it a worldview. It is as big as the cosmos itself, it explains space and time with all the trimmings and also frames the rituals of daily life. We could call this the great or transcendental meta-narrative. The myth tells about the origin and meaning of everything. The same goes for monotheistic religions, who gave up animism and turned an oral tradition into a written one but kept and reinforced the grand narrative. Judaism is based on a strong story—the whole history from creation till the end of the world is one big basic plot: paradise, fall, redemption—beginning, middle, end, so really a story, with many dramatic plot twists and subplots. Christianity took over that grand narrative, except that the Christian redemption was less collective: They will go to heaven, and now they wait, without really realizing it, for the second coming of Christ, because they are already saved. Most Christians are not even aware of this. Islam also knows this messianic narrative and fundamentalism is an aggressive form of this Messianism; just like the American fundamentalists believe that the end of the world is near. Strange symmetries, making theological allies of enemies. The moderns, since the Enlightenment, had a new grant story: progress, with the advancement in science as a model. Universal history: Humanity was on its way to perfection as a species. This belief also has its ecstatic variants: The Singularity is near; technology will supersede humans.[27] Transhumanism is a sort of techno-Messianism.

Lyotard had rightly observed that the narration of progress and that of myth have much in common, but while the myth finds its ground and legitimacy in the past and is an eternal repeat of the primal past, progress finds its legitimacy in the future—history is on its way to some sort of perfection, according to Kant. All those meta-narratives are always curves or lines. That is interesting in itself. However, the line or the curve seems to have been taken away from us, we have lost the thread. What now? We are in a kind of complex, non-linear time, a 'liquid modernity' (according to Zygmunt Bauman). Universal World History has exploded into a nonlinear multiplicity of local stories, the stories of the subaltern cultures, of the colonized. Lyotard and many others have argued that we should embrace this multiplicity of localized narratives. Agreed, but we will need a story for a global world, one that is more interdependent and interconnected than ever. In a globalized world we will need some story to make a *common* world. Latour is sharply aware of this. So is Chakrabarthy. Just a collection of local worldviews and local stories will not do. We will all end up living with our own 'alternative facts'. Above all, the epistemological challenge of the Anthropocene is to rethink history, to overcome the split between natural history and human history that was foundational for the modern conception of history. And it is here that these local, subaltern, animist stories can teach us a great deal.

Acceleration Versus Collapse

We may be living the end of the Anthropocene, we said, even if we don't know yet when it began. The sixth mass extinction and climate change are two major ongoing disasters, but what we are witnessing is rather a chain of ecological disasters. That is the most

technology is "nirvana" to man

unnerving aspect of our situation—the possible tipping points and the feedback loops that unlock as global temperature is rising, such as the methane that will be released if the permafrost melts. But also the wars that come with the collapse of ecosystems, and the humanitarian disasters, as famines and shortage of drinking water will be devastating. The end of the Anthropocene is its fulfilment: total predominance, meaning large-scale destruction beyond the capacity of recovery. But it is also announcing the end of this predominance of the human species. Humanity as a geological force will be forced to shrink its footprint, or just shrink. Indeed, even the end of the human species has become a possibility—with a temperature increase of five degrees centigrade the planet becomes too hot for most current life forms. This possibility has recently been called by scientists: 'Hothouse Earth'.[28]

However sober one tries to look at the forecasts of climatologists, overshoot and collapse (forecasted since *Limits to Growth, the Report to the Club of Rome* in 1972) seem inevitable. 'Collapsology' is a new discipline in radical ecology, introduced, or rather popularized in 2015 by Pablo Servigne and Raphaël Stevens in their book *Comment tout peut s'effondrer*.[29] We cannot avoid or solve the ecological disasters that are coming, only try to avoid the worst. But what we really need to do is learn how to *deal* with collapse. Servigne and his co-authors also insist on the psychological preparations and mourning processes this entails, for the most challenging thing is to look this apocalypse—based upon scientific evidence—in the face. The wave of climate denialism is partly due to a psychological shutting out of this inconvenient truth. However, collapsology is not a pessimistic or even apocalyptic theory, but a practical discipline for living and surviving in collapsing societies and ecosystems. It is not the end of the world but the beginning of something else that will be hellish at moments maybe, but we will have to do with it, like people survive in war times, often by self-organization and mutual help.[30] Urban gardening will soon prove to be much more than an 'eco-bobo' hobby: it will become essential for survival.[31] Hence their witty slogan: 'Another end of the world is possible.'[32]

And that is some good news: the Anthropocene is also the revelation of a cosmic dimension. We have to become aware of the cosmic dimension of all that we do and don't do. We must get humans out of the centre to give space and a voice to nonhumans (not only mammals, but also insects, oceans, rivers, the biosphere itself). The Anthropocene—whatever name you would give it, the term itself cannot be but an alibi—confronts us with gigantic questions and unseen urgencies. How will we deal with water and food shortages in an overcrowded world exposed to ever more extreme weather events, desertification, flooding, and sharply decreasing biodiversity? And what unspeakable responsibility do we bear towards all the nonhumans we are destroying as a side effect of our Great Acceleration and our eternal logic of growth? What unspeakable *ir*responsibility. And yet we must take up this challenge, even out of sheer sense of survival. That is maybe a flicker of hope: that we cannot save humanity without saving the biosphere and vice versa. Maybe collapse is our best bet. But it will most probably be rough. Self-organization and back to basics, rationing would be a solution, it will be most probably at some point. Like in war time. How to do that in a more or less democratic way? And who is we? Many, too many questions.

Collapsology, as Servigne and his companions are well aware of, is not only a tough exercise in mourning[33] but it also requires a lot of skills in new ways of telling stories, new ways of world-making. They took that gratefully from ecofeminism. Collapse can and will take a million shapes. Expansion and growth have reached ridiculous levels in capitalism but have been present in culture since the dawn of (Wo)Man, the rise of Anthropos as species: All technology is acceleration, every medium as extension of (Wo)Man is speeding up, that is its essence, according to what could be called McLuhan's Law.[34] Many known ancient civilizations had the urge to grow and expand. Acceleration means urgency. The more you speed up, the more you have to be aware of time to manoeuvre and anticipate. We are bad at anticipating, terribly bad. Diametrically opposed to collapsology is accelerationism. However appealing and spirited the accelerationist manifesto[35] may be, a leftist recapturing of technology from capitalism, an ecological post-capitalist technology remains a dream, and maybe even a dangerous one, as it feeds all sorts of political rather rightist optimism, like 'eco-modernism' or 'eco-realism'.

The fact that the atom bomb test may be the golden spike for the beginning of the Anthropocene is interesting not only because it coincides with the Great Acceleration, but also because the debate about nuclear energy is coming back with a vengeance. Nuclear energy is a symbol of the impasse and impact of our technology and at the same time it might, given the urgency to cut greenhouse gas emissions, be our saving grace, at least according to some. In studying the philosophical premises of this debate, one might discover the dilemma of our epoch, which I have called, maybe wrongly, *metamodernity*. In the debate on nuclear energy, accelerationism, and the degrowth-movement collide head-on. It shows how divided and uncertain we are in the emergencies we are facing.

Ending the Anthropocene

The 'solution' is near impossible, given our business-as-usual attitude on both macro- and microlevel. Yet, combining transition towards a zero-carbon, circular economy with global equity is the only possible solution and the ultimate quandary of our time. But as the time window for solutions is closing—more and more scientists agree it has closed already—we must prepare to survive in a chaotic world, an imploding *polis,* and an unstable, catastrophic environment. If we still are not sure when the Anthropocene began exactly, we might be living its end. We should end the Anthropocene. Ending the Anthropocene is the almost impossible task of our era.

The Atomic tests that will most probably end up marking the beginning of the Anthropocene coincided with the Great Acceleration, which somehow ironically enough was not driven by nuclear energy, but by fossil fuel. It is because of this 'construction mistake', or this 'path-dependency' of the thermo-industrial civilization, the unbreakable dominance and permanence of the combustion motor—we could say even because of this pathological Mowgli Complex—that we are in such trouble. But in any case, the Great Acceleration is reaching its end. We go into overshoot and collapse. The downfall has begun.

'The behaviour of the world system under the business-as-usual model', has indeed clearly proven to be that of 'overshoot and collapse', to paraphrase the dry announcement of half a century ago in the Report to the Club of Rome, *Limits to Growth.*[36] In retrospect, these words seem to have pointed at the necessity of collapsology all along. The limits to growth are now becoming tangible. Graham Turner, who with his team checked the report thirty years after its initial publication and found that it was correct in its predictions, stated in his afterthought: 'Instead of trying to avoid collapse, we should start to prepare for dealing with it.'[37] This is a daunting challenge for all of us. Whether one adheres to collapsology or not.

It is too late for eco-realism, eco-modernism, or accelerationism. A post-capitalist technology is not on the horizon. That is why the three other dates will always be in the running, maybe not as competitors for the golden spike, but as philosophical milestones in the build-up towards the Great Acceleration: The Agricultural Revolution that was the embryo of the much later agro-industrial one, the so called 'green revolution', colonialism as the rise of capitalism and of course, the Industrial Revolution, opening up our thermo-industrial civilization—all these markers are now topical, relevant if not urgent to think about. Even to live in and act against 'the Anthropocene'.

What we need is a cyberpunk philosophy for this cyberpunk age. The Anthropocene, the end of the Anthropocene, is the era of realized science fiction, the age of realized cyberpunk: a capsular high-tech society controlled by a few big corporations in an overcrowded, dualized, chaotic, heavily polluted world, sinking into lawlessness, often with 'off worlds' as escape. The Anthropocene is the age of cyberpunk. The Bubble is part of the Matrix, the archipelago of capsular entities in our security-driven, militarized urban space.[38] After the end of history comes the relapse into the state of nature. The condition of international lawlessness, of trade wars and proxy wars (Iraq, Syria, Afghanistan, Libya, Yemen, …) is becoming the new 'postmodern', 'posthistorical' condition. The collapse of the international legal order is one of the many silent disasters of our time.

This civilization is crumbling. Civility will be needed, but it might fail us. What I termed 'The Permanent Catastrophe' in 2001,[39] is now revealing itself in the possibility of collapse. *The capsular civilization*, I foretold in a book of that title in 2004, is coming: those who can, will hide in capsular entities. And what I termed—in *Entropic Empire,* the sequel of my projected millennium trilogy—'the relapse into the state of nature', in the form of the blackout, the latent universal civil war (with Beirut as model) or spreading lawlessness (many examples around the world), is the nightmare we have to avoid at all costs,[40] that is the ethico-political horizon of collapsology. Mutualism, mutual help, in terms of Pablo Servigne (and Kropotkin), the 'commoning', in the discourse on the resurgence of the commons, the common as political principle—all these practices could be a saving grace. In the Anthropocene, this ending epoch, this epoch of endings, an epoch of the end of the world as we knew it, safe havens for others, newcomers, migrants, will be crucial.[41]

The rise of populism does not help. Populism, as Latour has shown, is a sort of extra-terrestrial solution: climate change is a hoax, and yes, we can close borders, and cut ourselves loose from the world. Globalization, the magic word of the turn of the century, is unwinding, we live in the days of 'deglobalization': Brexit, new right, extreme right, xenophobia, climate negationism, fake news, alternative facts, and so on… As Latour explains in his exemplar pamphlet on Trumpism: against the new attractor of the *hors sol,* the outlandish, extra-terrestrial position of populisms, and beyond the local and the global axis of modernization, he pleads for the new attractor of the terrestrial.[42] We have to become terrestrial again. '*Cultiver son jardin'*, takes on a whole new meaning. Whether the *terrestrials* will win this war, as Latour calls it, against climate negationism and all the irresponsible, populist politics that comes with it, will depend on all of us, somehow. That is the existential challenge of collapsology, it seems.

And yes, all of us will have to work through this most awkward 'post historical melancholy'[43] and wake up to the reality of this cyberpunk age. Collective self-organization and mutual help will be needed at mass scale. Will our individualistic consumer attitude be up to it? May the Force of Swarm Intelligence be with us! And lots of Interspecies Love too. To learn and live with and

within 'contaminated diversity', as Anna Tsing called it.[44]
'Uncivilization' is maybe another name for what we need, as the *Dark Mountain Project Manifesto* has it.[45] Sweating out our civilization, its dualisms and extractivisms. We will have to learn to survive in the wild, in the blackout of our cities. In this urban chaos urbanity will be needed. The punks were early with their slogan: 'NO FUTURE', but now it rings a bell. In this day and age, the bells should ring, go off all at once. Greta Thunberg is right: 'I don't want your hope, I want your panic... our house is on fire.' The climate strikers and Extinction Rebellion do the right thing.[46] Rebel Against Extinction We Must.

Notes

1   Paul J. Crutzen & Eugene F. Stoermer, 'The Anthropocene', International Geosphere Biosphere Programme, Global Change Newsletter Nr. 41, May 2000, available online: http://www.igbp.net/downlo ad/18.316f1832132347017758000140l/1376383088452/NL41.pdf. For a short account of the history of the term (which was in use before Crutzen), see the good introduction 'Welcome to the Anthropocene', by T J Demos in *Against the Anthropocene*, Sternberg Press, Berlin, 2017.

2   Meera Subramanian, 'Anthropocene Now: influential panel votes for Earth's new epoch', in *Nature* https://www.nature.com/articles/ d41586-019-01641-5

3   Timothy Morton, *Dark Ecology,* Columbia University Press, New York, 2016.

4   We think of authors such as Donna Haraway, Starhawk, Anna Tsing, and Isabelle Stengers. For an early overview and synthesis of ecofeminism from the sixties to the early nineties, see the excellent article of Greta Gaard & Lori Gruen, 'Ecofeminism. Towards Global Justice and Planetary Health', in: *Society and Nature*, 2, 1993, p. 1-35.(available online: https://www.academia.edu/32438639/ Ecofeminism_Toward_Global_Justice_and_Planetary_Health)

5   For a chilling account on this event see: Eric Alliez et Mauricio Lazzarato, *Guerre et capital*, Editions Amsterdam, Paris, 2016 and also T J Demos, *Against the Anthropocene.*

6   Michael Franco, '"Orbis Spike" in 1610 marks date when humans fundamentally changed the planet', *C-Net,* online available: https:// www.cnet.com/news/orbis-spike-in-1610-marks-date-when-humans-fundamentally-changed-the-planet/

7   See the chapter on the commons in this book.

8   Karl Marx, Capital, available online: https://www.marxists.org/ archive/marx/works/download/pdf/Capital-Volume-I.pdf

9   Matthias De Groof, 'Congocene. The Anthropocene through Congolese Cinema' in: Marina Gržini & Sofie Uitz, *Rethinking the Past for a New Future of Conviviality: Opposing Colonialism, Anti-*

Semitism, Turbo-Nationalism, Cambridge Scholars Publishing, Cambridge, 2019.

10 Meera Subramanian, op. cit.: https://www.nature.com/articles/d41586-019-01641-5

11 See the graphs in Will Steffen, Wendy Broadgate, Lisa Deutsch, Owen Gaffney and Cornelia Ludwig, 'The Trajectory of the Anthropocene: The Great Acceleration', in *The Anthropocene Review* of March 2015, available online: https://www.researchgate.net/publication/272418379_The_Trajectory_of_the_Anthropocene_The_Great_Acceleration

12 I say this because some students ran off with 'the Mowgli Moment' and forgot the irony.

13 Donna Haraway, *Staying with the trouble. Making Kin in the Chthulucene*. Durham & London: Duke University Press, 2016.

14 T J Demos, *Against the Anthropocene*, Sternberg Press, Berlin, 2017. A must-read.

15 Rosi Braidotti, *The Posthuman*, Polity Press, Cambridge 2013; Donna Haraway, *Staying with the Trouble*.

16 See Gaard and Gruen, op. cit.

17 Benedikte Zitouni, 'Planetary Destruction, Ecofeminists and Transformative Politics in the Early 1980s'. In: *Interface: a Journal for and about Social Movements*, vol. 6, no. 2, 2014, p. 244-270. (available online)

18 One can think of the spiral dance of Starhawk and the erotizations of Nature by Annie Sprinkle.

19 'Form history to her story, in four stories', Isabelle Stengers in conversation with Lieven De Cauter, http://www.ny-web.be/transitzone/history-herstory-four-stories.html

20 See Anna Tsing, *The Mushroom at the End of the World, On the Possibility of Life in the Capitalist Ruins*, Princeton University Pres, Princeton, 2015.

21 The clearest criticism is contained in his theses on history, see Walter Benjamin, 'Ueber den Begriff der Geschichte', *Gesammelte schriften*, I, 2, Surkamp, Frankfurt am Main, 1974. (also available in English online: https://folk.uib.no/hlils/TBLR-B/Benjamin-History.pdf) A more extensive and fragmented critique of progress in contained the Passagenwerk (or arcades project, available online: https://monoskop.org/images/e/e4/Benjamin_Walter_The_Arcades_Project.pdf)

22 Jean-François Lyotard, *La condition postmoderne. Rapport sur le savoir*, Minuit, Paris, 1979.

23 Jean-François Lyotard, *L'inhumain. Causeries sur le temps*, Galilée, Paris, 1988.

24 Isabelle Stengers, *Au temps de catastrophes* (available in English: Isabelle Stengers. *In Catastrophic Times: Resisting the Coming Barbarism*. translated by Andrew Goffey. Open Humanities Press, 2015. Available online: http://openhumanitiespress.org/books/download/Stengers_2015_In-Catastrophic-Times.pdf)

25 Dipesh Chakrabarthy, 'The Climate of History: Four Theses.' *Critical Inquiry* 35.2 (Winter 2009), p. 197–222. It is also one of the main lines of Bruno Latour's pamphlet against climate denialism and Trumpism: *Ou atterir?* (translated as *Down to Earth*), a must-read.

26 Dipesh Chakrabarthy has made some attempts to spell out the difficulties of thinking humanity as a geological force as the subject of history in the article mentioned before and in 'Postcolonial Studies and the Challenge of Climate Change', *New Literary History* 43.1 (Winter 2012): p. 1-18.

27 Ray Kurzweil, *The Singularity is Near, When humans transcend biology*, Viking, London, New York, 2005.

28 See the recent multi-authored study 'Trajectories of the Earth System in the Anthropocene', in the Proceeding of the National Academy of Sciences of the United States of America (PNAS), August 14, 2018 , available online https://www.pnas.org/content/115/33/8252 (Pablo Servigne, one of the inventors of 'collapsology', explains this possibility of a hothouse Earth in a very clear way in one of his videos, called 'Un monde sans pétrol': https://www.youtube.com/watch?v=kSVA5Q79Urc)

29 Pablo Servigne & Raphael Stevens, *Comment tout peut s'effondrer*, *Petit manuel de collapsologie à l'ursage des générations présentes*, Seuil, Paris, 2015.

30 Pablo Servigne, Raphael Stevens and Gauthier Chapelle insist on this in *Une autre fin du monde est possible*, Seuil, Paris, 2018. Servigne has even co-written, with Gauthier Chappelle, a whole book about this mutualism: *L'entraide, l'autre loi de la jungle*, Éditions Les liens qui libèrent, Paris, 2017.

31 Pablo Servigne and compagnons, for instance show how during the Second World War urban farming was practiced on a large scale in the USA, even on the lawn of Capitol Hill: https://www.youtube.com/watch?v=kSVA5Q79Urc

32 Pablo Servigne, Raphael Stevens and Gauthier Chapelle *Une autre fin du monde est possible*.

33 Ibid. Particularly the first part talks extensively about this mourning, which is of course also the theme of my anatomy of political melancholy, the preceding text in this book.

34 Marshall McLuhan, *Understanding Media. The Extensions of Man*, Pinguin, London, New York, 1964.

35 Available online: http://criticallegalthinking.com/2013/05/14/accelerate-manifesto-for-an-accelerationist-politics/

36 Available online : http://www.donellameadows.org/wp-content/userfiles/Limits-to-Growth-digital-scan-version.pdf (p. 125)

37 Graham Turner, 'A comparison of The Limits to Growth with 30 years of reality'. Global Environmental Change, 18, 397-411 (available online: https://www.researchgate.net/publication/223746986_A_comparison_of_The_Limits_to_Growth_with_30_years_of_reality_Global_Environmental_Change_18_397-411

38   My book *The Capsular Civilization. On the City in the Age of Fear* (nai010 publishers, 2004) was an attempt towards a cyberpunk philosophy of the future read within the present.

39   'The Permanent Catastrophe', published in my book *The Capsular Civilization. On the City in the Age of Fear*, Nai publishers, Rotterdam, 2004.

40   See my book *Entropic Empire. On the City of Man in the Age of Disaster*, nai010 Publishers, Rotterdam, 2015.

41   See my text 'Other Spaces for the Anthropocene: Heterotopia as Dis-Closure of the (Un)Common', in Daan Wesselman et al., (eds), *Interrupting Globalisation: Heterotopia in the Twenty-First Century* , Routledge, London, 2020. Republished in this book.

42   Bruno Latour, *Ou atterrir?*, La Découverte, Paris, 2017.

43   See former text 'Small Anatomy of Political Melancholy'.

44   Anna Tsing, op. cit.

45   'The Dark Mountain Manifesto', a must-read: https://dark-mountain. net/about/manifesto/

46   Check them out! They have chapters near you. Maybe the most concrete proposal for action, in the form of large-scale civil disobedience, a manifesto for a climate Rebellion in general, and for Extinction Rebellion in particular, see: Roger Hallam, *Common Sense for the 21st century*, available online: https://www.rogerhallam.com/ wp-content/uploads/2019/08/Common-Sense-for-the-21st-Century_ by-Roger-Hallam-Download-version.pdf

II Dis-closures of the Commons

Common Places: Preliminary Notes on the Commons

The commons are under threat. Both 'Nature', the ecosystem we share, and 'Culture'—language, cultural tradition, art, cultural heritage, and media we use and share without ownership, knowledge, free research—are under severe pressure. The impending appropriation by states and multinationals of the North Pole for deep sea drilling is emblematic of the vulnerability of the 'natural common', as Negri and Hardt call it in *Commonwealth*. The patenting of seeds by Monsanto and other multinationals is equally emblematic: It constitutes the appropriation and privatization of what was shared by farmers for 10,000 years. The battle over the privatization of knowledge (and research) in the knowledge economy proves that the 'artificial common' is endangered too.

As the commons are under threat, we become aware of the commons. But we have forgotten what it is. Or we know what it is—it is pretty common, we have things in common— but it somehow remains alien; it is not an obvious category of our discourse. From newspapers to the history of philosophy and theory, discourse on the common is marginal. Even if it has become a buzzword lately, in sociological and media terms this attention would still have to be considered a marginal phenomenon—something for alternative people, ecologists, and leftist thinkers such as Agamben, Žižek, Badiou, Rancière, Virno, Harvey, and of course Negri and Hardt. The absence of the idea of the common, both our stuttering and our swooning when we use the word is therefore symptomatic. If we want to reactivate the common, we will have to start from its absence, its forsakenness, its oblivion, its abolition.

Particularly in relation to space, we are used to think in terms of public versus private; a space is either public or private. If we find a space that does not fit this dichotomy, we call it semi-public or semi-private. The common is a third category. But what is this forgotten third category, which we are rediscovering after it had almost completely been forgotten? As we have forgotten the common, and in order to approach the commons in spatial terms, the 'spatial' or 'landed commons', it is maybe wise to start with some basics, some commonplaces—in search of the link between common and place. If we look for the most commonplace definition of the common, it could sound like this: *The common is what is neither public (state-owned) nor private.*

But what does the word common actually mean, where does it come from? According to the *Online Etymology Dictionary* the adjective 'common' was introduced in English around 1300, and means 'belonging to all, general'. Easy: common is another word for general. It is not particular. Belonging to all in general also means belonging to nobody in particular. Interesting tautology and paradox at once... The word is derived from the Old French *comun* 'common, general, free, open, public' (that it dated around the ninth century, in modern French *commun*). It comes from Latin *communis* 'in common, public, shared by all or many; general, not specific; familiar, not pretentious', but originally it comes from the Proto Indo-European (PIE) word *ko-moin-i-* 'held in common', compound adjective formed from *ko-* 'together' + *moi-n-*, suffixed form of root *mei-* 'change, exchange', hence it means literally 'shared by all'.

'The second element of the compound', still according to the Online Etymology dictionary, 'also is the source of Latin munia "duties, public duties, functions", those related to munia "office". Perhaps reinforced in Old French by the Germanic form of PIE *ko-moin-i-* (cf. Old English *gemæne* "common, public, general, universal", corresponding in English to *mean*, which came to French via Frankish.' And then without further ado, the entry concludes: 'Used disparagingly of women and criminals since c.1300...' The linguistic revelation of this short entry is that common (in Latin languages and in English) and *gemein / gemeen / mean* (in Germanic languages) have the same root and are in fact another form of the same (hypothetical) 'ur-word' (*Komoini*)—so the French '*commune*' and the German *Gemeinde* (or Dutch *gemeente*) are not only equivalent—for village, or community—but in fact the same word, differently formed. Besides, we discover here that the common is always also the mean, the general, not only what is shared by all, but also what is despised as low and vulgar. The combination with duty (*munia*) points to a political task: taking up tasks in and for the community, based on mutuality, but it is too early to go into that.

The *noun* common(s) the dictionary dates as late fifteenth-century, 'land held in common'. That is of course the quintessence of what we are looking for: the spatial commons. In Dutch the common in its stark meaning of 'land held in common' would be '*meent*', but apart from the London commons, a street name in Rotterdam, and apparently some places in and around Bruges, and some other patches here and there maybe, very little is left of it. This is real proof that the commons in spatial terms have been almost totally appropriated, privatized, or nationalized. In addition, the dictionary signals: 'Commons "the third estate of the English people as represented in Parliament", is from late 14c. The Latin *communis* also served as a noun meaning "common property, commonwealth".' That is the concept of commons now used by the defenders of the commons. This dictionary entry seems a good starting point for our commonplaces, which may prove to be paradoxical platitudes.

The Enclosure of the Commons

The first common place, the commonplace of common places so to speak, would be that 'Nature' is common. Indeed, Nature is common by essence. It is the ultimate commons. It is that what we share, not only with all other humans, but with all living and inanimate creatures, organic or inorganic matter. The cosmos, literally meaning gem, ornament (hence cosmetics) has revealed Earth itself as the blue planet, since space travel. This once vast and overwhelming wholeness in which the human species one day appeared in prehistory is now a fragile and awfully finite ecosystem. It is precisely this human species that has become so predominant and so all-encompassing that it has given its name to a new geological era: the Anthropocene. It is in the Anthropocene that the common is at the same time precious in a new way and under stress, squandered and appropriated.

All this leads us to another platitude. The commons, in spatial or territorial terms, like the famous, paradigmatic London commons, are leftovers (of premodern law, like the Magna Carta and the Charter of the Forest, of nomadic cultures, of even the state of nature?). We can think of Rousseau's proto-anthropology of the 'good savage' (*le bon sauvage*). It is when somebody in an audacious gesture fenced off a patch of land, and said 'this is mine', and found people stupid enough to believe him, Rousseau writes in his 'Discourse on the origin and basis of inequality among Men' (1755), that private property, and after that regulated society and inequality started. Indeed, only for what anthropology has called the 'nature peoples' and for nomads, nature is truly common. For them it is common by nature, as it were. That is maybe the real reason behind animism. It expresses this deep awareness in the most perfect way possible, both children and rational philosophers, even scientists can understand this sometimes: the mystical 'given-ness' of it all. Given by nobody to everybody. Given to nobody by this ultimate body, Mother Earth, Gaia, Pachamama.

Deus sive natura, said Spinoza. God or nature, implying God is nature. Pantheism was a more modern way to express the unity of everything and the 'gift'. It is this 'given-ness', this gift that is taken away from us, or it is a respect or gratefulness that we have lost. In nomadic culture you use nature, but you do not own it. Life is a (sacred) give-and-take, a fragile process that requires restraint and respect, for land, trees, animals, and especially for the balance, the harmony of it all (which is more than a statistical equilibrium in an ecosystem). The shepherds are respectful of the land. The hunter is grateful and respectful to his prey. The common is primordial, archaic.

Sedentary cultures cannot move their turf, they can only expand by colonizing. Agriculture needs land. With the disappearance of nomadic culture—let's not think of it as a natural process but instead as wars, colonization, genocide—the commons shrink, it becomes more and more a leftover zone, often arid or at least non-arable land. From 1500 onwards the common in Europe becomes a reserve, like later the reserves for the nomadic Native Americans in the US and Canada. This idea of the common as 'protected' and imprisoned in reserves is something to stress. Of course, the oceans are still common, like air, but the North Pole is, as we write, under threat of exploitation, as states and multinationals want to appropriate and exploit it. The retreat of the icecaps is leaving the North Pole naked and vulnerable to rape, so to speak.

The common is weak. Seeds, water, and air have no defence. Even knowledge is not immune to privatization. Without property it is not easy to defend a territory, a space, place, an entity, a species. Wild nature is everybody's, so corporations can 'enclose' it, appropriate it, as they do with 'wild seeds'. In a sense only a world body politic, a radically reformed and strengthened UN could outlaw the privatization of seeds, like only a world body, like the UN, could really defend the Amazon forest, the North Pole, the ecosystem. That is of course what the UN, under the aegis of the IPPC (Intergovernmental Panel on Climate Change) tries with the Climate Summits (now re-baptized and somehow neutralized into 'COPs', Conference of Parties, as if nobody wants to know or mention what this conference is about), but… it remains all too little too late. The historical Paris Agreement was cast aside by Trump. But without an international legally binding framework, we will not get there. We will not be able to avoid unspeakable disasters.

That is maybe the great lesson of Peter Linebaugh's amazing book *The Magna Carta Manifesto*: The Charter of the Forest is a legal protection of the commons. The commons are in a sense instituted by law. The right to take dry wood from the forest, to take fruits and let a pig graze, all these practices of subsistence were stipulated in the charter. *The Magna Carta* (and its second part, the said Charter of the Forest) is a contract made up after a conflict between the sovereign and the people. The king promises the people fair trial by their peers, and in the second part access to the commons of the forests, and if he does not stick to the contract, it is stipulated by himself that the people have the contractual right to revolt. *Habeas corpus*, legal access to the commons, the right to revolt—it is all there in *Magna Carta*, a legal document of the year 1215. Alas, it has been forgotten.

Modernity opens with the enclosure of the commons. From the sixteenth century onwards the (spatial) commons, as 'land held in common', virtually disappear in Europe. Both Braudel and Wallerstein put forward 1500 as the beginning of capitalism. The rise of capitalism has been marked in an almost symbolical, but also very real way by the enclosure of the commons. Marx has documented this process in the last monumental chapter of the first volume of *Capital* on the 'Original Accumulation'. Besides the walling off of arable land for grazing for sheep—given the rise of the wool industry in Flanders—there was a massive destruction of houses and even towns. In one stroke the people lost their dwelling and their means of subsistence: ground around the houses, and the forests for wood and foraging. This expropriation was followed by a severe criminalization of the poor that lasted for centuries. Driven to the cities, they not only supplied the new proletariat for the first factories but also formed a new internal market, as they lost all means of subsistence. This is the basic mechanism behind the 'original accumulation'. But this erasure of the commons in Europe was just small fish in comparison with the great conquests elsewhere. Colonialism was one gigantic enterprise of original accumulation, of theft and destruction, of oppression and slavery, which formed the basis for the rise of capitalism.

One can say that in the course of five centuries capitalism has erased the common, both its reality and even the very idea of it. Like the history of colonialism and its horrors it was swept under the mat, until the present day. Particularly in spatial terms, we no longer think in terms of the commons. A massive appropriation of the commons has happened from two sides. First, the rise of capitalism has privatized the common and second, the rise of the (modern) state has nationalized the common. All land that is not privately owned is almost by definition owned by the state. It was not only capitalism that erased the commons, communism did so too, by nationalizing everything. Both capitalism and communism destroy or annihilate, abolish the category of the common: capitalism by privatization, communism by nationalization.

Both tend to destroy in their own, opposite, way the equilibrium of the three spheres: the public sphere (politics); the private sphere (economy); the cultural sphere (what we have called the heterotopian sphere). In capitalism everything is swallowed by economy: nature, culture, privacy, politics… Everything is subjected to a ruthless commodification and economization, a true metastasis of economy. In communism, or state socialism, as Negri calls it, or totalitarianism, the same happens by a metastasis of politics. Nature is ruthlessly appropriated, the private sphere is abolished, economy is subjected to political plans and culture is 'purged'.

Today the commons have indeed become a utopia; not only an illusion, but also a *non place*. Think of the commons in London, touchingly absurd cutouts, poetic nothingness, almost total absence. Not even a park, just a green, for nobody, for everybody. For everyone and therefore for no-one. This could well be the best definition of the common: *the common is that what belongs to nobody and therefore to everybody, or, what belongs to everybody and therefore to nobody*. This simple paradox spells out the fragility, the ungraspable, enigmatic character of the common quite well. The common is mysterious in a sense, just as language is.

The Common as Community, Communion and Communication

What can the cultural commons teach us for our investigation on the spatial commons? Can language help us? The most important lesson we can learn from language concerning the common is probably this—we use it but never own it. It is an always temporary appropriation of the common, When I speak, I use a language that is not mine, to say or write words that *become* mine. But even more than that, language is the symbolic order that we inhabit. It is in a sense the 'anthroposphere'.

How to find a spatial equivalent for language. Air? Maybe, since air is spatial but not territorial. It is the only element we cannot appropriate, domesticate, privatize (or nationalize). Oh yes, of course, we have tamed the skies. We have national airspaces, but not the air in it. Of course, even that is not quite true since the Kyoto Protocol. Clean air is translated into juridical and economic quantities, so countries can compensate their pollution by sponsoring clean air elsewhere. But if we muse on, are air and language linked? A clear hint—*flatus voci*: 'the commons' is an empty word, like the empty space it tries to name. Everything is common, nothing is common. The common is almost nothing that could become everything. That makes it so precious. Let us walk on Clapham Common again. It is an empty space in London, and because it is for everybody it is for nobody. Like language, in a sense. *The common is sheer but also mere potentiality.* Here language is again a potent paradigm, as the work of Giorgio Agamben has shown us.

What can the social common teach us, the communities that all of us are part of; from family over clan, to tribe, club, village, organization, neighbourhood unto the networks and e-communities? In search of common ground, while reading *Commonwealth* by Negri and Hardt with international students, I asked students to name the word for 'common' in their respective languages. Some of the Chinese students gave us a revelation as the ideogram for common looks somewhat like two separated hands eating from one bowl (共). This Universal symbol revealed a transcultural universality of communion, the sharing of food as the ultimate basic gesture of community and communication. It is this basic anthro-

pologic act of eating together and of sharing food that constitutes
the core of all acts of communing and communion. All 'practices of
commoning', as Peter Linebaugh calls it, have common meals as
crucial part of their process. They are often the festive moments,
after a task is done. It is the basis of hospitality, and the basis of
the feast and the festival. The Christian Eucharist is a ritualized
version thereof.

One could go as far as speaking about social animism in this
respect. The hypothesis of Durkheim that all religion is the forgotten self-adoration of the community is and remains extremely
beautiful and inspiring, beyond its positivist leanings; not necessarily in opposition to them. The common is the body without the
politic, it is the 'body natural' of the 'body politic', it is not mecha-
nical, not an artificial body, a machine man according to Hobbes'
baroque metaphor. The community always underlies the institution—the *polis*, the political, the public. There is always community before the *polis*, before the institution, and beside, underneath, and after it. It is the pre-political or 'zoopolitical' social body:
mother and child, family, kinship, the clan, the village, the circle of
friends.   circle of family → community

It is this community, this communalism of the commune, that
has been haunting all thinkers looking for an alternative to
capitalism. One example is Agamben's enchanting book on poverty,
De la très haute pauvreté, showing how in the medieval orders,
notably in the Franciscan order, there was a radical attempt to
think of use without and outside of property. The question remains
if the cloister can once more become a paradigm for utopia, as in
Thomas More's book. It can be inspiring but it can never become a
blueprint for society at large.

Here it is useful to remember the distinction between the
three spheres: the political or public sphere; the economical or
private sphere; and the cultural sphere as the common. There are
three forms of utopia. First, the metastasis of politics/public. The
private and the common are swallowed up by the public/political
sphere, the state. This is the totalitarian utopia. Then, second,
there is the capitalist utopia (neoliberalism is utopian, as clearly
shown by Hans Achterhuis) where the public and common are
swallowed up by the private; the privatization and economization
of everything as the ultimate solution. And third, there is the
heterotopian utopia where a cultural institution becomes the
paradigm and swallows up the public (political) and the private
(economic). The best-known example of this is the theocratic
utopia, and these days it is rampant in all forms of religious
fundamentalism, political Islam or Islamism being only its most
visible form.

In any case, the common is *not* the body politic. It is human
social formations as communities. The community is the common,

the common is community. It is this communication and this communion that make up the social common. The *polis* is always the other of the communities. It is the political form of these spontaneous communities. The 'state', the body politic is never spontaneous. It is instituted, it is a system of sovereignty, of law and order, of separation of powers, monopoly of violence, and so on. This is the big lacuna in the thinking of the common today—the absence of a political form, a 'state' or 'post-state' theory, even if the anarchist tradition from Proudhon to Bookchin tries to formulate a sort of confederalism, and Laval and Dardot in their *opus magnum* *Commun* try hard to prove that the common is the highest political principal and a viable alternative. But then as soon as the common finds a political institutional form, it could be considered as a betrayal of the commons, like nationalization of the commons by the state. The political form of the commons is its Achilles heel. But let's leave this big question for some other time and return to our search for the spatial commons.

Paradoxes of the Commons

In our time, we discovered, the spatial or landed commons are inexistent. As said, it is difficult to point to a real 'common place', a 'common ground', at least in the Western hemisphere. Land is either private or public, private property or state property. Except for the London commons, and then some patches here and there. As mentioned earlier, in and around Bruges, there would be some common ground (*gemene gronden*) left, and no doubt elsewhere as well. But these are relics, hardly relevant spaces.

Maybe there are some spaces that almost look like a common or feel like a common. I think of Tempelhof in Berlin. Tempelhof, a former airport near, almost in the centre of the city—built under fascism and, it has to be admitted, of still rather beautiful architecture—is now used as an open space for all sorts of informal activities. However, it only looks and feels like a common. There are some allotment gardens, there is skating, picnicking, even carpentry and other informal practices, but in essence it is not a park. It feels like an empty, open, vacant space. The pressure group 100% Tempelhof wants to keep it that way, but the City thinks otherwise. It wants to build over part of it with luxury dwellings in skyscrapers and transform the open space into a park, which will have a huge gentrification effect on the entire neighbourhood. As it is state-owned it is a common, which people can now visit from 8 a.m. to 10 p.m. But according to eyewitnesses it is still very special, a huge open space of four km². Visiting Tempelhof you get the feeling of the beach, a sea of space, or of a desert, the vastness of a gigantic urban void.

The common of Tempelhof is most probably just a temporary

mirage. And yet Tempelhof seems to be able to give an idea of the common as utopia. Realized utopia. Informal, for everybody but belonging to nobody. Heterotopia, not even the real common, the almost nothing of the common, and therefore awesome like nothing, a feeling of everything, like at the seaside or in the desert. Something almost cosmic, a gigantic void, a crater, a vastness of possibility, simply free space. But state-owned. Open from 8 a.m. to 10 p.m. A tamed, and soon no doubt, also a themed common.

There was a question—when I discovered Tempelhof in a long brainstorm session with two young artists doing a project on this space and its appropriation, transformation, and gentrification—if there could be political rallies at Tempelhof. My instinctive answer would be 'No politics on Tempelhof'. Common space is not public space. It is not the space for public, political acts. It is the space for informality, not for informed, formal action. Only a manifestation to defend Tempelhof would be appropriate, would belong in Tempelhof Common, so to speak. The common is and should remain this almost nothing, like air and language. The use of the Franciscans, a minimalist approach, a temporary appropriation, not possession (I again refer to Agamben on this). In another discussion—after a walk with the activist architecture group Stalker—somebody came up with another beautiful platitude: 'The most important thing you can share is time.' Again, this almost nothing. Like the common should be defended against the econo-mization (boiling down to privatization), it should also be defended against politicization. You cannot and should not politicize, let alone have state control or any other political control, on language, culture, nature, air, and so on. But then again, there is no other way to govern the commons…

Tempelhof contains a paradox. If you let it happen, it will become a park with high-rise along the side and this will mean a gentrification of the entire neighbourhood. If you defend it, by mobilizing Berlin, like 100% Tempelhof tries to do, it will mean a gentrification of the neighbourhood just the same, because you will draw attention to something that should just be there. The common is threatened as soon as you draw attention to it. The good news is of course that in the meantime—it is by now, as I do the final editing of this text of 2013 for this book—the action group 100% Tempelhof won and Tempelhof remains unchanged.

The Universal and the Particular Commons

We maybe should make a distinction between the universal commons and the particular commons. The universal common is what really is owned by nobody and therefore everybody. Like air or language it can only be used, not appropriated. The particular common is a community, a community property, or collective property. One could call it the 'cooperative property', like in the idea of a cooperative corporation, a factory run by the workers, for instance, or even a collective ownership of an industrial building divided into lofts that are collectively owned (although that is somehow less heroic, it is just a way to share the burdens). The squatter movement has always been an exercise in 'commoning'. It is appropriation by use, by living together in a vacant or abandoned building. The communal gardens and urban farming in popup parks have lately become the textbook examples of this particular common, which of course has a link to the universal common of the ecosystem.

Not all commons are the same. Every feast is a practice of 'commoning', a celebration of the communion, the community as such, but when all is said and done it often is a private party, like a family party or a party of friends. The festive communal meal shared in many French villages once a year, with attractions and *bal populaire*, is in a sense a better instance of this particular common. The universal common is not something you can celebrate, not really, unless in a more religious or animistic way. We can invent water day, air day, language day, open-source day, and so on. But they remain artificial. Maybe religions have served this purpose. Religion is another appropriation of the common—God owns it all. We even went so far—in a class with besides atheists and social Christians, also Muslims and a Hindu girl—as to define God as 'the name for the universal commons' (and Giorgio Agamben liked my definition when I tested it with him, so there must be some truth in it...). The Common is elusive and fragile, almost nothing. Even if it is almost everything.

You might think I am getting in some mystic trance here, repeating some mantra. No. Take the example of the city, the liveliness of the city and its very heart—who produces it? Common inhabitants, artists, bohemians, shopkeepers, cafés, the lot. Who captures it and capitalizes on it? The market, the real estate market, developers, and let's not forget the tourist industry, only to destroy the original spirit. Greenwich Village, Soho, are textbook examples of this process of gentrification. And even Brussels' Oude Graanmarkt, my local square, will be overtaken by commerce and tourism one day.

The commons can and will be appropriated time and again. But then David Harvey is right too in his book *Rebel Cities*: The urban commons are created time and again. We collectively produce a nice neighbourhood, a nice *ambiente*, which then most of the time is gentrified. This vicious circle of original accumulation, of appropriation, privatization, enclosure, if not theft of the commons should be broken. Even if all acts of enclosures of the commons are answered by new 'dis-closures'.

Maybe in the digital age at least the artificial commons are ultimately beyond privatization—we can and will hack them and share them time and again… Wikipedia, the largest and most used encyclopaedia ever, is for free and is for all, made by anonymous commoners. It shows how monumental the digital commons and the open-source movement can become. It gives a very good idea of how a universal common of knowledge and information is made by particular acts of commoning, of sharing knowledge, in this case.

Conclusion

The spatial common is difficult and temporary, more a moment than a space—a moment of space. More a use than a property. It has vanished, has been appropriated, read: has been mostly stolen—through the colonization of the territory by big farmers, the state, multinationals, and so on.

As we are all becoming nomads in some way or other: migrant, commuter, refugee, global student, business class, etc., but also digital nomads, internauts, cyber shepherds—the human herds a tweeting swarm—we might have to reconsider the commons. We should maximize the commons because open-source knowledge will be crucial against the ongoing privatization of knowledge and research. Defending the cultural or artificial commons is just as important as defending nature or the natural commons against exploitation and appropriation. I gave the examples of the North Pole and the privatization of seeds.

To overcome or bypass the dualistic distinction between artificial and natural commons, we should insist on this distinction between the universal commons (air, water, seeds, in short nature, language, traditions, art, and so on, in short culture) and the particular commons, the sharing as practice in a society or community or network, the governing of a concrete commons, like a fishing ground, an irrigation system or an alp meadows—the examples of Elinor Ostrom—or just an allotment garden for urban farming. Practices of commoning are always particular, there is no such thing as a concrete world community. Humanity remains always abstract. This distinction between the universal commons and the particular commons (a squad, a feast, an action, a place) is more important than the distinction between the natural commons and the artificial commons (of Negri and Hardt), for the privatized seeds for instance are both: nature and patented genes (hence technology). We should, in a sense, give up the idea of Nature, as Latour tells us in his *Politics of Nature*.

Is this new distinction helpful? Maybe it is. What is at stake in the tenty-first century is to defend the universal commons, in particular the eco-system, the freedom of seeds, open-source knowledge, by the proliferation of particular practices of common-ing. We have to take lessons from the *Magna Carta Manifesto* and the Charter of the Forest: the protection of the commons should be enshrined in law.

The case of the privatization of seeds proves that the 'original accumulation', the theft that starts the capitalist process is not, unlike some phrases in Marx' chapter on it suggest, something of the beginning of capitalism but is *ongoing*. Even land grabbing is ongoing, like in South America where huge soy fields of the agro-industry, called 'green deserts', have taken the place of small farms.

However, we learned from David Harvey that the process of commoning is as continuous as the process of enclosures. It is an important point. One can think of the open-source movement or even the illegal downloading and uploading of about anything from music and films to entire books. But Harvey is thinking about the city, the urban commons. And it is indeed true that there is a certain metabolism—besides gentrification there are a thousand practices of commoning, from a simple picnic in the park to urban activism. Acts of 'commoning', of re-appropriation of the commons are needed. Use, not property, is what counts. Like the people spontaneously cleaned up and swept the ground after the revolu-tion on Tahrir Square. A public roundabout had become their shared space. Indeed, a paradigmatic act, real and symbolic at once. We re-appropriate the common every time we reclaim the streets. Every time we turn a park into a community garden. The common is commonplace each and every time we make a space common, a common place. Just as acts of commoning are the core of the creation of the spatial or urban commons, civic activism is the true core of democracy. It is the re-appropriation of democracy, as the ideal of the rule of those who are not entitled to rule, eternally those who are not in power or in parties, as Rancière points out in *The Hatred of Democracy*.

All this has convinced me more than ever that one of the deeper meanings of the common is indeed, as the etymology dictionary suggested, *munia*, a duty to the community. The struggle for the commons will be one of the most important struggles of the twenty-first century.

Utopia Rediscovered

Ending the Anthropocene

The Many Meanings of Utopia

'Utopia' is a confusing concept. The word has too many meanings. The first meaning is a literary genre that depicts an ideal society. That is just about the only meaning everybody agrees on, as it is the title of the most famous book in the genre, *Utopia* by Thomas More. A second meaning would be the real blueprint for an ideal society, not fictional or artistic, but as a programmatic theory for a practice, like the ones designed by many anarchists, from Pierre-Joseph Proudhon to Murray Bookchin.[1] Third are the small-scale but real experiments in communes over the last centuries, from the phalanstery of Charles Fourier or the *familistère* of Jean-Baptiste Godin to the hippie communes of the 1960s and the urban commons and squats of today.

The fourth meaning is the most notorious one. In political discourse the realized ideal societies of the twentieth century are also considered utopian: communism and fascism. We could call these the 'grand-scale political utopias'. They all turned into dystopian, nightmarish societies, as they were totalitarian from the beginning. This fourth meaning has taken predominance, as these were considered the realizations, on the level of societies, of the utopian tradition. We will come back to this totalitarian essence of utopia.

The fifth sense is more derived: the utopias of architecture. This tradition of utopian architecture runs from the late eighteenth century—Claude Ledoux and Étienne-Louis Boullée—to the 'megastructures' of the 1960s. Architecture was the ideal discipline to give a concrete form to the utopian impulse in modernity. Related attempts were those aiming to realize the aesthetic utopia of art by 'bringing art into life', with the Russian constructivists as the textbook example, but utopian impulses can also be detected in artists like Gordon Matta-Clark or Joseph Beuys. Equally derived, though close to the first meaning, are science fiction novels and films, comic strips, and the like. In science fiction, utopias and especially dystopias are omnipresent, mostly in some form of technotopia.[2]

The seventh, and from a philosophical viewpoint perhaps the most interesting meaning, is utopia as a name for the collective dream images of a better, emancipated world. This is the meaning we find in the works of Ernst Bloch, Walter Benjamin, Theodor Adorno, and Herbert Marcuse. Here utopia becomes the philosophical name for a longing, a mimesis of the possible, the anticipation of 'the not-yet' (in the terms of Bloch).

These different meanings—some would come up with other classifications, no doubt—all the shifts between them and the open vagueness of the term 'utopia' make it difficult to use the term, because confusion starts as soon as one mentions the term. The reader is therefore free to make his or her own classification of these meanings. Nevertheless, the connections between the meanings and the phenomena they point to, the causal chains between them, form a cluster, a constellation, which will keep the debate going.

Let us first have a closer look at the disastrous 'grand-scale realized utopias' (the fourth meaning), 'utopia' in the most familiar and most disastrous sense.

The Three Grand Utopias

We can conceive of the City of Man, the Polis—inspired by but differing from Hannah Arendt[3]—as a complex interaction of three more or less autonomous spheres: the economic/private sphere, dominated by work and labour and the essentials of life; the political/public sphere, characterized by action; and the cultural sphere as a common space of play and ritual.[4] This ideal-typical diagram has it limits, for in a functionally highly differentiated network society the boundaries of these spheres seem to blur, but nevertheless it can clarify a few things. Grand-scale utopias can be conceived of as the absorption of these separate spheres into one. That absorption and the abolition of the other spheres is the essence of the totalizing, totalitarian aspect of utopia.

There are three grand-scale utopias as such. First and foremost, amongst the grand-scale utopias is the totalitarian utopia—in the strict sense of the word—of communism: everything becomes political, public, state-owned. Both the private sphere, the household and private sector of the economy, and the cultural sphere, art, and intellectual life, but also social rituals and religion, are abolished and absorbed into the political sphere. The total abolition of private property and of the family is typical of this utopia. Likewise, it needs to abolish the autonomy of culture: purging art and academia is obligatory, and abolishing religion commendable. It is precisely this that makes it 'total' and thus totalitarian. Most classical utopias are totalitarian or will end up becoming so. This goes for most classical utopias, from Plato over More to communism. Almost all scholars of utopia have discussed this at length—I mention Hans Achterhuis' monumental study on the subject, which explicitly has this totalitarian side as its ultimate focus.[5]

Second, as its opposite, comes the neoliberal utopia. It is most clearly embodied in the work of utopian writer Ayn Rand. In her novels she evokes the utopia of entrepreneurial heroism.[6] This utopia has been realized as the neoliberal society, marked by an omnipresent competition, by competitivity as the highest virtue, enhancing individualism and the economic egotism of calculating subjects. Everything should be privatized. Everything becomes economic.[7] This utopia, often in the shape of 'market fundamentalism', is permeating contemporary capitalism. The political and the cultural sphere have been abolished as much as possible and absorbed into the economic sphere. Politics has become good management and art part of 'creative industries'. Although this second grand-scale utopia seems innocuous compared to the totalitarian utopias, it too turns into a dystopia as it privatizes the commons, it destroys 'human resources'—child labour all around, the sweatshops of South-East Asia, the labour camps of Dubai, but also leads to an epidemic of burnouts and work-related depressions caused by the universal rat race. And of course, it destroys 'natural resources' to the extent that the entire ecosystem is now in danger. The logic of growth to which this neoliberal utopia is addicted, in a finite (eco)system amounts to a flight forward towards disaster. In short, the capitalist or neoliberal utopia of the 'free market', is, like the other grand-scale utopias, doomed to turn into a dystopia. The neoliberal utopia leads to a growing inequality in society and hence to security capitalism: a system of omnipresent surveillance and repression, mostly of the poor. A less dramatic but nonetheless clear sign of absorption is the fact that academia loses its autonomy and becomes a supply factory for the knowledge economy. The management newspeak that surrounds us is a sure sign of this 'brave new world' brainwashing by manipulating language. This hegemony is sealed by the famous TINA mantra (originally from Thatcher): There Is No Alternative.

Third comes the religious utopia. This utopia can be conceived of as the regression towards theocracy. Like in ancient theocracies the economic/private and the political/public are to be subsumed under the all-encompassing umbrella of culture/religion, and will be devoured by it. The private sphere has to be controlled and infiltrated, purified, purged by religion. Hence strict sexual politics, strict dress code, and no free speech, no alcohol, no music, no dancing, and so on. The political sphere on the other hand loses its autonomy, for the religious leaders are the true leaders, they hold the power. One could also argue that religion here in fact loses its core identity and becomes a kind of political system and that religion is just as much impoverished in the process as is the political. Nevertheless, it is important to see how this is an expansion of one sphere, a dominance of one sphere over the others, with the aim of abolishing them as autonomous spheres. One could say that this 'cultural' or 'cultic' utopia is archaic. Since theocracy might be older than the separation of the spheres in Ancient

Greece, it is at least as old as monotheism. But monotheism has theocracy as its utopian past and future (paradise and redemption). This utopia is back with a vengeance: ISIS, the Islamic Caliphate, being its most visible version. But the Israeli colonists too are increasingly fired by holy religious hatred of the Other, and the American (and some European) Christian fundamentalists hope and believe that the end of the world is near, which means that ecological policies should be blocked as they would only delay the 'end time tribulations' and the rapture.[8] The regressive utopia is indeed often mingled with end time creeds and crazes, like in the case of Anabaptist Munster in the sixteenth century and in ISIS today. It is precisely the belief that the world is about to end that makes these movements so radical, iconoclastic, and violent—it implies the need for an all-out cleansing before the second coming of the Messiah (or Mehdi).

In the cultural sphere, only religion seems to have the power to become a source of utopian politics. The idea of 'art into life', the utopia of art, has never really worked, even if we can see and admire its utopian impulse, from the Russian constructivists to Joseph Beuys and beyond (see our sixth meaning of utopia). The artistic utopias remain short-lived. There will always be a Stalin, a mullah, or some managers to abolish it. But art should remain, with a term borrowed from Michel Foucault, 'heterotopian': a space that is other, a space of otherness; a space of play, not a sphere of action.[9] Art can only flirt with politics, and all too often in the past this flirtation has turned sour.

To conclude, a grand-scale political utopia often is the metastasis of one sphere, absorbing and annihilating the other spheres. This absorption, abolition, or annihilation of the autonomy of the spheres is the totalitarian essence of all grand-scale utopias. Therefore, all those who have been warning us against utopianism (and they are many) are right. Or at least have a point. *Exit utopia?*

Revisiting Utopia

The book *Utopia* was written against the backdrop of the 'enclosures', the fencing off of huge pieces of land, sometimes also entire villages, to turn woods and farmland into grazing grounds for sheep (fuelled by the booming wool industry in Flanders). This event, the violent and illegal expropriation of peasants, which took place before the eyes of Thomas More, was the very beginning of capitalism in England. Linked to it was the criminalization of the poor. More's ventriloquist dummy, the storyteller Hythloday, criticizes the disproportionate and counterproductive hanging for theft as a judicial scandal. And he makes it clear that both are linked: it is the absurdly severe repression of those who were first deprived of their means of subsistence. This most obvious of facts in and about the book has often been forgotten.

This is quite remarkable, as More takes great pains to make clear to his audience that he is writing as a man of law, as under-sheriff of London. This is done in an unusually explicit way. At the beginning and the end of the book, More gives his title. The hint is clear: he wants us to pay attention to a crime. And indeed, his famous description of 'sheep eating man', of destroyed villages and a banned population, is almost graphic:

'Your sheep', I replied, 'which are usually so meek and modest in their diet, have now, so it's claimed, begun to be so voracious and fierce that they swallow up people: they lay waste and depopulate fields, dwellings and towns. It's a fact that in those parts of the kingdom that produce the finest and thus most highly priced wool, the nobles, the gentry and even some abbots—godly men— are no longer content with the annual profits that their estates yielded to their predecessors. It's not enough for them that while living in idleness and luxury they contribute nothing to society, they must do it active harm. They leave nothing to the plough but enclose everything for pasture; they throw down homes and destroy communities, leaving just the church to function as a sheep fold. And, as if there were not enough land in your country wasted already on chases and game reserves, these good men turn all habitations and arable fields into a wilderness. Consequently, just so that one insatiable glutton, a grim plague to his native land, can merge fields and enclose thousands of acres within a single boundary, the workers of the countryside are driven out. Some are stripped of their possessions, whether they are cheated by fraud or intimidated by force or, simply, worn down by wrongs and forced to sell them. So, one way or another, it turns out that these unhappy people have to leave—men, women, husbands, wives, orphans, widows, parents with small children, a company more numerous than rich since rural occupations require many hands—all these, as I say, have to leave their known and familiar homes without finding any place to take them in. They are evicted so briskly that all their household effects, which wouldn't fetch much even if they were able to wait for a buyer, are sold off for next to nothing. Since such a small sum is soon used up in the course of their wanderings, what alternative do they have but to steal and be hanged— according to the forms of law, naturally—or to continue their travels and beg? But in that case they are liable to be thrust into prison as vagrants since no one will employ them, although they are all too willing to work: since there are no crops to be sown there is no call for their particular skills.'[10]

This arresting description reminds us today of a crime that had no name until recently: ethnic cleansing. The enclosures More talks about constitute some sort of 'economic cleansing'. Marx has made this double crime the focus of his chapter on the 'original accumulation' at the end of volume one of *Capital*. But even he only dedicates a minor footnote to More,[11] which seems a bit unfair given that Marx used the double mechanism of expropriation and subsequent criminalization of the poor as the basic framework for his fresco of four centuries of original accumulation. 'And the history of this, their expropriation', Marx remarks, 'is written in the annals of mankind in letters of blood and fire.'[12]

So, to make my point clear, one could say that the true message of More's book has been forgotten. Maybe the author himself is, at least partly, to blame for this. The description of an ideal society and the organization of this 'proposed constitution' (to use Aristotle's word for the utopia of Plato in his *Politica*) in the so-called 'second book' have received all the attention, but the real issue at stake may be in the 'first book'. In fact, in the second book More simply revives a well-known genre of antiquity, as is clear from Aristophanes' comedy of the women's parliament, which is a parody on Plato's utopia of the *Politeia* and other well-known utopias of his day like the ones by Hippodamus and Phaleas, all three discussed and criticized in Aristotle's *Politica*.[13] So More has not invented a new genre—he has simply given it a name. Even the form is not new: it is a platonic dialogue. It is his response to the enclosures and the criminalization of the poor that remains important: the description of a 'proposed constitution' without private property, inspired by Plato, but much more egalitarian, albeit still very patriarchal.

It is interesting to note that More takes a cultural place as heterotopia, as paradigm for his utopia: the monastery. So, in a sense, underneath the platonic 'proposed constitution' there is in fact a religious paradigm—the monastery is fundamentally the model of More's ideal society. No private property, common meals, one piece of clothing for summer, one for winter, a strict day order, all cities, like monasteries, having the same typology, and so on. In short, Utopia is a society of mixed monasteries.

It is this detailed picture of an ideal society in the second book that has obscured the critique of his time in the first book. But this oblivion of the true issue at stake in the book, the naming and denouncing of the double crime of expropriation and criminal-ization of the poor as the primordial act of early capitalism, is not so remarkable at second sight. The commons have been erased over the centuries and the enclosures were swept under the carpet of history, despite More's world famous book or Marx' efforts and those of several others. Most discourses on utopia do not really focus on the enclosures or the criminalization of the expropriated poor, let alone on the commons.[14]

Redefining *Utopia* in the Light of the Rediscovery of the Commons

What is more—and this makes the rereading of More's book all the more relevant—these enclosures, this 'original accumulation',[15] this 'expropriation', this 'silent theft'[16] is on-going. The privatization of all things public and common has reached its apogee in our time: the privatization of everything. Not only energy, public transport, public communication, education, prisons, and so on, but also nature is privatized, water being a classic example. The privatization of seeds, through genetic modification and patents, has proved archetypical of our time with the manipulation and appropriation of so-called 'wild' nature. But seeds are not wild nature, they are the product of 10,000 years of collective work. This cannot and should not be privatized. It is a common basic resource of humanity. Now it is privatized by multinationals like Monsanto.[17]

It has also boosted the critique of and resistance to the economization of universities and the privatization of knowledge, leading to a 'slow science movement'.[18] Because also knowledge, the 'artificial commons', is privatized. Knowledge now forms the basis of the economy and is therefore patented and privatized. This 'silent theft', the private plundering of our common wealth, the neoliberal wave of privatizations of what had always been considered public or shared goods—from language to knowledge, from public services to our natural habitat and the ecosystem, from water to air—has been called the 'second enclosure movement',[19] but it could also be called the third wave.[20] It is a relentless flood in any case. We need to revisit utopia, both the book and the concept, to rediscover the crime of enclosures—a crime against humanity and against nature.

This new wave of enclosures has triggered a counterreaction: the rediscovery of the commons. Elinor Ostrom has defined 'a commons' as consisting of three elements: a community, a common-pool resource, and a set of rules—of the community to take care of this common resource.[21] Besides her somewhat archaic cases of Alp Meadows, fishing grounds, and irrigation systems, Wikipedia can serve once more as a simple and obvious contemporary example: the resource is existing knowledge, the community is a worldwide internet network of volunteers, specialists as well as amateurs, and the rules are the editing rules and the way in which the whole endeavour is organized. Wikipedia also shows what the commons can do. The biggest encyclopaedia ever is made neither by a private corporation for profit, nor by the state for political reasons, but is a product of collective commitment and intelligence, by volunteers, and it is free for all. It points towards the commons—both virtual and material—as a forgotten and excluded third.

This much discussed 'rediscovery of the commons' was quite sudden, a complex constellation, an 'emergence', a 'resurgence':[22] from the open-source movement to the alter-globalist protest waves; from 'the battle of Seattle' to the *Indignados* of Syntagma Square and Puerta del Sol and the Liberty Plaza of Occupy Wall Street unto the climate strikers. In addition, we have witnessed the spreading of a myriad of practices such as urban farming, repair café's, cooperatives of all sorts, peer to peer economies, 'fablabs', and so on. As the open-source movement might suggest, this rediscovery had something *sui generis*, the old forgotten category of the commons seemed a paradigm well-suited for the World Wide Web and IT technology as 'digital commons'. It is from the perspective of this rediscovery of the commons that we have to reread *Utopia*, both the book and the concept.

It is by going back to the source, the book—from this double angle, the new wave of enclosures and the rediscovery of the commons—that we can find a new definition of utopia. It has been there in the first book of More's *Utopia* all along: *Utopia* is a radical, imaginative response to the enclosure of the commons. The first book of *Utopia*, as explained, is one long attack on the enclosures and the criminalization of the expropriated poor, and this and only this is the focal point of the contrasting image that More evokes in his second book, a non-existent alternative world, based on Plato and the monastery, where the source of all evil the first book ends with, private property, is abolished. The aforementioned rediscovery of the commons was, at least in part, a radical response to the second wave of enclosures. Radical and imaginative responses to the enclosure of the commons are often of a utopian nature. Utopia or utopianism(s) can therefore be redefined as a plurality of experiments and endeavours in 'practices of commoning', in the defence of the commons against the ongoing and apparently never-ending enclosures. This might supply a post-totalitarian conception of utopia. Is every radical and imaginative response to the enclosure of the commons utopian? I believe we may say so. We could go as far as defining, today more than ever, as utopian all attempts to save the commons from enclosure. In any case, we will need radical, activist, optimistic, and imaginative responses to the enclosure of the commons to face the overwhelming challenges ahead.

To make this rather abstract redefinition of utopia a bit more concrete, let's look at an urban common as an example. Parckfarm, a people's park in Brussels focused on urban farming and sharing, may be considered a concrete utopia. It is both an ecological experiment in short food supply chains and a meeting place for a super diverse neighbourhood, mixing people from very different backgrounds via basic anthropological activities such as growing vegetables, cooking, and eating together. Both ecological and cross-cultural encounters will be needed urgently with the increasing urbanization of mankind.[23] These small-scale experiments should be expanded across our cities and across the planet.[24]

We need to explore the old and new, the real and digital commons. This is the way ahead: in each practice of commoning a spark of utopia is realized. Piecemeal utopias, experiments with the commons, from open source to urban farming, all these movements against the neoliberal globalization are the utopian forces of our time.

Towards an International Legal Order Under the Sign of the Commons

However hopeful, all these bottom-up social innovations—urban activism, the 'small revolutions', 'revolutions in reverse',[25] tiny acts of resistance—could remain only small diversions. We need to intervene today at the almost cosmic level of the biosphere. True politics today is cosmopolitics (cosmopolitan in a super diverse world and cosmic in an ecological sense).[26] We need to reread history, brush it against the grain (as Benjamin advised us).[27] In the 'Charter of the Forest', a forgotten appendix to the Magna Carta, the right of the commoners to use the forests of the king was stipulated: People could collect firewood, apples, nuts, they had the right to let their pig graze in the forest, and widows had special rights to wood. We need a new Charter of the Forest and a new Magna Carta.[28] In short, what we need, and urgently so, is an international legal order under the sign of the commons.[29]

The commons cannot do without the law. An international legal order was Immanuel Kant's utopia in his text on the idea for a universal history from a cosmopolitan viewpoint.[30] It has been partly realized 150 years later. Only partly, but we have an international criminal court, which is a miracle in its own right—not to say that it is perfect, but the miracle is that it exists. In the same vein we should be able, 500 years after More, to juridically qualify and prosecute the crime of the enclosures.

The 'dis-enclosure', both protection and governance of the 'universal commons'— air, the North Pole, the Amazon forest, seeds, the biosphere, biodiversity, and so on, but also knowledge and language—is what we need at this point in history.[31] The declaration of the universal rights of the common good, a text written in the slipstream of the otherglobalization movement, could be considered a first draft, a first proposal for a legal document towards the realization of this new international legal order.[32] However, Dardot and Laval, in their monumental study on the commons, fear that these efforts—like so many efforts and theoretical elaborations on the commons, starting with Elinor Ostrom's Nobel Prize winning seminal work—remain based on a 'naturalism' of the commons, as if it is in the nature of some resources to be common, to be a commons (with -s). They claim that it is instead in the human praxis that the common (without -s) is instituted, and that it does not lie in the nature of things, as if air or the internet would have some sort of essence that makes them common by nature. Hence, they write 'common' without -s, as a commons is not an object. They promote the common as mutual duty (from the original root of the word *co-munia:* mutual duty), as practice, as the most basic, fundamental political principle. The risk however is that by dropping the -s, the common remains a completely anthropocentric endeavour, always based on a community and its institutions. And today it is exactly the global or universal commons, what one could call 'the commons without community' (like the North Pole or the oceans, the air, the biosphere itself), that need protection. That is exactly why we need this new international legal order under the sign of the commons.

Today this remains a utopian dream, more than ever, as what we witness is in fact a dismantling of the international legal order. The climate summits are small and slow steps in the right direction, but too small and too slow. Even so, such an international legal order would at the same time be anti-utopian, as it is not totalitarian, but rather an endless process under always imperfect democratic conditions of trying to reach it. In this dream of a new international legal order under the sign of the commons More meets Kant and The Charter of the Forest meets the World Wide Web.

Notes

1 For the work of Murray Bookchin, see http://dwardmac.pitzer.edu/ Anarchist_Archives/bookchin/Bookchinarchive.html; David Harvey discusses his anarchist self-organized 'confederalism' in *Rebel Cities,* New York & London: Verso, 2013, 84-85, *passim.*

2 This entire tradition is studied in Frederic Jameson, *Archeologies of the Future. The Desire called Utopia and Other Science Fictions*, New York & London, Verso, 2007 (2005).

3 Hannah Arendt, *The Human Condition,* Chicago, Chicago University Press, 1998 (1958).

4 To Arendt's private sphere and public sphere, we added a third one: the cultic/cultural sphere. Lieven De Cauter and Michiel Dehaene, 'The space of play. Towards of a general theory of heterotopia', in Dehaene and De Cauter (eds.), *Heterotopia and the City. Public*

Space in a Postcivil Society, Routledge, London, 2008, 87-102.

5   Hans Achterhuis, *De erfenis van de utopie*, Baarn, Ambo, 1998. Unfortunately, not translated into English.

6   This utopian side of neoliberalism and its roots in the work of Rand and her clique have been dissected by Hans Achterhuis in what could be considered a long footnote, or even a correction to his classic work (see former footnote): Hans Achterhuis, *De utopie van de vrije markt*, Amsterdam: Lemniscaat, 2010. (Unfortunately, not translated into English either).

7   Already in 1944 Polanyi called this 'the great transition': Economy should be embedded in society, now instead society is being embedded in the economy. Carl Polanyi, *The Great Transformation. The Political and Economic Origins of our Time*, Boston: Beacon Press, 2011 (1944).

8   'The Rapture Index has two functions: one is to factor together a number of related end time components into a cohesive indicator, and the other is to standardize those components to eliminate the wide variance that currently exists with prophecy reporting. The Rapture Index is by no means meant to predict the rapture; however, the index is designed to measure the type of activity that could act as a precursor to the rapture. You could say the Rapture index is a Dow Jones Industrial Average of end time activity, but I think it would be better to see it as prophetic speedometer. The higher the number, the faster we're moving towards the occurrence of pre-tribulation rapture.' (http://www.raptureready.com/rap2.html) I have written on the end time craze of born-again Christians and the coalition of neocons and fundamentalists in 'The Tyrant as Messiah', in *Entropic Empire*, Rotterdam: nai010 publishers, 2012.

9   'Heterotopia' is a concept coined by Foucault, for other spaces as spaces of otherness, the theatre and graveyard for instance. See for an English translation of Foucault's lecture, Dehaene & De Cauter, *Heterotopia and the City, op. cit.*, pp. 13-29. For our general theory of heterotopia as cultic space of play and ritual, see 'The Space of Play', our own contribution to the aforementioned book. And, of course, the text 'Other spaces for the Anthropocene' in this book, which contains a summary of this 'general theory' of the three spheres.

10   Thomas More, *Utopia*, available online: https://www.gutenberg.org/files/2130/2130-h/2130-h.htm

11   Karl Marx, 'Die sogenannte Ursprüngliche Akkumulation', *Das Kapital*, I, *Marx-Engels Werke*, band 23, Berlin: Dietz Verlag, 1993, p. 747, footnote 193 (English version *Capital*, Part 8, online: https://www.marxists.org/archive/marx/works/1867-c1/index.htm).

12   Online: https://www.marxists.org/archive/marx/works/1867-c1/ch26.htm (German original: Ibid., p. 743.)

13   Aristoteles, *The Politics*, Cambridge (MA): Harvard University Press, 2005 (1934), II, 1264b26-1269a28; Aristophanes, *The Knights, Peace, Wealth, The Birds, Assemblywomen*, London, New York: Penguin, 1978.

14 It is for instance no theme or term in Achterhuis' *De erfenis van de utopie*. He corrected this in his third book on utopia: *De Koning van Utopia*, Rotterdam, Lemniscaat, 2016. (inspired by my contribution to a collective book published on the occasion of the 500th birthday of the publication of Utopia (1516), a version of this text. I wish to thank him for this honour).

15 Karl Marx, op. cit.

16 David Bollier, *Silent Theft. The Private Plunder of our Common Wealth*, New York, Routledge, 2003.

17 See 'The Potato War and the Slow Science Manifesto: on the GMO event in Flanders', elsewhere in this book.

18 See slow science manifesto, http://www.petities24.com/slow_science_manifesto and for further reading Isabelle Stengers, *Une autre science est possible! Manifeste pour un ralentissement des sciences*, Paris, la Découverte, 2013.

19 James Boyle, 'The second enclosure movement', quoted in Pierre Dardot & Christian Laval, *Commun*, Paris, Editions La Découverte, 2014, 98-103.

20 One could speak of three waves of enclosures: under early capitalism (15th-18th century), liberal capitalism (19th century), and under neoliberal capitalism (since the 1970s), but essentially it is a constant, primordial process of capitalism.

21 David Bollier, *Think Like a Commoner. A Short Introduction to the Life of the Commons*, Gabriola Island: New Society Publishers, 2014, p. 175. I opt for a broader conception of the commons, like most authors on this subject do (e.g., David Harvey, David Bollier, Antonio Negri and Michael Hardt, Pierre Dardot and Christian Laval, Peter Linebaugh): not only the commons as specific organizational form to manage a specific resource (a common-pool resource as Ostrom calls it), but all practices of bottom up sharing and shared goods, such as language, knowledge, the biosphere, and so on. The urban commons, the quality of life in a certain neighbourhood is a good example (taken from Harvey's chapter on the 'creation of the urban commons' in *Rebel Cities*): it is co-produced by all inhabitants and users, but the 'value' thus produced is privatized by the real estate market as 'location'.

22 David Bollier, Ibid. The first chapter of this excellent introduction is called 'The Rediscovery of the Commons'; Part one of the monumental study of Dardot and Laval is called 'The Emergence of the Common' (Dardot & Laval, *Commun*). Stengers too tries to decipher the constellation of the IT open-source movement and the otherglobalist resistance against enclosure in this rediscovery of the commons, in *Au temps des catastrophes*. In collaboration with Serge Gutwirth she subsequently published specific articles on the commons and they call the rediscovery with an interesting term a 'resurgence', referring to ecology and resilience. Serge Gutwirth and Isabelle Stengers. 'Le droit à l'épreuve de la résurgence des commons' in *Revue Juridique*

de l'Environnement Iss. 2016/2 (2016) p. 306–343.
Online available at: http://works.bepress.com/serge_gutwirth/119/

23   See my text 'Parckfarm as Concrete Utopia' elsewhere in this book,
under 'Blogs on Urban Activism'.

24   The practice of the AAA, 'Atelier d'Architecture Autogérée' has
exactly this spreading of urban farming commons as its programme;
see also the writings of Doina Petrescu, http://www.urbantactics.org/

25   David Graeber, *Revolutions in Reverse. Essays on Politics, Violence,
Art, and Imagination,* London & New York, Autonomedia, 2011; also
books like Pinxten, R., *Kleine revoluties* or Hens, T., *Klein verzet* focus
on such small-scale alternatives.

26   See my text 'The Negation of the State of Nature' in *Entropic Empire,*
where I use the term, borrowed from Stengers.

27   Walter Benjamin, 1968. *Illuminations.* [1st] ed. New York: Harcourt
Brace & World, p. 257. See also 'Monadological Messianism. History
as Construction', chapter 5 of my *Dwarf in de Chess Machine,
Benjamin's Hidden Doctrine,* Rotterdam: nai010 publishers, 2019

28   Peter Linebaugh, *The Magna Carta Manifesto. Liberties and
Commons for All,* Berkeley, University of California Press, 2008. See
also the work of Serge Gutwirth and the work of Ugo Mattei on the
commons and the law.

29   'Postscript to the future. Afterthoughts on posthistory', in my book
Entropic Empire.

30   Immanuel Kant, 'Idee einer Geschichte in Weltbürgerlichen Absicht',
in Kant, I., *Schriften zur Antropologie, Geschichtsphilosophie, Politik
und Pädagogik I, Werkausgabe,* Band XI, Frankfurt am Main:
Suhrkamp, 1977, pp. 33-61.

31   See next text on the concept of 'Dis-closure of the Commons'.

32   See http://www.dewereldmorgen.be/blog/lievendecauter/2014/04/22/
proposal-for-a-universal-declaration-for-the-common-good-of-
humanity. This proposal was made by a South American group
around the Belgian activist priest François Houtart; the ideas behind
it are also discussed by Dardot and Laval in *Commun.*

Dis-closures of the Commons (Proposal for a New Concept)

In the chapter on 'The Creation of The Urban Commons' in his book *Rebel Cities,* the social geographer David Harvey admits that commons might need enclosure: 'There is much confusion over the relationship between the commons and the supposed evils of enclosure. In the grander scheme of things (and particularly at the global level), some sort of enclosure is often the best way to preserve certain kinds of valued commons. That sounds like, and is, a contradictory statement, but it reflects a truly contradictory situation. It will take a draconian act of enclosure in Amazonia, for example, to protect both biodiversity and the cultures of indigenous populations as part of our global natural and cultural commons. It will almost certainly require state authority to protect those commons against the philistine democracy of short-term moneyed interests ravaging the land with soy bean plantations and cattle ranching. So not all forms of enclosure can be dismissed as bad.'

We would argue that enclosure has become a technical term for land grab, of what Marx called original or primitive accumu-lation and for privatization in general—from the sixteenth century onwards. With the advent of neoliberalism there has been a new wave of enclosures: the privatization of all things public, such as public transport, communication networks or power plants; and the commodification of everything, even knowledge, but also plants and seeds. Even if we are fully aware that a great Marxist scholar like David Harvey knows all this (and even better than most), we deem it a bad idea to use the same term for the necessity to defend commons against overuse or 'freeriding' (as Ostrom calls 'profi-teering') or depletion, with overgrazing the allegorical example as the tragedy of the commons. We propose the term dis-closure.

To disclose means 'the action of making new or secret information known', according to the Oxford English dictionary. However, besides the colloquial meaning it has in English, this disclosure has to be broadened by the meaning of the Dutch word *ontsluiting* (i.e., 'unlocking') often used for listed buildings. Dis-closing them means to protect, maintain, and open them up to visitors in a sustainable way. To emphasize this shift, I propose to use a hyphen against the enclosure of the commons—the dis-closure of the commons. Dis-closing the commons then is not only the revelation or sharing of something that was secret or privat-ized, but also the protection and caring for a common. In any case we should keep the clarity of the concept of enclosure of the commons, which is their demise and destruction as commons. In fact, the enclosure of the commons and the nationalization of common land—which in Belgium for instance happened as late as the first half of the nineteenth century—led to the forgetting and erasure of the very concept of commons from our collective memory. Dis-closure of commons can have very different forms. We will have a look at some of them to give the term we propose some substance. We start with world heritage. Some heritage can only be preserved and protected by complete closure. An classic example of a common good of mankind is the cave of Lascaux with its magnificent cave paintings, that has been closed off for the public after it became apparent that the respiration of more visitors would eventually destroy this heritage. So, it was closed and a replica was made: Lascaux II. To cater for the mass of tourists that make a pilgrimage to this site, subsequently also Lascaux III and IV were made. This shows we can both keep the treasure and visit it. When the cave paintings at the 'Grotte Chauvet' were discovered in the early nineties of the last century, the first decision was to close it to the public and immediately start to make a replica or simulacrum for visiting. This radical closure gives an idea of what dis-closure can mean for the debate on the commons and their protection. So, this radical closure covers very well what David Harvey has in mind when he gives the example of the protection of the Amazonian. As for Van Eycks world famous altarpiece *Lam Gods* in the Sint Bavo Church in Ghent, a different solution was found. The original painting from 1432 remains in the same church, well protected behind thick glass, and since 11 July 1986 is located in a different part of the church, i.e., the Villakapel. At the original location, in the Vijdkapel, tourists can look at a colour copy of the fifteenth-century polyptych. This enables showing both the interior as well as the back panels of the altarpiece, without denying visitors to also get a glance of the original. Whilst it is presented as a measure of precaution and protection of this world heritage as a sort of global cultural commons, it has also made it possible to receive even more paying visitors. It is perhaps useful to remember that in the cases of Lascaux and Chauvet, I do not take the touristic exploitation into consideration. I just take them as pure examples of closure as protection.

An almost opposite example is hacking. In the tradition of hacking, the colloquial meaning of disclosure as revealing a secret and the meaning of the creation and protection and caring for the commons by sharing almost coincide. Hacking is a practice that reveals and gives back to the public information or tools that are withheld from it. This constitutes the beauty of activist hacking. The many leaks of late are good examples: WikiLeaks, the Panama Papers, Luxleaks, and so on. All of these have contributed to stirring the debate in society on profiteering and dark political and military schemes, such as the invasion of Iraq and the subsequent torture practices at Abu Ghraib, for instance.

Hacking does not always have to be spectacular. I give the example of our book *Heterotopia and the City*. For this book I collaborated with my friend and colleague Michiel Dehaene, collecting the texts of a colloquium on the theme. All authors were paid by their institutions, as participating in colloquia and publishing in books and journals is what academics do, so they were more or less all paid by the taxpayer. We cleared the rights for the illustrations in the book and even designed the cover. So, it was a free book, so to speak. Then Routledge published it and sold it for £ 120 a copy. Of course, most of the copies were bought by university libraries, so this Routledge book was subsidized by the taxpayer a second time, as most university libraries are paid for with public money. This is a good example of the so-called market logic in academia: enclosure of public funds. Socialization of costs, privatization of gains—the golden formula of capitalism. That business plan is of course repeated book after book. I just contributed to a new book on heterotopia and it will also cost 120.

With this business plan Routledge made the book almost inaccessible for the common reader/buyer. And even for the editors—ten copies at half the prize is still 600, quite an investment to hand out the book to friends and colleagues. Until an anonymous instance just hacked it and made it available for free, so now anybody, including myself and my students, can use our book for free. Just type 'heterotopia and the city' in your search engine and it is all yours. That for me is a fine and fitting example of hacking as dis-closure. Re-appropriation of what was enclosed for private gain. The battle for open-source knowledge sharing in academia is an epic in itself. The slow science movement has criticized this privatization of knowledge, as knowledge should be a common.

Another, different example of dis-closing, also in the sense of opening up, revealing, is *Trage Wegen* [slow paths], a Belgian organization that works on networks of ancient neighbourhood paths in the countryside to roam. *Trage Wegen* is working on a network of these roaming paths, and it is literally opening up privatized small paths harking back to the right to cross, habitual law, and so on. So, this sort of opening up is certainly a good example of a dis-closure of a common.

The co-housing or common living is another example of dis-closure of landed commons. Particularly the Community Land Trust or CLT is a truly landed commons: the ground is property of the trust, or the government and the apartments are property of an intensely coached group. The trust also involves the neighbourhood, which is represented in the board. It has several aims: To go against gentrification, as the ground remains fixed and, due to the split between ground and building parts, the apartments are cheaper and therefore accessible for lower incomes, and in the process a sort of community is formed that makes sure the wider neighbourhood is involved.

A wilder form of appropriation for dwelling is of course squatting. Squatting is, like hacking, a radical form of commoning: a re-appropriation of private property, a re-use of empty houses or buildings. Unfortunately, in recent times in most countries, also in Belgium, squatting has been criminalized, even if the needs for housing have considerably risen, not only in terms of number but also, and even more so, in terms of money as the rents and real estate prices have risen to dangerous levels in almost all major cities. This combination of enclosure and subsequent criminalization of those who infringe upon the enclosure is somehow comparable to More's example: First the commoners were bereft of their common lands and therefore source of subsistence, and subsequently they were heavily punished. Vagabondage was severely repressed and the punishment for theft was hanging. This double crime Thomas More witnessed was the true point of ignition of his book *Utopia*.

A popular form of dis-closure since the sixties, but with a significant rise recently, is temporary use. You could call it squatting with permission. The idea is that all sorts of socio-cultural organizations are given the time and space to experiment and provide all sorts of events and services to the neighbourhood during this temporary use. *Toestand* and even more so *La Communa* in Brussels are good examples. They fill empty buildings with intense social activities of local groups and curate all sorts of events. Dis-closure here means trying out possibilities, preparing the neighbourhood for transformations, trying to give the youth of the neighbourhood a place to do graffiti, skate, organize concerts, film screenings, debates, and so on. 'NEST' in Ghent was another example. Time Lab made a sort of self-organizing work and event space in the empty old public library for a year. It was a great success.

All these urban commons try to be open or half-open, for closure is almost inscribed in the traditional commons. In the conception and cases of Elinor Ostrom commons are for a particular community, like irrigations systems, alpine meadows, or fishing grounds. Free access and Free use would deplete the common-pool resource, as she called it.

Closure is indeed, besides scale, the Achilles heel of the commons, for you do not want gated communities to count as commons, or even worse—commons starting to resemble the logic of gated communities. This is not an abstract problem, as we have seen in the CLT's—the community land trusts—where the ground itself remains the property of the cooperative trust. They try to involve the wider neighbourhood by having a third of the board consisting of people from the neighbourhood, precisely to avoid that this form of co-housing becomes a sort of gated condominium.

Besides all the local commons and the different forms of dis-closure people use to simultaneously open up and preserve a commons, it is of course imperative to protect the global commons. Dis-closure as protection by an international legal order under the sign of the common good will be of the utmost importance in this era called the Anthropocene, the era in which humankind is not only the predominant species, even in geological terms, but is also in the process of destroying the ecosystem. Particularly at the largest scale, dis-closure should be high on the agenda: the dis-closure of the biosphere. It is this sort of gigantic protection that Harvey was thinking of when giving the example of the Amazonian in his quote. Dis-closing the Amazonian would mean closing down the massive mechanisms of deforestation as well as protecting both the biodiversity and the livelihood of the local population and indigenous tribes.

The legal commons (as distinguished from the cooperative commons) that were founded in the 'Charter of the Forest', the appendix rediscovered by Peter Linebaugh to the founding text of Anglo-Saxon law, the Magna Carta, can give an idea of the grander dis-closure we will need to protect and give access to the universal commons of the ecosystem in the Anthropocene. This has been called climate justice. The Charter of the Forest gave all com-moners access to lose wood and fruits of the royal forests, the right to have a pig grazing, and so on, but they were forbidden to hunt. This sort of right of access for subsistence and protection will be crucial to avoid the worst overuse and depletion, resulting in the intrusion of Gaia as ticklish assemblage, to refer to Stengers and Latour. We must break away from 'extractivism' and 'agrilogistics'.

To conclude, I hope the term dis-closure can help avoid confusion in the debate on the struggle against the enclosure of the commons. In the Anthropocene, which is now turning into a constellation of ecological disasters such as climate change and loss of biodiversity, protecting the global commons and the biosphere will be of utmost vital importance. Protection by closure of the Amazonian, as Harvey suggests, is the scale of dis-closure we will need.

(with thanks to Annette Kuhk for her critical feedback and additions)

Notes

1   David Harvey, *Rebel Cities. From the Right to the City to the Urban Revolution*. London–New York: Verso, 2012, p. 70.

2   I of course refer to the classic tale by Garret Hardin on depletion of an ungoverned open land by overgrazing and freeriding: Hardin, G

(1968). 'The Tragedy of the Commons' in: *Science*. 162 (3859), pp. 1243–1248.

3   https://en.oxforddictionaries.com/definition/disclosure. Accessed February 2019.

4   Dehaene, M. & De Cauter, L. (eds), *Heterotopia and the City. On Public Space in a Postcivil Society*. Oxford–New York: Routledge, 2008.

5   Slow Science Manifesto: https://slowscience.be/the-slow-science-manifesto-2/

6   Sofia Saavedra Bruno, Claudia Parr, Frank Moulaert and Pieter Van den Broeck. 'Reclaiming space, creating a landed commons. Negotiating access through the Hoofse Hoek'. In: Van den Broeck, P., Leubolt B., Kuhk A., Moulaert F., Parra, C., Delladetsimas, P., Hubeau, B. (eds), *Governing Shared Land Use Rights: Conceptualising the Landed Commons*. Cheltenham: Edward Elgar publishing, 2019.

7   For more on CLT's see: https://cltb.be/fr/ accessed February 2019

8   See 'Utopia Rediscovered' in this book.

9   Elinor Ostrom, *Governing the Commons*, Cambridge: Cambridge university Press, 2015.

10   Peter Linebaugh, *The Magna Carta Manifesto. Liberties and Commons for All*, Berkeley, Los Angeles, London: University of California Press, 2008.

11   Isabelle Stengers, *Au temps de catastrophes. Résister à la barbarie qui vient*, Paris: La Découverte, 2013. Bruno Latour, *Face à Gaia, huit conférences sur le nouveau régime climatique*, Paris: La Découverte, 2015.

12   Naomi Klein, *This Changes Everything, Capitalism vs the Climate*, London/New York: Allen Lane (Penguin Books), 2014.

13   Timothy Morton, *Dark Ecology*, Columbia University Press, New York, 2016.

Political Postscript to the Rediscovery of the Commons

If the renewed interest in the commons remains based only on an apolitical idea of active citizenship and participation, it will not change much. It may, some fear, even lead to 'depoliticization', and in that respect become part of post-politics. Or even worse: the commons may be captured and absorbed in capitalism. If the circular economy of sharing, the peer-to-peer movement, the stress on care and the return of the concept of craft are absorbed by capitalism, they will not change anything. Facebook, Uber and Airbnb show how bottom-up self-organization, sharing and 'commoning' can be hijacked by powerful multinationals. That is why for many political theorists, such as Dardot and Laval, Negri and Hardt, and Harvey, the crux of the matter is: Can the commons become the backbone of a true alternative political paradigm? That remains a matter of debate and one of the stakes of our political theory and practice today. The rediscovery of the commons can in this regard be considered as a revival of anarcho-communism.

In the world of real politics, of pluralistic democracy, we will need a dialectical theory and practice of the commons, where the state, often in the guise of local authorities, and private initiative, often in the shape of social entrepreneurship, find each other in and via the commons. This means a collaboration of the three instances—private, public, and common. These hybrid experiments of cooperatives of commoners, helped by public and private support like crowdfunding, already take place in many forms of cultural production, circular economy, bio-farming, urban gardening, and urban activism. However inspiring, these 'small revolutions' are not enough to protect and govern the global or universal commons. Indeed, as David Harvey has stressed in his beautiful chapter on the creation of urban commons in his book *Rebel Cities* (2012), the Achilles heel of the commons is scale. This is why we need an international legal protection of the global commons.

But even if the commons may never become a political paradigm in and of itself in the sense of a ready-made alternative 'system', then the rediscovery of the commons may still break the neoliberal, neoconservative hegemony by putting a different worldview and a different view of man into practice. This is urgent now. Man is not an egoistic competitive individual but an empathic social being. Additionally, the world is not an unlimited territory to colonize and exploit in a logic of eternal growth and profit, but a finite and fragile commons that needs to be managed and cared for with caution and restraint. This new subjectivity and this new ecological or even cosmic awareness is of literally vital importance today. That is why every common, however small, is a concrete utopia, because it contains the idea itself of common good, of commoning, as the essential trait of humans as political animals (as *zoön politikon*). At the same time it embodies and puts into practice a different attitude towards 'nature' (the nonhumans, the ecosystem). One could even reverse this: only eco-social practices today truly deserve the label of being a common.

The study of the commons could therefore be called a 'Gaia scienza': not just (in line with Nietzsche) a cheerful or uplifting science—because those who dare to look at the world today threaten to fall into deep political melancholy—but also a science that, with trial and error, teaches us how to deal with Gaia, with the biosphere. Therefore, the re-emergence of the commons is, could and should be one of the most promising events of our time.

III Identity and Heterotopia in the Anthropo-cene

Beyond Identity (Statement for a Public Debate[*])

Upon close inspection identity is a dangerous fiction. For three main reasons. Firstly, simply put: you *are* not, you *become*. The term 'identity' tries to fix this 'becoming' into 'being'. Hegel understood this well. In his 'Logic' he rediscovered the ancient dialectic that it is true that day and night are complete opposites but, equally true is: day is on its way to become night and night is on its way to become day. Dialectical becoming. Seeing the identity (on a higher level) of the contradictions between matter and spirit, between the ephemeral and the eternal, between male and female, etc., is what since Lao-Tzu is called insight. But even there, in the deepest and highest regions of thinking, identity is still dangerous. Contrary to Hegel, Adorno has made 'the non-identical' one of the key concepts of his thought: in all identifications the concrete, the different, the deviant, the marginal is silenced. In that respect Adorno anticipates Derrida's philosophy of Difference.

So, for the sake of clarity, it is good to choose. In this debate about identity, I consciously choose the becoming, the non-identical, the deferring of the difference (with Derrida): the delaying of the difference, the refusing to fixate the difference into an identity. Men are…, women are…, the Flemish are…, the Dutch are…—these kinds of identities, based on differences, deliver nothing but clichés and nonsense. Utter gibberish.

This contradiction between 'being' and 'becoming', is reflected in the almost equally ancient and heated discussion on Nature and Culture. Of course, there are the genes (nature), but there is equally as much history (culture). In debating nature versus 'nurture', we must choose nurture because many of the stereotypes are naturalized for instance in the question of gender: male/female patterns are mostly cultural constructs and the result of a process of socialization. Identity is the naturalization, the projection and fixation in a 'nature' of cultural socialization and of processes of becoming. Of course, this is not absolute, there are natural differences, like anatomical differences.

This brings us to the second point: Identity—I don't change every day, so there is indeed a continuity, a 'being' underneath the 'becoming'—is 'multi-level', so more of a plurality. Identity is not a unity, not singular, but a layered and even fractured multiplicity. It seems almost superfluous to explain this on the basis of an example, but okay, here we go: Besides being a man, I am a father, but also *bon vivant*, maybe even libertine, or at least rather 'liberal'. I am an atheist but see no reason to erase my Christian roots as I consider it a rich heritage, full of inspiring moralities, and a key to understand other monotheistic religions. I think in a 'Flemish' way—as I am formed by the patterns of my mother tongue and habitat—but also in a Greek way, as a philosopher, and even a Jewish way, as I studied many Jewish thinkers as well as the gospel, the Kabbalah, and have read hundreds of pages of Scholem, and finally Marx and Freud, and Benjamin and Adorno and Derrida. In addition to being an activist I am also an aesthete. While I am heterosexual, I have an eye for the bisexual in all of us and in all our relationships. And so on. In short, it is not about fixating identity, but about enriching it. Identity is a palimpsest, a text in several layers on top of each other; some would call it a lasagna. In a sense, enriching your identity is overwriting your identity and seeing the tensions and contradictions in it.

This is why 'identity' is also a relational concept. It is construed in relation to others, which is emphasized by Alain de Benoist, well known within this Delta Foundation*, in his lecture 'On Identity'. Identity is basically a social mask. Therefore, I say to the youth: 'Do not seek your identity but set yourself free from it by enriching your identity as much as possible, by assuming other identities and turning your identity into a plurality. Do not try to become the image that others have of you but break through the social mirror. Resist conformism, even your own tendency to conform to your models, fashion, gender, ethnicity, nationality, etcetera.'

Collective identity is, according to the same Alain de Benoist, unconscious until the advent of modernity, which blots out the old traditions. Modernity, with its universalism and progress, means a loss of tradition, loss of identity. So, in modernity identity primarily the collective identity becomes a problem. Alain de Benoist points to capitalism as a major culprit of the loss of (collective) identity. It is difficult to deny. Capitalism has a deep tendency to erases all difference through the universal equivalence of money. This has been aggravated due to globalization as there will always be a loss of identity in globalization. This is why the wave of identity politics that we now experience is a reaction to globalization as a uniformity. We are indeed seeing a sort of epidemic of identity politics. And this brings us to our third point: identity is a dangerous word because it is the basis of identity politics.

The unconscious identity is deliberately used in identity politics for political purposes and thus becomes a caricature of itself. Sociological or anthropological plurality, or plural individuality, is politically forged into identity, in many cases national but it may as well be a religious or ethnic identity, through fictions and fixations. Fixations: the hardworking Flemish versus the lazy Walloon, the Burgundian Belgian versus the stingy Dutch. Fictions: the heroic national history and its own greatest cultural products are 'nationalized' — Bruegel for instance lived long before

Belgium existed and he has therefore little or nothing to do with Belgium or even Flanders, for he was from Brabant, not from 'the Flanders'.

When identity and politics start romancing, it usually doesn't bode well. Identity politics does not want a broadening but a fixation onto a largely fictional national, religious, or ethnic identity: the invention of tradition, the invention of a grand history with heroes like Jan Breydel and Pieter Deconinck. They are two legendary, largely fictional leaders of a historical uprising, recast as a 'Flemish' uprising against the 'French', in the nationalist classic novel *The Lion of Flanders* by Hendrik Conscience. It is forbidden to laugh about it. Tom Lanoye, our famous writer, is, according to Bart De Wever, leader of the separatist party, not allowed to say that '*The Lion of Flanders* is a shitty book'. And the proposed name change of the Deconinck Square in Antwerp (from 'Pieter' to 'Herman' — alluding to famous poet who recently died) infuriated him. It was a good joke, though.

Art does not readily lend itself to national myths and constructions of identity. Because, to stick to our example, novels are precisely the genre par excellence of inner life, ambiguity, complexity, doubt. Nationalist novels are like the history paintings hidden in the cellars of our museums—bad art. Art in service of cultural national identity is fake art. Cultural identity politics is trying to silence artists and intellectuals for the sake of their political purpose. And that is objectionable. Arts and culture are no lubricant for politics.

One could minimalize this. Historical myths and famous figures of the past are used politically to create a continuous, transhistorical identity throughout the centuries. Nothing wrong with that, you might say. But identity becoming political is extremely dangerous. All politics is based on adversaries facing each other, identity politics however not only thinks in terms of 'us' and 'them', but gives it a sort of deep ontological, religious, and often ethnic root that precludes all dialogue. Political Islam, fundamentalism, is a caricature of Islam, but this is what makes it dangerous—pagans or renegades, these 'others' have to be killed to establish the pure identity of the religious utopia, the Caliphate. Identity politics becomes murderous very quickly (after the wonderful essay *Les Identités meurtrières* by the great novelist Amin Malouf. And as a Lebanese Christian Malouf knows this topic very well). One can also think of the Ku Klux Klan or the ruthless fanaticism of Jewish colonists, which is at the same time nationalist, racist, and religious.

Identity politics is feeding civil war. Examples: Rwanda, Iraq, Syria. And that, precisely that is the last thing we need at this moment in history. Once identity becomes political, it ends up in a murderous logic. In Iraq, Sunni and Shia were marrying each other, but once identity politics, introduced by the Americans by the way, got the upper hand, these couples had to divorce as civil war began. This civil war is still latent, or according to some, continuing—ethnic cleansing, systematic abduction and killing of Sunni academics, and so on. That is the problem with civil war: Once the evil genie is out of the bottle, it simmers latently. Think of Beirut. It could go wrong at any moment. In each house there are weapons... To make a long story short, politics is about avoiding civil war.

The difference between Shia and Sunni is almost incomprehensible or at least minute to outsiders. This is what Appadurai (with Freud) calls 'the narcissism of the smallest difference'—I hate the other because he is not entirely what I am. He is so similar to me that he threatens my identity. The difference between the Flemish and the Walloons? I would not know. Then what is the difference? Try to explain it to a foreigner. Good luck with that. I'm not saying that we should erase differences, but we should avoid reifying or naturalizing them as fixed, by thinking, not in terms of identity but in terms of 'deferring': differentiation is not only a difference but especially a *delay,* as Derrida suggested.

A similar debate as the one between becoming versus being or nature versus culture, is the one between Romanticism and Enlightenment. Enlightenment defended universality and progress towards a brighter future, Romanticism stressed the loss and the value of particularity, the charms of the past, and in doing so invented national identity. What we need is a dialectic between Romanticism and Enlightenment. The one cannot exist without the other. We should not desperately cling to a lost identity that we project in an idealized past or a utopian future out of romantic sentiments (as a recovery of history, such as nationalism or mutatis mutandis the fundamentalist Caliphate). We should multiply our identities by embracing the diversity and affirm the genesis of globalization. We do not need to say farewell to our identity, but we have to go beyond it.

Therefore, three conclusions, three programmatic targets: 1) against identity thinking (or identity philosophy); 2) in favour of 'plurality-thinking' (not thinking in 'identity' but in 'becoming', 'differentiation' and 'plurality'); and 3) radically opposing any form of identity politics! Identity politics must be, especially at this moment in history, philosophically (!) exterminated. Or else we will exterminate each other.

PS: In my polemic statement at the time I overlooked the fact that feminism, the LBTGQ movement, the anti-racist movement, and so on, are also called identity politics. I think it would be safer and better to call these 'politics of difference'. Much better.

Note

* Translation of a statement for a debate held in Leuven on 19 November 2013 with Peter De Roovere, Chief-Politic of Doorbraak (Breakthrough) and Honorary President of the Flemish People's Movement (co-opted in the meantime by NV-A) who has become fraction leader in Parliament, and Adreas Tires, from Liberales, a (neo)liberal think tank, in the Delta Foundation—a think tank inspired by Alain de Benoist, one of the main thinkers of the so called 'nouvelle droite', the new right.

Other Spaces for the Anthropocene: Heterotopia as Dis-closure of the (Un)Common

For Michiel,
in fond memory of one of the most joyful
intellectual collaborations of my life.

Introduction

The rediscovery of the commons sheds a new light on the concept of heterotopia.[1] Against the enclosure of the commons, and primitive accumulation through appropriation and privatization, heterotopias appear as what I would propose to call 'dis-closures of the commons'[2] or, rather, as I will explain, dis-closures of the (un) common, the common uncommon. Dis-closure is both the necessary closure and protection on the one hand, and opening up and sharing of the common on the other. Dis-closure is not only the sharing, the revelation of a secret, like in hacking, but can also mean closure for protection, like we do with monuments to preserve them. Heterotopia, also according to Foucault's principles of 'heterotopology', functions exactly according to this dynamic of opening and closure. In all cultures the sharing of the uncommon happens in special, enclosed spaces, where otherness is given its place.

'Commoning'—to use the crucial neologism that has become the core of the commons discourse to indicate the commons as practice, as a verb, not a noun[3]—is nothing but this practice of sharing which makes up the core of the commons. Besides the community, the resources and the rules to govern that common, it is this praxis of sharing and self-organization that defines the essence of any commons. The less organizational sharing of culture is also based on that sort of commoning, and heterotopias in particular have the function to share the uncommon, the strange, the weird, the forbidden, the other. Heterotopia can be redefined as the 'commoning' of the uncommon.

We just have to glance at the examples of Foucault to intuitively grasp this redefinition: from nude beaches to saunas, both radical revelations of nudity; at the temples where the sacred is kept, protected, and revealed; at the theatres and cinemas where the horrors of Oedipus and Medea and all their descendants are revealed and shared; not to forget the cemeteries where the very common and totally uncommon reality of death is given a place—all are special places where this 'otherness' is shared, 'commoned'. The first aim of this text is to make this redefinition of heterotopia from the vantage point of the idea of commons plausible.

The second aim concerns the urgent questions of our time: What can heterotopia mean in times of uncertainty, in 'liquid modernity'[4] and, more broadly, in the Anthropocene? Hence, the question of heterotopia today could be phrased as 'other spaces for the Anthropocene'. More precisely, I will try to show how hetero-topia can play a crucial rule in the practices of commoning the uncommon in relation to one of the central figures of the Anthropocene: the refugee.

When we tried to clarify the concept of heterotopia for our book *Heterotopia and the City*, Michiel Dehaene and I took Foucault's text 'Of Other Spaces' very seriously, almost word for word, and tried to really make a coherent concept out of it, in line with his six principles and in line with almost all of his examples. To have some firm ground to look back on heterotopia from the vantage point of the rediscovery of the commons and to be able to face the question of heterotopia in the Anthropocene, I start with a summary of our general theory of heterotopia (as we called it with some irony) as exposed in our book, notably in our text 'The Space of Play: Towards a General Theory of Heterotopia'.[5]

The Third Sphere: The General Theory of Heterotopia in a Nutshell

Heterotopia literally means 'other place' (*hetero-topos*). Foucault introduced the concept in a lecture for architects in 1967 but did nothing with it in his major works. The text did not appear until 1984, shortly before his death.[6] He himself regarded it clearly as a rough sketch. Foucault's examples give a good idea of the otherness of the places of alterity called heterotopia: the honeymoon, saunas, hammams, holiday villages, museums, theatres, cinemas, library, cemeteries, homes for the elderly, psychiatric institutions, gardens, parks, fairs, brothels—these are all heterotopias. What do they have in common? They are 'different', 'other'. They interrupt the continuity of the everyday.

To outline these other places Foucault sketched six principles of what he called somewhat tongue-in-cheek a 'heterotopology', a 'science in the making'.[7] It is useful to briefly recall them here. The first principle is that all societies have heterotopias but that none are universal. So, Foucault inscribes them as central in all societies. This is crucial because for a long time, commentators had a tendency to situate heterotopia in the margins, on the threshold, even in the realm of the invisible.[8] The second principle is that they can change function; for example, the cemetery was initially the garden of the church, where much of burial practice was collective, later shifting to the outskirts of the town and giving rise to the nineteenth-century pompous neoclassical cult of individual monumental graves. The third principle is that heterotopia can contain several spaces in one, the theatre stage being the key example here. It evokes the complexity of heterotopia in its mirroring and inverting relation to the ordinary world. The fourth principle states that heterotopias are linked to another time, that they are always also heterochronic. Here the extra-ordinary comes to the fore and points, as further discussed below, to rites of passage and liminal space. The fifth principle is closure, for all heterotopias have to be set apart as another space-time. This principle is of course very relevant for my idea of dis-closure. Finally, all heterotopias have this mirroring/inverting function to the rest of society, theatre being a mirror of society and the city of the dead being our destiny even if opposed to the city of the living. It is clear that Foucault is outlining a sort of anthropology of extra-ordinary places. We should take this anthropological view of Foucault seriously. His heterotopology clearly points towards extra-ordinary places, set apart from the continuity of ordinary life. It is usually also a space that is not entirely public and not entirely private, but lies in between, mostly semi-public.

For our book, Michiel Dehaene and I tried to make the concept more consistent, since it pointed to something very interesting but remained a little bit hazy. Because many concepts about space, economy, and politics originate from antiquity and are derived from classical Greek, we thought it was imperative to return to the Greek *polis*. So, in our attempt to further define the contours of the concept of heterotopia, we started from Arendt's analysis in *The Human Condition*[9] and along the way discovered a gem of a revelation in Aristotle. In addition to the sphere of the *oikos* (literally the household, both the private sphere and the private sector, the economy) and the sphere of the *agora* (literally the square, the public space, the space of politics), Hippodamus, an urbanist mentioned in the *Politika*, envisions a third space, which is neither economic nor political: the 'hieratic', sacred or cultural space. In his utopia, the city (state) is divided into three domains: communal land (*koinèn*), private land (*idian*) and a part for the gods (*hiéran*).[10] This tripartition can also be found in his city plan for the city of Milete: There are markets, agoras and 'sanctuaries', sacred squares, which also contain hippodromes and theatres. We called this the discovery of the third space.

The holidays were called 'hiéromenia' (derived from *hiéran*, holy). This time of the sacred is still clearly evident in the English word holiday: holy day. In other words, the third space of hetero-topia corresponds to the sacred day, which interrupts and even suspends the everyday of economics and politics, very much in line with Foucault's principle of heterochronism. Heterotopia is therefore initially an event (in time) and only in the second instance a place, a building (a space). In other words, heterotopia is a time-space, a 'sphere.' We therefore called the collection of all heterotopias the third sphere, which consists of a cluster of heterotopias, other spaces, from the theatre, to the temple, the gymnasium, the stadium and the hippodrome or the bathhouse.[11] The temple complex at Delphi could serve as a glorious visual example. Temporally we also see analogous clusters: during the *hiéromenia* not only rituals took place and religious parades, but also games, in the form of competitions, such as horse races, athletics and music and theatre competitions.

Even in our time, where the distinction between the holy-days and the ordinary days is becoming increasingly blurred, we still recognize the same contours. We still go to the temples of culture on Sundays, or during the weekend or on city trips; we go to stadiums, concert halls, hammams, nudist beaches, cinemas—to almost all of Foucault's examples.[12] The holidays are still the time for culture, sports, arts, and religion. Heterotopia is the space of the cleansing, the feast, of the sacrifice and the ritual, of the gift, of the abundance and the wastefulness of the game, of representation, of the mimetic and the performative.

While we were working on our book *Heterotopia and the City*, at some point my eldest daughter burst in and told us about her Chrysostomos party. Chrysostomos is a secondary school ritual, a veritable rite of passage for secondary school students to mark the last 100 days of school. In my daughter's school, the main event was a masked ball. To make her point, she said the following: 'Whoever is not masked, cannot get in.' This phrase was, for us, unforgettable because it marked in an utterly clear way the specific closure of heterotopia (the fourth principle of Foucault's hetero-topology), and at the same time it contained the essence of the heterotopian in an almost graphic way. To be masked is to be other, masking is 'othering'. That is why children, who are by nature heterotopians, like it so much because heterotopia is the realm of the mimetic and the performative. And because it is a party, it is of course also one of the highest practices of commoning: the feast, the festive. Almost all heterotopias are festive.

It is by giving the other, otherness, alterity, a place that heterotopia is socially and therefore also politically relevant. In short, religion, art, sports, and games are all markedly social activities that we undertake outside the economic and the political, or, phrased more cautiously: It is not the economic or political, but the anthropological, the sacred and social, the common uncommon that drives our activities in art, religion, sports, and games. Work and labour are the characteristics of the private sphere (of the economy) and action is the nature of the public sphere (of politics), according to Arendt.[13] One could say that the activity of the third sphere, which Arendt somehow overlooked, is play or ritual behaviour. Huizinga's *Homo Ludens of* 1938 remains a monu-mental contribution to this (re)discovery; like nobody before or after him, he laid bare the essentially playful dimension of human culture. An awful lot of human behaviour is game-like and the game is a good metaphor to understand all things human, (think of Wittgenstein's language games).[14] Heterotopia is the time-space of play in the broad sense: everything that is not work and not action. This is not only free time, but also ritual behaviour and study, as the term *skolè* indicates: school is essentially free time, time free of work and action. Likewise, artistic creation and performance take a central place in this ritual/playful realm of alterity. You see *plays* in the theatre and you *play* music. This heterotopian sphere, the secularized space of the 'holy days', which we now call culture, or the cultural sphere, is just as important as the economic or the political sphere, but in a different way: as other space, as space of otherness.

In every society these spheres enter into a dialectic—heterotopia is a space of mediation between private and public, nature and culture, the realm of the living and the realm of the dead, between people and gods, between the rules of morality and the disturbances of desire. We took tragedy as an example. Women are invisible in the Greek *polis* in public and certainly in the political space of the agora, but on the scene of the theatre they can be represented as strong figures: Antigone, Medea, Elektra. In the third space a conflict can be brought up that cannot be shown in the public (political) space of *agora* or in the private space of the *oikos*. In Sophocles' *Antigone*, for example, the law of the *oikos*, 'you will bury your dead', comes into conflict with the political regulation of Creon that her brother may not be buried because he has attacked Thebes and is therefore outlawed. In this tragedy, therefore, a conflict between private morality and public policy erupts. The conflict of Oedipus is also something that can be played out better on the stage than in the living room. But it does not always have to be tragic, it can also be comical, as in Aristophanes' *Assemblywomen*. The main character Praxagora—literally she who acts (*praxis*) on the agora—violates the rules because she leaves the private sphere. She and her friends, dressed as men, assume control over the assembly in the early hours of the morning and immediately annul private property and declare free love. In Aristophanes' play, heterotopia becomes utopia and then degenerates into a comical dystopia, with people who do not pay their contribution, beautiful youngsters who have to make love with old ugly women, and more.[15]

Heterotopia thus gives a place to that which has no place—from the taboos of nakedness, from Oedipus to the utopias of free love, from the numinous of the sacred and the mysteries of death to the gratuitous innocence of mere senseless play: sports. It is the 'otherness', the extra-ordinary of heterotopia that represents and shows what else should be hidden. It is also the place of transition, of the body (sauna, brothel, motel) and eroticism. Foucault gives the example of the honeymoon. This brings heterotopia close to the ritual of transition, as it was conceptualized by Arnold van Gennep in 1909: All traditional societies have rituals of transition, from thresholds in space upon entering a house or a temple, to transitions in life (birth, adulthood, marriage, death). In his classic book *Les Rites de Passage* Van Gennep studied the unstable thresholds of these transitions which have to be stabilized by specific rituals.[16] In the case of the honeymoon the transition from stable state 1 (virginity) to stable state 2 (being married) has to be performed through a ritual (the marriage), but there is an unstable transition space (the honeymoon) that situates the problematic transition outside the community, beyond the daily. The honeymoon is this 'elsewhere' of the defloration, the honeymoon is the 'nowhere' (often a hotel) where *it* happens, as Foucault jokingly says.[17]

In 1967, the same year in which Foucault gave his heterotopia lecture, Victor Turner, directly inspired by Van Gennep, named this transition space, 'liminal' (from border, *limen*) if a real transition took place, and *liminoid* if only an interruption of the daily takes place, for example a rock festival.[18] Heterotopia is thus a threshold space or even a 'borderline' space. Because it places the stable state of the everyday between brackets, it must also be demarcated and protected, by the playing surface, the boundaries, the seclusion, the limited access.

Therefore every heterotopia is a space set apart from the continuity of the normal by a system of thresholds and (dis)closures, to protect the space of ritual and play. During a game or ritual, the playing field or the temple is, in a sense, absolutely closed. Somebody entering a football field is in a sense just as much in transgression as a tourist entering a church during a holy mass. It interrupts the game and harms the ritual. *Temenos* means temple in Greek, but literally it simply means: cut-out. Every temple (of culture) is a cut-out from the continuity of the everyday.[19] It is this closure that is so important to set heterotopia apart from ordinary space/time, and this closure and opening determines, as we hope to show further on, the dis-closure of the (un)common in heterotopias, especially in times of crisis.

Our attempt to clarify and limit the concept of heterotopia had a clear programme: Museums, libraries, universities, art schools, theatres and other temples of culture, which are all being reduced to enterprises, these places of otherness in the *polis,* which are also places of deviation, dissent, eccentricity and excess—these places should be critically defended against the experience economy, against the economization of heterotopia and against the political pressure to control them.

Heterotopian Practices as the Commoning of the (Un) Common

Against the background of our general theory of heterotopia, the rediscovery of the commons sheds a new light on heterotopia. What is shared in heterotopias basically is this special common: it is the commoning of the uncommon, the sharing of the meaningful and profound that we should but somehow cannot come to grips with. The common uncommon is that which is absolutely essential to the community and at the same time totally uncommon: nakedness, death, and all other unspeakable things, such as the gods, the ultimate meaning of culture and life, and so on. It is this function of heterotopia that I would like to call the dis-closure of the (un) common: bare life, death, drama, the sublime, fear, the sacred. If this sounds farfetched and abstract then Oedipus and Antigone make it concrete, but it could also be Van Gogh or Rothko. And almost all of Foucault's examples of heterotopias are the localizations of the unlocalizable, with nakedness and transience, love and death at their core. This dis-closure of the (un)common, the common uncommon is the function of ritual and play, of arts, sports, religion. But also the festive sharing of the group itself as the appearance of the common, communion and community as such. Of course the common(s)—of nature and culture—cannot be reduced to heterotopia, but I do believe that heterotopia is the place where the common appears as alterity, and alterity appears as common. Heterotopias are the places where this fascinating and threatening otherness—bare life and death and every other inexorable, inexplicable and/or important and unacceptable thing in between—is housed, tamed, adored, kept, defused. Both the cemetery and the theatre, the two only recurring examples in Foucault's text, are and remain excellent concrete examples of this fundamental anthropological operation.

The term of the 'common uncommon,' which Michiel Dehaene and I used intuitively and rather tongue-in-cheek, could be enriched by more recent uses. Blaser and de la Cadena argue that commons tend to overlook the conflict between the anthropocentric common good argued by governments to exploit resources and the commons as an environment including non-humans, or even spirits, as might be the case in how indigenous people approach the same resource. For instance, the uncommon in approaching a river as a community living beside it, a source of hydraulic energy and a habitat of biodiversity, entails realizing that different actors see a different common good.[20] They argue that we have to become aware of the 'equivocations'—a term they borrow from Eduardo Viveiros de Castro—to fully understand the 'uncommonalities' that are part and in fact constitutive of the commons. The authors also use the spelling '(un)common.' The main thing we can learn from this unexpected and refreshing approach in anthropology is that equivocations and ambiguity are vital in all things cultural, most tangibly in art, which makes them both common and uncommon. For this reason, art is both adored as the epitome of culture and despised as useless luxurious nonsense for the rich. That is both the magic of art and its Achilles heel: it is an ambiguous game with signs and images, which also explains why artists are descendants of shamans and medicine men. Some artists, such as Dali, Warhol, or Beuys, have taken up this role explicitly. As outsiders they deal with what really matters but they are also always charlatans and clowns holding up a distorted mirror to society. Artists are inhabitants of heterotopia—like priests and theatre people, heterotopians par excellence—and because of that they are both revered and despised.

Like the religious sacred, art is both attractive and intimidating. The sharing of art is similar to all other anthropological rituals surrounding the sacred, and it is barely a metaphor when we speak of 'temples of culture'. Even their often deplored 'high thresholds' are not accidental. The ambiguous, open, playful, self-critical nature of modern and contemporary art has fuelled this distrust and has made the equivocations and the mismatches only worse. But all these ambiguities are essential: the fact that all 'commoning of art' is always an unending process of interpretation points towards this cultural (un)common, similar to the iterations of the 'recursive ethnographer' to deal with reciprocal translations of the uncommon inside the commons.[21] Just like we have to decipher what we have in common when we see nature as a common cause from different perspectives and from different paradigms (scientific, activist, animistic), we have to share our impressions of films, theatre pieces, and artworks to find out if we have actually seen the same thing. Heated exchanges are inevitable, like in sports, by the way. Interpretation is the life nerve of all things cultural, since language—a conventional system of ambiguous, 'polysemic' signs—is the core of culture as human element.

Heterotopias are the laboratories, the breeding grounds of these ambiguities and equivocations, of this feast of mystery and meaning (ritual), of senselessness and gratuitousness of the rule itself (play). Therefore these places, all of them, since the dawn of civilization to the last man, are crucial for anthropogenesis: it is in heterotopias that we become human. It is the unending inculturations and acculturations into and out of the human element—culture; and the unending cleansing and mediating with our inhuman element—nature. In heterotopias culture and nature, spirit and body meet and mate. Even Aristotle thought highly of dance in his *Poetica* and he ends his *Nichomachian Ethics* with musings on the softening effects of music.

Other support can be found in the work of Stavros Stavrides, who almost painstakingly tries to solve the problem of closure in the commons.[22] Indeed most commons in the sense of Ostrom are closed. You are either a member of the community governing the irrigation system, the fishing ground, or the alpine meadow or you are not; free-riding is fatal to those commons.[23] Stavrides tries to 'expand the commons', by stressing 'porosity' (a term he borrows from Walter Benjamin) of what he calls 'shared heterotopias': 'Heterotopias can be taken to concretize paradigmatic experiences of otherness, defined by the porous and contested perimeter that separates normality from deviance. Because this perimeter is full of combining/ separating thresholds, heterotopias are not simply places of the other, or the deviant as opposed to the normal, but places in which otherness proliferates, potentially spilling over into the neighbouring areas of "sameness". Heterotopias thus mark an osmosis between situated identities and experiences that can effectively destroy those strict taxonomies that ensure social reproduction. Through their osmotic boundaries, heterotopias diffuse a virus of change.'[24]

But at the same time, a specific closure of heterotopia protects the otherness and the other and it is precisely this 'apartness' that can make it a laboratory for change. This dialectic of osmotic porosity and protected apartness we have called dis-closure. In contrast to the enclosures of the commons—the original appropriation by privatizations of the commons from the time of Morus to the present neoliberal wave of privatizations—we could call these practices of commoning the common uncommon: dis-closures of the (un)common.

Heterotopia in Times of Crisis: Safe Havens for the Anthropocene

Exactly because of such dis-closures, I believe that in extreme situations heterotopia can play a crucial role in a society and a community, to maintain a kind of gathering spaces and even to deal with trauma. It can help reshuffle the balance between the spheres and can be an instance where a weak or non-existent public sphere needs to be strengthened or criticized. It can, in a sense, be a *stand-in* public sphere, without being immediately political, not exposed to the control of politics: apolitical or indirectly political maybe but far from party politics, policy, and the police. As the public sphere came into existence in strange places such as the Palais Royal in Paris or the free mason lodges in England and elsewhere, as Hetherington (1997) brilliantly analyzed, in a similar vein, the public sphere has been kept alive in all sorts of salons, bookshops, theatres and the like whenever freedom and democracy are under stress. It is in heterotopia, where artists and intellectuals flock together, that the critical spirit finds its origin and its hideout.

Here though I want to focus on situations of distress, which characterizes our current situation during this long ending of the Anthropocene, the moment that the predominance and footprint of the human race has become so massive that it is destroying the habitat of humans and non-humans alike, which Stengers and Latour have called 'the intrusion of Gaia'.[25] Combined with ruthless capitalism, neocolonial exploitation, failed states, wars and civil wars, and the ongoing demographic explosion, people are forced into massive migration. Migrants are often considered as unwanted, surplus humanity.[26]

Some years ago 'illegal migrants', undocumented people or *sans papiers* occupied churches in Belgium to claim their rights. The Beguinage Church in Brussels, for instance, hosted several occupations between 1999 and 2014.[27] Because they were safe havens outside the private and public sphere, they had a different, ancient status of hospitality, of refuge. It is no accident that those who have no place to go, who are stripped of their rights (*bios*) and reduced to bare life (*zoē*), in the words of Agamben,[28] take to churches as protected ground, where the police cannot go, because in a sense the *temenos*, the 'cut-out' of the holy place, lies outside the political sphere, the sphere of policing. It is equally no accident that some theatres and universities took over from the churches by hosting protest occupations and hunger strikes by illegal migrants. They are not really private grounds, nor public in the sense of state-owned and controlled, and universities are age-old alien bodies ('corporations' in the old sense) in the city, with their own uniforms, rituals, rules, and freedoms. In that sense universities are heterotopias and should not forget their origins.[29]

This sort of refuge is the opposite of the camp as paradigm. The concentration camp has recently become a paradigmatic space of the extreme condition, of the localized state of emergency; one can refer to Agamben but also to Guantanamo. In our text Michiel and I have cast heterotopia as the opposite of the camp, a safe haven against the state of emergency.[30] It can oppose hyper-politics of emergency, occupation, war, civil war. The camp is characterized by an implosion of the spheres: the absence of the public, reduction of the private (to mere life: *zoē*), the lack of place for the common. But refugee camps too struggle with a weak differentiation of spheres: a lack of public spaces and cultural spaces.

What the refugee camp needs is maybe not so much 'public space' along the lines of squares, open spaces, and spatial representations of politics, but rather heterotopias. The cultural centre Al Finieq in the Dheisheh refugee camp in the West Bank (Bethlehem), provides a colossal example of what heterotopia can mean for a community under stress: it is a bottom-up heterotopia. Built by the people from the camp, it supplies the people with a theatre, a library, a garden, a gym, after-class study rooms, a concert and wedding hall, and so on. It is a true civic centre of the camp and social gathering place but it is also a source of pride and collective self-respect. It is furthermore a laboratory for political education via culture and conviviality.[31] Since it is situated outside official politics it can be political in an oblique, diagonal way: not the way of open confrontation in the political arena—which in the case of the occupied Palestinian territories is absent, in a sense—but in a contemplative, artistic, heterotopian way. Campus in camps and the Garden by DAAR are projects that have enhanced this emancipatory conviviality and empowerment.[32]

Heterotopian practices are not activism but playful transgressions, opening up possibilities. The practices of return that Sandi Hilal and Alessandro Petti have enacted in workshops and exhibitions are doing this. The exhibition, the museum space (Foucault's example of heterotopia as heterochronism) is a way to experiment with these returns. Like the initiative to declare Dheisheh Camp UNESCO World Heritage is at the same time real and fictitious, the process itself is contrasted in exhibitions and in Petti and Hilal's book *Permanent Temporariness* with the razed villages where the inhabitants of the camp, who have dreamed of returning for 70 years, come from.[33] So besides stressing that this camp is a heritage of humanity, it also alters the fixed dream about 'the right of return' of the inhabitants, symbolized by the keys of their houses they have kept all those years, as if one day they would just go back and open the door. But the reality is that these villages were razed and often turned into natural reserves by the Israeli state, to prevent any possibility of return. The museum can host this double movement of heritage and return, which cannot be practiced, but it can be exhibited and debated, also with camp inhabitants and officials. In fact, as heterotopia is always several places in one (think of the theatre), it is ideal for practices of return to forbidden/inaccessible places.

Of course the 'real' declaration of Dheisheh Camp as UNESCO World Heritage would go beyond these micropolitics, to become a hard political fact. Here heterotopia almost literally becomes the dis-closure of an (un)common: an inconvenient truth that neither the camp residents, the Israeli state, nor the outsiders seem to be able to come to grips with, but that needs sharing all the same. Heterotopian places and practices contain and exercise scenarios for the 'decolonization of the mind', as was the initial battle cry, borrowed from Frantz Fanon, of the practice of Sandi and Alessandro (and Eyal Weizman) which was aptly called DAAR: 'Decolonizing Architecture Art Residency' (*Daar* also means 'hearth' in Arabic and I will come back to this hospitality).[34] Or at least: heterotopias supply a protected environment, a laboratory, a stand-in public sphere, in anticipation of a true political differentiation of the spheres. When the house is not a home and the agora is absent, or the school is lacking, heterotopia (the other space of culture and leisure) can be both a safe haven and a laboratory for hope.

A further example of heterotopia in times of distress would be 'Campus in camps,' another initiative by architects Alessandro Petti and Sandi Hilal, a university campus in this same Dheisheh camp. It is a heterotopian school for camp youngsters, opening up the world for them via discussion and art, and transforming the deadlock of frozen 'permanent temporariness' of the Palestinian refugee camps.[35] That is in a sense what they try to do in all their work via practices of heterotopian conviviality. After their many projects in Palestinian refugee camps, they transposed 'the living room' to Sweden: in Boden they organized a sort of bottom-up meeting place for refugees by refugees, based on the idea that hosting gives agency, reversing the role of guest, who should integrate, into that of host, who can add to the culture where he is newcomer.[36] This transformation from guest (refugee) to host proves the healing power of practices of heterotopian commoning. The common meal is the utmost symbol and embodiment of the common and the utmost practice of commoning. Hospitality is the sacred idea of sharing food with a stranger, to bring the uncommon (the stranger) into the common (the own community), by affirming the humanity and the need to eat and drink and share. This sort of micropolitics is an aim in itself, but can be paradigmatic for a larger approach of these problems. Indeed, just like a heterotopia can be the embryo of a public sphere, like Al Finieq in Dheisheh camp, or Campus in Camps, in a similar manner a heterotopia can be a stand-in for the home. Initiatives like 'the living room' are needed and practiced in many forms.

I give the example of Cinemaximiliaan in Brussels, a cultural initiative working with refugees, often without papers. The asylum seekers or undocumented people involved speak about the 'Cinemaximiliaan family', indicating that for them these cultural houses really function as temporary homes and as improvised kinship. Cinemaximiliaan arose from screening films in the improvised refugee camp of the Maximilian Park at the Brussels North Station that caused much commotion in the summer of 2015, as a visible disgrace and symptom of the 'refugee crisis' in Belgium. Besides blankets, tents and food, there was also a need for culture and conviviality. It was an excellent idea to show films because it brings a moment of relaxation, but at the same time it stimulates social life. The initiators, Gwendoline Lootens and Gawan Fagard, continued to show films after the park was evacuated, in asylum centres and later also in private houses, the so-called home screenings.

In the meantime, the initiators moved to a large house that has become a real reception centre for 'newcomers'; not only a living community for exiles, but also a production house. Now these newcomers make films, which are tutored by big names like Bela Tàr and a bunch of local personalities from the film world (Hans

Van Nuffel, Michael Roskam), in which they can often give shape to their traumatic stories. These films are already being screened at film festivals.[37] Through these productions they give these young people a voice, or even agency, empowerment, and emancipation, chances of processing their traumas. These young undocumented people, 'illegal migrants', are also guided in pursuing education and are assisted with their files and papers. But above all they have a warm home and a place in Cinemaximiliaan to drop by and hang out.

This is a laboratory for working together and living together across linguistic, cultural, and religious boundaries (as I could see with my own eyes, as I was philosopher-in-residence there for a few months of personal exile). It is literally an exemplary, paradigmatic experiment, a heterotopian laboratory in globalization, a breeding ground of a new global culture for the Anthropocene. Here the meaning of the formula of heterotopia as dis-closure of the uncommon acquires a new, more concrete ring: It is by opening up familiarity, convivial space and a network that the refugees, with their uncommon, alien, traumatic experience are brought into a new common and that the large community of white intellectuals, artists, and cultural folk involved can in turn become acquainted with a new cross-cultural richness. Disclosing a new common by overcoming the uncommon could be the magic formula for this kind of initiatives.

These examples point to the power of cultural spaces, of heterotopias, to give a place to the common, without being private (economic) nor being public (state owned). Heterotopian politics is symbolic politics, diagonalizing the private and the public. It reclaims the common—education, culture, memory—while giving the private and the public a new place. Or it can be a space of preparing the ground for public space and a politics to come: a space of hope. Through cross-cultural hospitality and sharing, these practices dis-close the uncommon of migration and displacement by turning it into a common, even the embodiment of commoning par excellence.

Other Places for the Anthropocene (Conclusion)

What is the relevance of heterotopia in the Anthropocene? All the examples I have given deserve more attention and explanation, but I have neither the space here nor is it my point. My intention was not to excavate cases, however paradigmatic. My point is exactly the plurality of them, for the reader could no doubt think of others. One could say that the book of Stavros Stravrides is one long attempt to 'expand the commons' by studying 'shared heterotopias', also in the face of the Greek crisis after 2008. Even if it expands the concept of heterotopia towards dissolution, the entire book tries to think this *dis-closure* of the urban commons.

All this proves the topicality of heterotopia for the Anthropocene. It is not difficult to see that heterotopias will be most important in the chaos of this end of the Anthropocene: during the long collapse, there will be an immense need for these other places and places of otherness. We will need these heterotopias as laboratories to invent ways of dealing with the inevitable collapse of our system as the climate catastrophe is unfolding. In contrast to the enclosures all around us, we should pay attention to the dis-closures of (un)common in and during the heterotopian practices of commoning. One could say that in the uncommon situations of the Anthropocene, with the refugee crisis as its almost allegorical symptom, heterotopias more than ever have the task to embody and make the common, often by simple gestures such as common meals, hospitality and by forming basic solidarity networks.

One could argue that heterotopia is too anthropological, too transhistorical, too archaic and fixed for this liquid modernity, for this (neo)cyberpunk age that will be the ending of the Anthropocene. But I on the contrary believe that places such as the museum, the exhibition, the special school like Campus in Camps, cultural centres like Al Finieq, but also the special 'houses' like 'The living room' in Boden and Van Abbe museum, and Cinemaximiliaan and so many 'other spaces' all around the world, will keep their role as *hetero-topias*: as protected safe havens where otherness and alterity are hosted and at home, where the uncommon is shared and 'commoned', both in artistic practices, which always deal with the equivocations and ambiguities of the (un)common, and in basic practices of hospitality. As the places par excellence of sharing otherness, heterotopias have an important, maybe irreplaceable role to play, particularly in the inhospitable landscape of the Anthropocene.

Notes

1　See: Elinor Ostrom. *Governing the Commons*. Cambridge: Cambridge University Press, 2015 (1990); Michael Hardt and Antonio Negri, *Commonwealth*. Cambridge, MA and London: Harvard University Press, 2009; David Bollier and Silke Helfrich, eds. *The Wealth of the Commons*, Amherst MA: Levellers Press, 2011; Pierre Dardot and Christian Laval, *Commun, Essai sur la révolution au XXI siècle*. Paris: Editions La Découverte, 2014 ; Stavros Stavrides, *Common Space: The City as Commons*. London: Zed Books, 2016; Massimo De Angelis, *Omnia Sunt Communia: On the Commons and the Transformation to Postcapitalism*. London: Zed books, 2017; and many others. And see, of course, part II of this book.

2　See elsewhere in this book (first published as Lieven De Cauter. 'Disclosures of the Common(s)'. In Lessons in Urgency, blog on *De Wereld Morgen,* 2019).

3   Peter Linebaugh. *The Magna Carta Manifesto: Liberties and Commons for All*. Berkeley, Los Angeles, London: University of California Press, 2008, p. 279.

4   Zygmunt Bauman, *Liquid Times: Living in an Age of Uncertainty*. Cambridge: Polity Press, 2007.

5   Lieven De Cauter and Michiel Dehaene, 'The Space of Play: towards a General Theory of Heterotopia'. In *Heterotopia and the City. Public Space in a Postcivil Society*, edited by Michiel Dehaene and Lieven De Cauter, London: Routledge, 2008, pp. 87-102.

6   Michel Foucault, 'Of Other Spaces.' (1967) (Translated by Lieven De Cauter and Michiel Dehaene), in: *Heterotopia and the City. Public Space in a Postcivil Society*, pp. 13-30. Most probably Foucault never corrected the transcript from tape. There is even a mistake in the text that survived into *Dits et Ecrits*: speaking in a sequence on the cemetery Foucault speaks about 'le vent de la cité'—the wind of the city; in an attempt to translate this, we discovered it should of course be 'le ventre de la cité'—the cemetery as 'the belly of the city' (see Michiel Dehaene and Lieven De Cauter (eds), *Heterotopia and the City*, (Introduction) footnote 19, p. 26.

7   Michel Foucault in the radio programme on heterotopia quoted in Dehaene & De Cauter, op. cit., p. 6.

8   Kevin Hetherington, *The Badlands of Modernity. Heterotopia and Social Ordering*, Abingdon, New York: Routledge. 1997, p. 23-38; Dehaene and De Cauter, *Heterotopia and the City*, pp. 5-6.

9   Hannah Arendt. *The Human Condition*. Chicago, and London: The University of Chicago Press, 1989.

10   Aristotle, *Politics*. The Loeb Classical Library, Cambridge, MA, and London: Harvard University Press, 2005, 1267 b 30–b 40.

11   De Cauter and Dehaene, 'The Space of Play', in *Heterotopia and the City*, pp. 88-91.

12   Except the prison of course, that was, so to speak, a Foucauldian lapse by the author who tried for once to stay clear of all the rest of his work. It has to be stressed that Foucault never called the panopticon, the hospital or the prison heterotopias in his classical works on these institutions.

13   Hannah Arendt, op. cit., passim.

14   Johan Huizinga, 1938. *Homo Ludens, Proeve Eener Bepaling van het Spel-element der Cultuur*. Haarlem: Tjeenk Willink en Zoon, 1952.

15   De Cauter and Dehaene, op. cit., p. 93.

16   Arnold Van Gennep, *Les Rites de Passage*. Paris: Picard, 1981 (1909).

17   Foucault, 'of other spaces', in *Heterotopia and the City*, p. 18.

18   Victor Turner, *From Ritual to Theatre: The Human Seriousness of Play*. New York: PAJ Publications, 1982. See also a most interesting article by James Faubion in our book on this constellation between Foucault and Turner, (James D. Faubion, 'Heterotopia: An Ecology.' In *Heterotopia and the City. Public Space in a Postcivil Society*, pp. 31-40).

19 De Cauter & Dehaene, op. cit., p. 95.

20 Mario Blaser and Marisol de la Cadena, 'The Uncommons: An Introduction.' *Anthropologica* 57, 2017, p. 185-193.

21 Blaser and de la Cadena, op. cit., p. 190.

22 Stavros Stavrides, *Common Space*. Zed Books, 2016, pp. 65-94.

23 See Ostrom, op. cit.

24 Stavrides, op. cit., p. 73. A similar attempt to preserve a certain openness to the commons, can be found in the book by De Angelis, *Omnia sunt communia*

25 Isabelle Stengers, *In Catastrophic Times: Resisting the Coming Barbarism*. translated by Andrew Goffey. Open Humanities Press, 2015 (French original 2009); Bruno Latour, *Face à Gaia, Huit Conférences sur le Nouveau Régime Climatique*. Paris: La Découverte, 2015.

26 Bauman, *Liquid Times: Living in an Age of Uncertainty*. The chapter on migration is blood-stirring.

27 See for example the newspaper De Standaard: http://www.standaard. be/cnt/3r1pfvmc or national television: https://www.vrt.be/vrtnws/nl/2014/08/12/opnieuw_ asielzoekersinbrusselsebegijnhofkerk-1-2058591/

28 Giorgio Agamben, *Homo Sacer: Sovereign Power and Bare Life*. Stanford, CA: Stanford University Press, 1998.

29 In that tradition, academic freedom should provide intellectuals the freedom to speak up against the powers that be, without fearing repression. The 'temples of culture,' and the 'temples of science' are supplying a free space that can and should assure the right to protest from sacred ground. This academic freedom is constantly under pressure.

30 De Cauter and Dehaene, op. cit., pp. 97-98.

31 Alessandro Petti and Sandi Hilal, *Permanent Temporariness*, Stockholm: Art and Theory Publishing, 2018, p. 178; p. 275.

32 See: https://www.unrwa.org/newsroom/features/common-display-campus-camps-initiatives and http://www.decolonizing.ps/site/present-returns-al-finieq/ (both accessed July 2020)

33 Petti and Hilal, *Permanent Temporariness*, pp. 250-260. The exhibition was on show in the Van Abbe Museum, Eindhoven, in spring 2019.

34 Decolonizing Architecture Art Residency/ Alessandro Petti, Sandi Hilal and Eyal Weizman. *Architecture After Revolution*. Berlin: Sternberg Press, 2013.

35 http://www.campusincamps.ps/ (accessed July 2020)

36 Petti and Hilal, op. cit., pp. 359-369.

37 http://www.cinemaximiliaan.org/ (accessed July 2020)

Toothpaste and Taboo (Letter to the Newcomers of Cinemaximiliaan)

Dear Cinemaximiliaan Family, I wish to thank you all for the warm welcome and hospitality you extended towards an exuberant and straightforward philosopher, by writing you an exuberant and straightforward letter, to explain myself and my philosophical approach a bit more, on things that might concern you as 'newcomers'. Let me start with the situation that led to this letter.

On the second day of my residency here at Cinemaximiliaan, as an asylum-seeking philosopher, as it were, I suddenly got fed up with having no toothpaste. I had asked you to buy some when you, Goran, passed by to go to the shop earlier and asked me kindly if I needed anything. But you said there was a lot of toothpaste upstairs, but later you forgot of course, then I asked you, dear Fatma and you also forgot. I could not go and steal toothpaste myself, could I? So, after more than 24 hours without toothpaste I said, half-jokingly, that I was fed up, and when I finally got some toothpaste, we started a meditation on culture and cleanliness.

Lubnan—then a still undocumented Iraqi refugee—you said that culture is about being clean, about an idea of cleanliness. Inner and outer cleanliness. Purity of the body and purity of the soul. Yes, I said, the other is always dirty, nature is dirty. Culture, my culture is clean, halal, kosher, pure, right. Of course, there is truth in it: everything that lives stinks. Metabolism is dirty business. So, the human animal needs a lot of hygiene—because naked ape very sweaty. Fatma, you added that in warm countries like Somalia, this is essential.

Then we came to secrets, because culture is also about hiding, about hiding all that is natural, starting with nakedness. Let alone all our desires. I quoted one of my favourite phrases: 'Give up your secrets and become an untouchable.' Dangerous, foolish wisdom. Madness, really. I explained that it is your secrets that make you weak, vulnerable to social control, to public exposure, to your enemies who can blackmail you with your secrets. But it is of course also ambiguous, as untouchable also means pariah, outcast, outlaw. To be an outcast is an ugly position. Fatma, you objected fiercely that you could get killed in Somalia and many traditional cultures, if you did not hide your secrets. You challenged me if I was willing to die. Well, to reply I started a philosophical speech with bits and pieces I subsequently turned into this overlong epistle.

You need to be with many to change anything; that is an important lesson from all the emancipation struggles in history. You need to be with many to emancipate and break open the oppression of a culture. The Iranian women fighting the veil came to my mind but I decided not to mention them—so as not to shock you, my beloved Fatma, wearing the veil—or the Saudi women fighting for driving licenses. They won. I believe I mentioned the suffragettes, who marched on the streets, went to jail, burned houses, vandalized paintings, to get the vote. And lo and behold, they got the vote. So, yes, emancipation of the oppressions, conventions, secretiveness, and taboos of a culture is a collective task.

But there is also personal work to be done. You need a philosophical attitude towards your own culture, its conventions, prohibitions, and creeds, to free your inner thinking. That is emancipation. Kant's famous 'dare to think'. Philosophy knows no taboos. It breaks down, criticizes, 'deconstructs' common sense, dogma, convention, and taboo. That is why so many philosophers were prosecuted, starting with Socrates, who had to drink the poison chalice for not recognizing the gods and leading the youth astray. There are no holy books for philosophy, no dogmas, or taboos. For philosophy, all books are holy in a sense and everything is worth questioning. Culture means seeing the relativity of cultures. Civilization means seeing the relativity of civilization. There is, as far as I know, no other discipline that has made this highest demand so much its very own as philosophy. If we do not become somehow philosophical about cultures, we will kill each other. Identity is a killer.

Give up your identity to become what you are called to become: a human being, a human, a humanoid. More or less. Anthropogenesis, the process of becoming human, is a never-ending task, both in the phylogenetical and ontogenetical sense. Sorry for being difficult. Just a joke, to tease you with difficult words and to prove to you they don't bite. It means both for the development of the species (phylogeny) and the individual in his/her development (ontogenesis). But what I'm trying to say is this, in all possible senses and directions: There is only one culture and it is human culture, humane culture, humanoid. More or less.

We are all newcomers, in a sense. We are not all without papers, but we are all 'in bad papers'—a Flemish expression for being in a difficult, dangerous, ugly situation—with climate change, the ongoing demographic explosion, and the many wars of capitalism against Mother Earth and its inhabitants, human and nonhuman, and the mass migration that comes with it. Mother Earth does not really exist, Gaia is just a name. But because we gave up believing that she was our mother, we are now destroying her.

In the face of the permanent ecological disasters and mass migration caused by the combination of carbon- and waste-based capitalist growth, ruthless wars, and the ongoing demographic explosion, I would almost call for a new mystical pantheism or a sort of neo-animism. We must start a new civilization now. There is simply no other way. Let us at least play the best we can. Just imagine that with the commons movement we start to colonize the world in an inverted way: dis-closures of the un-commons, undoing of the enclosures. Heterotopian environments such as Cinemaximiliaan can, with open-mindedness and hospitality, be testing grounds for this new world civilization, this new civility. Maybe love can save us, the love of the commons, the common of love, which we all have in common. If we dare to share. Hospitality is vital today more than ever. Sounds cheesy, I know, but you do it. People of Cinemaximiliaan, Respect.

When there is true love and true respect, taboos are no longer necessary. Some rules, maybe. 'Do not do unto others what you do not want others to do to you', said rabi Hillel. Buddha, Christ, Mohammed, Kant, they all agreed on this. So? It is crystal-clear what we must do.

Cross-cultural encounters can be wonderful and enriching. I will never forget how a Hindu student, Rajani Balasubramanian, gave my first course on the commons an entirely new spiritual meaning. I could give you other examples, like the Chinese students who taught me the ideogram for the commons: two separate hands eating from the same bowl. The essence of commoning. Of course, we sometimes will have differences, or even quarrels. 'Future shock is culture shock', is my phrase for it. Shall I tell you the story of Anissa? One day she—a grown-up Belgo-Moroccan woman in her mid-thirties, leftist with lots of commit-ment for the Palestinian cause, mother of two, not wearing the veil—at some point in class and I don't remember how we got there, said: 'The Qur'an is written by an illiterate, dictated by an angel and is literally the word of God.' I replied: 'Dear Anissa, illiterates do not write books, angels do not exist, and God cannot speak for he has no vocal cords.' She claimed I did not have the right to say that. I looked at her and said: 'Anissa, I am a philosopher, I have a duty to say what I think. This whole story of Mohammed being illiterate and the angel dictating him the true word of Allah means only one thing: It means to tell in a metaphorical way, that this book, the Qur'an, is a most important book, a holy book.' We got over it. The Palestinian cause, mutual respect, and liking helped us to move on. You could also say that it was love that helped us to overcome this incident.

But you see, the shock of the future in a globalizing world will be a bombardment of culture shocks. We will have to learn to live with it. Exercises in culture shocks is what we need. We will have to live with these culture shocks of meeting across different nationalities, religions, and cultures. Not always easy. But just look around, the Cinemaximiliaan family is doing fine. And it under-scores my point, that it is in heterotopias such as this one that this new civilization I was dreaming of, can be experimented with. Let us think and drink and eat and dance together, and make beautiful things together, like the amazing films you, 'illegal migrants', make here. You, beautiful people. Let's be brave and face this ugly world with all the love and energy we have in us. And we will have to include nonhumans too, in this holy communion. A superhuman task. Intercultural interspecies animist commoning is badly needed, but actually quite simple when you look at it. It is what we've been doing for ages. Think of Lubnan and his kitten. She is following him everywhere in the house and in the courtyard and he is watching her every move, feeding and cuddling her. He calls her 'my daughter'. Interspecies love is a way towards animist commoning. Intercultural love and hospitality are what you practice here every day. We must start this new civilization somehow. That is what I try to do in my courses, by making them festive. By making the common both form and content of every-thing we do. With three dimensions, three ecologies: a new subjectivity, new social relations, and a new attitude to the biosphere and all that is in it. Here and Now. (See you at dinner).

IV Considerations on Activism

Mary Poppins and the Climate Strikers

The concept of politics of the French philosopher Jacques Rancière is brilliant, but difficult to grasp. For him, politics is a moment in which the natural order, in which everyone knows his or her place, is interrupted. A moment when a group that is excluded from governing demands a voice. This is accompanied by a misunderstanding. The goal is to undo an injustice. In that moment where noise becomes voice, the new group, as a new political subject, proves the principle of equality and that is the only real meaning of democracy for Rancière. All the rest, just about everything we consider to be real politics, he calls 'police', governance, so to speak.

That remains abstract. To illustrate his theory to my students, to make it concrete and palpable, I referred to *Mary Poppins* one day. In the film, the character Winifred Banks, the mother of the unruly children, is not only a chattering and submissive wife, but also a suffragette. She knows full well that she helps make history by taking to the streets for women's suffrage. 'Our daughters' daughters will adore us', she sings. Hilarity when we watched the video...

That was an eye-opener for the students. Winifred Banks is a new political subject, that's obvious. She literally turns her noise, women's chattering, into a voice, the voice, the ballot, and wants to undo an injustice (*le tort*)—that women are only half adults. There is also a misunderstanding (*la mésentente*): Mister Banks, the banker with the bowler hat, doesn't understand anything or thinks it is all just nonsense. And the natural order is broken—the woman at the fireplace caring for the children, the man at work. It is just a mirage, now that the woman becomes an emancipated activist. The entire Rancière is in there. (In fact, it is Mary Poppins who is called in because of course Winifred has little time for her children, who became unruly in the process. That could be the less feminist side of the film, but that is not my point here, and then again, she is a strong woman, independent like few women are, and she gives them a most unorthodox education).

In my attempt to make it clear to the students that the suffragette movement was more than a funny side plot in a musical for children, and to fuel their feminism, I referred to Mary Richardson, who in 1914 vandalized the Rokeby Venus of Velázquez in the National Gallery. I said I found that political vandalism just as impressive, even as an art historian, and had someone google the vandalized painting so that they could see for themselves, and feel what it is like, carving into that painting, into that body. In it you can see the radicality of the suffragette movement: How it mutilated that naked female body to address the eternal aestheticization and eroticization of women and to give a voice to the female anger about it. With her outrage, Mary Richardson almost singlehandedly, so to say, put an end to the eternal *'sois belle et tais-toi'*. In any case, she was a raging suffragette.

This year I found an even better example: Greta Thunberg, Anuna De Wever, and the other climate strikers. Children who do not yet have the right to vote give us a wake-up call. They are both subjects of debate and the bearers of a new hope. They interrupt the natural order, in which minors should legally attend school and as children do not exist in politics. Therefore, they become political subjects par excellence. They address the greatest fiasco of our time; that for decades we have failed to intervene to prevent ecological disaster. The misunderstanding? It manifests itself in the disdain of right-wing politicians and opinion makers and their followers and trolls on social media. They just want them out of the way. They want to silence them by contempt.

The example of Thunberg and De Wever, my new heroines, shows us how refreshing Rancière's concept of politics remains. What a stark contrast with the lame spectacle that party politics stages every day. As proof of equality, we could take the lesson Greta Thunberg taught the great of the earth in Davos: 'I don't want your hope, I want you to panic. I want you to take action, as if the house were on fire, because it is.' And her anger is as beautiful as that of Mary Robinson. Winifred Banks would be proud of this granddaughter! The tiniest, frailest world-historical personality (to speak with good old Hegel) since times immemorial, I would think. For that is what she has become: a world-historical personality. What a girl!

Those climate strikers, these non-voting, school-age minors who skip school to raise their voices—that's a real political moment. The only meaning of democracy, in Rancière's terms. Now let's hope the so-called adult politicians listen and finally do their homework.

(De Standaard, May 9, 2019)

Theses on Art and Activism in the Age of Globalization

0

Politics, in the broad sense, is the discussion about and the practice of the good life in the *polis* (Aristotle). In a narrow sense, it is the process by which those who are not entitled to govern—by birth, rank, riches, class, gender, colour, religion, ethnicity—are coming to the fore (Rancière). The political moment, the essence of democracy, is the moment when they leave their assigned place, and turn their noise into voice. In doing so they correct a misunderstanding and undo an injustice. Politics is about this exclusion/inclusion. Democracy is the empowerment of the powerless. The making of a common world. The rest is 'police' or policy.

What is action? Action is speaking and doing things (mostly together with others) in the public sphere as 'space of appearance'. This action itself makes and shapes the public sphere, often by turning public space into a political space (Arendt & Butler).

What is activism? Activism is a form of civil action outside of party politics for the common good, to fight injustice, to make the world a better place. Ideally, all activism takes place on three levels: on the ecological, the social, and the subjective level. It should create a new environment, a new social bond, and a new subjectivity (the three ecologies of Guattari).

1

There is only one real form of activism and that is political activism. Action, being a deed in the public sphere, the space of appearance, should take place in the political sphere. Therefore, political activism is the only real form of activism. (By 'real' I mean effective, efficient, purposeful). Artistic activism is almost never real, for it is not action but 'acting', a play in the cultural sphere, the sphere of the mimetic and the performative.

2

Art and culture, the cultic: ritual and play, arts, religion, and sports, constitute a sphere outside, besides, between, the private sphere, the economy, and the public sphere, the political. It is the sphere for sharing the uncommon, the otherness: the commoning of the common uncommon—think of birth, death, the cosmos and every other weird thing and encounter with strangeness and estrangement between. Art is communion of the uncommunicable.

Artists reside on the threshold of politics, by mediating the all too private in an explicit, public way. That is why politicians so often want to silence them.

3

Imagination is rich, ambiguous, amoral—action is moral, straightforward, poor (in imagination). Therefore, good committed art is rare and problematic, committed artists are common and necessary, as alert citizens. The political has an aim—art is aim in itself.
    The task of art is not to change reality but to show and evoke it. The mimetic of art is the true power of art, its true task: reshuffling the sensible (Rancière). The 'performative' in art is the sharing of the 'common uncommon' (from Oedipus to the present) as mediation between the private sphere (the space of hiding) and the public sphere (the space of appearance). The performance of art—the art performance—has very little political performativity.

4

However, the rare moments when the imagination of art and purposeful activism truly mate, are to be cherished as the locus of an activist imagination. In that particular spot, that niche, activist artists can do wonders for social movements, for they inject creativity and imagination into social action. By bringing a playful element to an action and injecting activism with aesthetics, artists can surely contribute a great deal: by making actions fun to do and subversive too (think of the clowns army invented by the Laboratory for Insurrectionary Imagination, for instance, and other work by them). The playfulness subverts the 'police', the artistic performance creates public awareness and forces institutions to change, to undo a wrongdoing (like Shell being a sponsor of Tate Modern). And most of all, artists can make actions mediagenic.

5

The public sphere is today more than ever the virtual space of the media. Street protests and all forms of action turn open space into truly public, i.e., political space, only if they are reported in the media. 'Publishing', making things public, mostly by texts, can change the game. Here artists and all cultural actors can prove most useful, as public intellectuals. The first task of public intellectuals in the post 9/11 era is 'meta-activism': acting against the criminalization of activism.

6

Activism is always local, at most 'glocal'. Global activism is a long shot. But, in the age of globalization, it is where we have to get to. You cannot stop the American invasion of Iraq, but you can stop your university from collaborating with the Israeli police. You cannot save the Amazon, but you can save a few trees near you. And, if all trees near us are saved, and all universities stop collaborating with Israel, the world will have changed.

7

Art is part and parcel of the cultural middle-class spectacle. All attempts towards 'exodus' (away from the institutions and temples of culture into real life) have proved pretty vain—commitment as gesture. However, as every monument of culture is at the same time a document of barbarism (Benjamin), art can hugely contribute to the cultural critique and (ecological, feminist, postcolonial) awareness. One of the tasks of art is to digest, deconstruct, decolonize the past. That is the antitraditional in the tradition of art, the transmission of recalcitrance, the habit of 'brushing history against the grain' (Benjamin). The avant-garde, as 'the self-criticism of the art institution' (Peter Bürger), might be dead as a dodo, but the transmission of anti-traditionalism, the culture of the self-criticism of culture, is alive and kicking, and will hopefully never die.

8

New alliances between socio-political work and culture are charming, but they tend to be amateurish, inconsequential forms of social work, mostly unpolitical. However, social-artistic work with the disenfranchised, the poor, the discriminated (because of colour, gender, ethnicity, religion), the migrants, the newcomers, the 'illegal migrants' or 'undocumented persons', and so on, can have immense emancipatory force of empowerment and agency. At the moment, this social-artistic hospitality gives a place and voice to the disenfranchised, it *becomes* political. This becomes tangible when these cultural places of refuge are repressed (by police raids for instance).

9

Urban activism is a laudable form of activism for it brings enthusiasm and creativity, conviviality, and social ecology to urban interstices. It combines mixing of cultures with urban ecology (urban gardening, short chains). It gives citizens agency.

But alas, for the most part it has been instrumental to the neoliberal urban agenda. Urban activism has been used and abused to make neighbourhoods swallow neoliberal cleansing operations—the creative city for the creative classes—and for gentrification, if they were not engines of gentrification themselves. And if they save a building, for instance, it is turned into corporate plus value anyway. So, urban activism, relational art, process art, and so on have proved, when all is said and done, almost always, to be dangerous liaisons with the powers that be.

10

Retreat into *Heterotopia?* Yes! Why not? Art and culture should be defended against the neoliberal logic of marketing and management. Temples of cultures are not enterprises.

As art and cultural institutions constitute a sphere outside, but also between, the sphere of the private (economy) and the public (the political), all sorts of experiments are appropriate there.

11

Art can change perception only in a sort of slow motion, almost in retrospect. Art's political value is extremely indirect. The function of art remains its 'functionlessness' (Adorno). The visual arts can, maybe, reinvent themselves as an anthropological practice, mapping and documenting processes and events in poetico-political ways.

Some artists (very few) leave the art world, often with beating drums and slamming doors, to become part of movements, insurrections, occupations, and become activists-artists who give talks and workshop about their actions in cultural institutions and art schools, surviving by eating out of the hands of the institution they left.

12

The university is more and more regarded as a base for the knowledge economy. But knowledge and cultural experience should be common. Slow science now! The battle for art schools is on. Let us defend their heterotopian character.

13

The Struggle for the commons is the most urgent struggle of our time. To stop the enclosure and destruction of the commons is the ultimate task of activism today. Even art cannot remain indifferent here. Artists, as concerned, informed, alert, free, well-known, sometimes even famous citizens, have a special task here, as public figures they should speak out much more.

14

The beauty of the common is its sheer potentiality. It becomes actual in every practice of sharing and re-appropriation. We re-appropriate the common every time we reclaim the streets. Art can contribute to spreading the spirit of self-organization and the awareness of the universal, global commons. Above all it can embody the idea that commoning of the universal (un)common is an aim in itself. Art can evoke its potentiality; art is this opening of polysemic potentiality. Think of poetry: showing the 'linguicity' of language (the work of Agamben, in the footsteps of Benjamin). Or just think of the platitude about poetry of Verlaine: '*de la musique avant toute chose*'. Artists, make music before anything else (*mausikos*: all art is of the Muses)!

15

'Let it be us, Artists, who save the world by celebrating life.' Karel Appel was maybe overstating it in an ecstatic way when he said this (if he said it at all), but there is truth in it. Turning life into an artwork will never really work (life is not an artwork). Artists, however, cannot but attempt to do so.

Art should never forget its heterotopian festiveness, its belonging to the cultic, the other space-time of the 'holy days'. Artists are by nature heterotopians, inhabitants of other space-times, representative of alterity. That is why they are at the same time despised as useless, eccentric fools and revered as generous geniuses. Their political message is to make music with the noise of the uncommunicable, of the nameless; to give voice to the terrible noise that surrounds us. It will therefore often, and maybe forever and a day, be for the few.

Politics on the other hand is sober and for everybody and for every day. If the global commons can be saved, it will not be with intoxicating dreams of a 'posthistorical' utopia but with real politics.

Da capo: there is only one real form of activism and it is political activism…

Blogs on Urban Activism in Brussels*

From Hotel Central to Picnic the Streets: A Panorama of Urban Activism in Brussels
(*De Wereld Morgen,* March 25, 2014)

In the 80s Brussels was a quiet, slowly decaying city, having a hard time coping with the emptying out of the city, the so-called 'city flight' or 'urban exodus', which started in the 60s, with the advent of the car and the suburbanization of Belgium. The city didn't seem to have a clue how to make the transition from an industrial to a post-industrial era. A London friend of mine was charmed by this slumbering metropolis of the second or third tier. 'Let it slowly crumble' was his mantra. And he wasn't entirely wrong: it was charming.

I arrived here in 1986 as an unemployed philosopher living in the block of Hotel Central, a dilapidated establishment in the Ortsstraat, right across from the 'Theatre of the Stock Exchange', the for foreigners unpronounceable but admirable Beursschouwburg, an important spot in the cultural landscape of Brussels. I had a view from my balcony towards the Stock Exchange, 'De Beurs/La Bourse'. It was glorious to live in the heart of the city.

A few years later, the block where I lived was evacuated, unfortunately. By this time, the cockroaches from a fast-food joint's abandoned kitchen came looking for food and rats crawled up the stairs. When the rumour was confirmed that the whole block would be torn down to be replaced with a new and hideous building in nondescript corporate postmodern style, a coalition was forged of current residents, residents from the neighbourhood, people from Sint-Lucas Architecture, RITS media school, and of course the staff of the Beursschouwburg, which would become the epicentre of the whole action: the squatting or 'occupation of Hotel Central'. There was a lot at stake. A complete residential block in the heart of the city would be razed, yet another example of 'Verbrusseling' or 'Brusselization', inflicting another scar on an already molested city. The action was deemed a lost cause. Everything was already arranged, from demolishing permits to plans to building applications—everything. The people involved were aware of the historical importance of this occupation. At stake wasn't only the architectural heritage, but also urbanity, 'the right to the city, the right to centrality', in the terms of Henri Lefebvre. More concretely, it was the defence of residential accommodation next to hotels, shopping accommodation, bars, and restaurants. The aim was mainly that the residential function would be kept.

It was the atmosphere of the Big Days: street parties, squatting, negotiations, police raids... Those who were there will never forget. The cinema right in front of the Beursschouwburg was one of the occupied spots. 'Urban Squat Dance', as I remember, was one of the activities that took place in the cinema. The poster with the witty word play was still hanging outside the building a long time after.

The battle for the block of Hotel Central was a turning point. According to some it was the start of urban activism in Brussels. It led to the occupation of the Luxemburg Station and to City Mine(d), an organization of urban activists. The occupation of Hotel Central, as primordial event, should at some point be documented, now that somehow most of the participants are still alive.

The activists gloriously won the battle. The residential block of Hotel Central is still standing and this is an absolute triumph, since at the start it looked like a lost case. But unfortunately, the Marriot Hotel, which now takes up a big part of the block of the former Hotel Central and cinema, isn't really the thing that we as activists were dreaming of—a corporate hotel. It seems to be an iron, devilish law that urban activism leads to gentrification. At the same time, though, architecture is patient. Who knows, maybe this block will find another, new destination in a far-off future.

The later occupation of the Luxemburg Station unfortunately shows a similar pattern. The historical station at the Luxemburg Square has a central position, right in front of the ugly colossus of the European Parliament and it closes and crowns the square, which was built as one unified ensemble. It was saved by the occupation, which constitutes an undeniable victory for the urban activists. But it is now the 'Belgian Press Centre', not really the thing one imagines when thinking of the connection between Europe and the city of Brussels. Here as well we must perhaps have patience and see the saving of this architectural piece of heritage as an achieved aim in itself.

From this and other, similar actions emerged City Mine(d)— an urban activist group who have been engaged in actions, events, and experiments all over the city for several years now. Besides in Brussels they are also active in other cities, such as London and Barcelona. Cinema Open Air, an outdoor film festival held in abandoned spaces of Brussels was one of their best-known and popular events for years. This in turn was the starting point of a squatted alternative cinema, Cinema Nova. Most of the projects of Citymine(d) are aimed at more in-depth interventions and are small-scale, attracting little media-attention: for example, when they were focusing on water in the European quarter.

'Brussels 2000', European Capital of Culture, was an important milestone in a conscious, activist way of dealing with the city. Although the overall project was strongly hindered by Brussels 'communitarian' Francophone-Flemish infighting, the activist approach remained intact. Ever since, 'De Zinnekeparade', a legacy of Brussels 2000, is a bi-annual parade that is prepared by different neighbourhoods and groups of multicultural Brussels for two years, then leading to a moment of collective festivity, a feast where many different communities come together.

Although the squatter movement in Brussels never was as expansive as in Amsterdam, there were several experiments with the idea of 'collective appropriation' that are worth mentioning. The biggest one of the early 2010s was the Jesu church, where over a 100 people lived, including families, ending with a dramatic evacuation in 2013. But there is still the squat 'Koningstraat 123' and 'La Parfumerie' (near Ninoofse Poort, now gone too) and lots of different bottom-up 'cultural institutions' where the verb 'commoning' ('communalizing', sharing) is central. Living, eating, composing, watching movies, debating, painting... doing all of this together. 'Toestand' and 'La Communa' took over this tradition in a more official way and at a much larger scale in the form of temporary occupations in consultation with the authorities.

The craze about urban gardening, also guerrilla gardening and urban farming, has in the meantime arrived in Brussels (at the time of writing in 2014 it was a discovery, now it is well-established). An early example is the collective garden on the roof of the Royal Library. Also, at places such as Ninoofse Poort, Park Canal and La Parfumerie people are experimenting with urban gardening. Although most of the projects are small-scale, temporary, and slightly touching, it is the symbolic value that counts: the activity of the common care for food that has been forgotten in our society. In times of ecological awareness, food shortage, economic crisis, urbanization of humanity, the necessity to 'vegetarianize' our diet, these are potentially very important initiatives. Cooking and gardening together are obviously basic activities of community building and each of them is an act of 'collective appropriation'.

There is the example of Parkdesign, an initiative of the Brussels Institute for the Environment. After last year's experimenting with landscape interventions in abandoned places nearby the canal area, this year (2014) they will start working in Thurn and Taxis, between the two bridges at the end of the old customs house. Here too, urban farming will be the core of the project.

Another important experiment is the so called CLT, Community Land Trust, in Molenbeek. This is a form of collective living, whereby the ground remains the property of the city, but the buildings, mostly old factories or warehouses, are used to live in collectively. Besides that, in the first place, it makes living much cheaper, it also stimulates a new way of living, the so-called collective living, and counteracts the gentrification as the ground remains the property of the rust (or the city).

Between the station of Evere and the Avenue Lambermont near the Josaphat Park, there is a huge, empty, open space, an old railway yard, about 24 hectare or as big as 46 soccer fields. Although the region has plans for it, a group of activists, under the ambitious title 'Josephat Commons', is busy brainstorming to demand designating this giant open space, or at least part of it, as 'commons'—as common ground, as city garden, for several activities such as people's allotments for urban gardening, and so on. Furthermore, there is Cyclo Guerrilla, a group of activists who paint cycling paths where there are none, and Park Ludic, Park Kanal, the Facebook group 'I love Molenbeek', and others. Too many to name, and probably loads that I don't even know exist.

Of course, we still have Picnic the Streets, an action of civil disobedience, encouraged by the Belgian economist and philosopher Philippe Van Parijs. In an opinion piece that was published in newspapers and went viral on Facebook, he had launched an appeal to occupy the 'Beursplein' square in front of the Stock Exchange, to make clear to the city that this should be a car-free zone. It became an overwhelming success as 2000 picnickers came together at 'the square de la Bourse' in June 2012 to remind the city council that ten years earlier they had promised to make the square a pedestrians-only area. The mayor couldn't do anything but give permission for the action. Making the area pedestrian would happen soon (and happened in the meantime and is a story in itself…).

And thus the circle is complete: Hotel Central and Picnic the Streets are literally neighbours as the Hotel Central block is located at the Beurs. Both prove that urban activism not only takes place in the abandoned parts of a city, the *'terrains vagues'*, the wastelands, the 'interstitial spaces' of the city, but also right in the middle, in the centre of a city. As we know since Henry Lefebvre, the right to the city is also the right to centrality.

Reclaim the Steps: On the Depoliticization of Downtown Brussels
(*De Wereld Morgen*, September 9, 2014)

For many years I looked out on the 'Beurs', the Brussels Stock Exchange, from my balcony in the Ortstraat. I could witness an event almost every day: soccer fans after a match, union actions, protests and demonstrations. It was as if the daily events of history found their stage there. Yes, I really had the feeling that I was looking at a political and social theatre, a glimpse of the world, not just a nice street view. The stairs and the forecourt of the Beurs almost literally form a theatrical space where politics and history assume a tangible and visible shape. It was a beautiful and useful backdrop for the television cameras. Later in my life I often participated with short, improvised speeches. But that is all over now…

When I arrived there in the late summer of 2013, on the 28th of August to be precise, joining an emerging manifestation against a then possibly imminent Western military intervention in Syria—in 24 hours we got 200 people and the attention of national radio and television—I was shocked that we were denied access to the stairs and the square of the Beurs by the police. Their excuse was that it had become the entrance of a museum and therefore political manifestations no longer belonged there. I couldn't believe my ears. They obliged us to continue our demonstration on the other side of the street, between the concrete flower boxes. A pathetic place, no visibility, no amphitheatre, no political stage. The camera crews of the television also had a hard time finding a good angle there.

It is important to realize what was happening here: the most public space of Brussels, maybe even Belgium, a true amphitheatre of social and political life in our country is being taken from us. For many years this was the place where one could not only measure the true temperature of our time but also track the daily events. Loud soccer fans, angry unionists, or outraged activists—all chose the steps of the Stock Exchange as their stage. And they knew why. It was simply the place to be.

Anyway, all this strongly illustrates the subtle expropriation of our public space in the strong sense of the word—as a political stage. And this is obviously not at all a coincidence: The neoliberal city does not like political expressions. The Belgian beer temple, the future destination of the Beurs, should become a place to boost Brussels as the place to be for tourists. As in a shopping mall or a theme park, let's keep it cozy. 'We don't do politics here.'

But that cannot be an excuse.

By the way, tourists like a little spectacle so that they can witness with their own eyes that Belgians are actively engaging in democracy. I even want to help the tourist services draft a complete marketing plan to transform this into a true 'must-see': The Brussels 'Speakers' corner' at the steps of the Stock Exchange. You can imagine tourists would be disappointed if they didn't see a group of people with signs, a megaphone, and the media on the steps of the Beurs on the day they pass by. Anyway, maybe I'm taking this too far, but you know what I mean.

Neither the temple nor the tourists have to fear any nuisance from demonstrators. Even more so now that it's been announced that the beer temple will have its entrance at the side of the building. So, an undisturbed entrance is guaranteed. Now the steps are certainly available, they are ours, they are everybody's and nobody's.

The steps of the Beurs are also more than just a platform for protest. It's a fixed meeting point for very diverse people. From the homeless to businesspeople or tourists. You meet at the Beurs and if you have to wait you sit down on the steps. It is just an amazing meeting point. Especially now that it will soon become a car-free zone. But at the same time, we have to make sure that implementing this car-free zone will not be used as a cover-up to frame the centre as an even more unpolitical theme park. Honestly, I am pessimistic.

Most cities would envy a place like the steps of the Beurs: the ultimate spot of democracy. Because in addition to the daily visitors, newspaper stands, sounds of joy and protest, it's a domain for freedom of speech, a true symbolic realization into a material space of 'the public sphere' that represents itself in newspapers, television, radio, internet… basically a virtual space. This is more impressive then 'Speakers' corner' in Hyde Park. That is why I think that the city council should reconsider its decisions or instruct the managers of the building to hold themselves to their civil duties. It is about a true duty to democracy, maybe not according to the law but *de facto*. As inhabitants of Brussels and even as Belgians we cannot let them take this unique place from us. Hereby I call up the Picnic the Streets network, in collaboration with the trade unions and several activist organizations, to organize a 'Reclaim the steps!'

Postscript

But that isn't all. My open letter to 'Picnic the streets and co' last year was too focused and therefore a little short-sighted. All the demonstrations I participated in since then, and there were a few, started traditionally at the North Station but were guided away from the usual route to Brouckère and Beurs. So now the procession runs around the city. All screaming towards nothing, towards nowhere. No audience. The demonstrations are almost literally deprived from their public character—a protest without passengers or spectators might as well just pass through some empty fields.

A demonstration has its place at the heart of the city. A political action belongs in the heart of the city. Right? In my opinion there is method in the madness. The steps of the Beurs are only one sore point—yes, it's painful to me—but it actually covers the whole downtown area. They want to safeguard the city against all political expression. The inner city has to be a peaceful theme park for tourists and one big shopping mall. Like 'Winter pleasures', that horrible Christmas market transforming Brussels into an unbearable light show and a no-go zone because it's flooded by tourists for several weeks, but then the whole year through.

Political protest does not fit in that image. So, we should zoom out from the steps of the Beurs to the whole downtown area if we want to defend the 'right of centrality' for protest. In other words, we should start yet again crossing the city explicitly with our manifestations to preserve it from total depoliticization. Hence this message to the inhabitants, a call to the entire civil society, to all organizations who will organize demonstrations: They should march straight through the centre. Tell that to the police. A forbidden area around the parliament, fine… but no blocking off downtown! The city is ours. Reclaim the steps? Also. But more importantly: reclaim the city!

The opening of the KunstenfestivaldesArts 2015, an action curated by artist Anna Rispoli and architect Koen Berghmans, took this message to heart for it was a re-enactment of 50 years of protests on the steps. From miners to Catalans, from the Palestinian question to the Iraq war, it was all there. I was there too with the 'BRussells Tribunal' that, together with the peace movements, organized a protest marathon against Bush coming to Brussels in 2005. This re-enactment was quite magnificent as a mass theatrical event, and it had a beautiful energy and brought urban activists together. It was beautiful because it was totally impossible to decide whether this was art or a political manifestation, or both or neither. And therefore a good example of what cultural actors can do. The message was clear: 'Reclaim the steps!'

Parckfarm as Concrete Utopia
(*De Wereld Morgen*, November 17, 2014)

During the summer of 2014, a wasteland transformed into a public park that is situated on a railway bed behind the mighty Thurn and Taxis site became one of the most beautiful places in Brussels: Parckfarm. The artificial railroad valley makes for a beautiful post-industrial landscape, situated in a bend on the border between Laeken and Molenbeek. It is crossed by three old bridges, monuments with all the charm of industrial archaeology. A piece of neo-nature. From underneath the foremost bridge, the 'Jubilee Bridge' (on the lane of that name), you get an enchanting view of the skyline of the Noord Quarter…

The creation of the park has embellished and opened up the site. A long, winding access path, near a well-used playground just outside of the park, slowly leads the visitor from the side down to the flat part under the bridges. Important to know is that the site is part of a planned linear park that will stretch from the canal to the city hall of Laeken. This gives the Parckfarm site its strategic position.

Architects would call it a 'residual space' or rather an 'interstitial space', an in-between space, like a dead end or an impasse in the urban fabric, a crack or gap in the territory, a *terrain vague*, an undefined terrain, and thus, a place of endless possibilities (or why not, an interface). At places like these a lot more happens than you might think. There was, for example, well-hidden on the top of the slope past the first bridge since several years, a self-organizing allotment garden initiated by the non-profit organization *Les Débuts des Haricots*. Some homeless people found their shelter—yes, their home—in this wasteland; one near the first bridge, another underneath the third bridge. And for children and youngsters from the neighbourhood the area was a natural playground. And the little signal tower of the old customs Thurn and Taxis has had a lot to endure, but even after a fire, three homeless people now live here... Sex, drugs and other rock'n'roll that shouldn't see the light of day will probably have been at home there, like in any other wasteland.

Parckdesign 2014, the second edition of a city festival about public green space initiated by the Brussels Institute for Environmental Management (BIM, also known as *Bruxelles Environnement* or *IBGE: Institut Bruxellois pour la gestion de l'environnement*), was curated by the architectural firms Taktyk and Alive Architecture and a couple of artists. Under their direction, the local residents and activists worked together with landscaping architects, artists, and all kinds of collectives and many, many volunteers, to transform the residual space into a real public park, no, sorry: an *urban farm garden*, a *park for urban gardening*. In short: Parckfarm. Later, an access was added, a wooden slope from the level of the first bridge. During the summer of 2014, this almost idyllic post-industrial landscape was the setting of a unique initiative in which government, professionals such as artists and architects, volunteers, and local residents found each other.

To give an idea of what was going on, let me sketch an incomplete overview. Ruth, a local resident, together with an architect and many helpful hands have built Kotkot, a henhouse of clay with an organic form, at once prehistoric and modern. Abdel built an oven, in which anyone can bake bread or a pizza; an oven that with its spherical shape and a ball on top echoes the onion-shaped ends of the pillars crowning the big bridge. He also let a sheep or two graze near the Kotkot. Next to the first bridge, a new ensemble of allotments was made, situated near Abdel's oven. There was a dry toilet, not unimportant in a public space, but especially crucial here: a playful ecological toilet, with slides as exits, that transforms human waste into useable compost. Truly a vital invention for the survival of an overpopulated urban human species. In short, closed ecological circuits is what we need to make.

Collective Disaster, the architects' collective that built the impressive toilet, initially wanted to call their first edifice 'The Temple of Holy Shit', but none of these three keywords were acceptable for the neighbourhood, so it became 'L'usine du Tresor

Noir' (The Factory of the Black Treasure). On September 20, during the end of the festival, the collective stirred the composting manure for hours on end. It reminded me of Walter Benjamin's saying that the 'new barbarians' face the future of humanity, however perilous it may be, laughingly. Ecology, but with a serious dose of *esprit dada*. In the late hours after the festival, I immediately offered myself as prospective member.

But not everything can happen simultaneously. During the preparation of the Parckfarm project, the tea house of Mo-Mo, which gives out onto the park at the back, was a meeting space and during my first visit the rear terrace was one of the most beautiful places of the whole park. You had a nice overview in the shade between Moroccan men who smoked and drank mint tea and were happy to see a Caucasian visiting. (In retrospect, I think the smell of cannabis was at the origin of the closure; I liked it, too bad).

Parckfarm is not only an ecological laboratory but also a social laboratory, a place to mix cultures. Because mixing is something we humans are not good at. It is in a park, in a 'hetero-topia' as Foucault would say, in a place that is extra-ordinary, outside the everyday, in that 'other space' (*hetero-topos*) that things become possible. Things such as smoking and drinking tea together with Belgian Moroccans one doesn't know. There are several Moroccan terraces around the corner, but I do not go there, no time, I can't make it, these are not magical places...

A greenhouse, a reconstituted readymade, became the centre of the entire park, The Farmhouse, a cafeteria with local produce. Tessa and her husband, also locals, were important driving forces. Beside it, a huge table with edible bushes in the middle, built by members of the curatorial collective, where visitors could meet. There also was a beekeepers' collective and even our students built something there. In the evening, the Electric Rainbow Farmfair lights up, a beautiful lighting under the Jubilee Bridge, and so on...

Today, at this moment in history, eco-social heterotopian practices are vital. Creating a melting pot of different cultures is not easy, there must be a special place. Parckfarm did the trick. It really was an exercise in globalization, superdiversity, and ecological transition, which deserves our attention and our respect, because obviously it was and is very intensive for those involved. Beware, there was ambition. A van introduced the products cultivated in Parckfarm or ready-made products into markets and elsewhere. The Farmtruck was a mobile kitchen and a place for events... What this in turn shows is that such a project is an economic utopia of workable co-operative production. DIY farming, DIY processing, DIY selling—all locally and everything in co-operation. Small wonders are badly needed.

Most touching was that one of the homeless people, who at first was not happy seeing all these people in his backyard—even the homeless potentially suffer from NIMBY syndrome, and who can blame them—is now a day-and-night guard and handyman for the whole site, which earned him the nickname Super Marcel. Now this I call integration!

The good news came late September 2014 during the final colloquium: Parckfarm would not end with the end of the summer festival but got another year and minimal supervision. Hurray! We can only hope that Parckfarm survives. In one way or another. It can be an important link, even the node, but also a model for the linear park that will stretch from the Canal all the way up to the Bockstael square.

Places like Parckfarm where the ecological, urban agricultural, the social, multicultural, superdiverse, the global and the local come together in a unique way in a *commons* which really deserves that name, a true *urban commons*—places like this we should cherish. Cherish them as small, fragile laboratories of the future; micro-politics for a sustainable urban policy. That is why we need to give such initiatives every possible opportunity to continue. If only, as I have done here, by looking at them in an optimistic frame. Even if I am often branded as a doom thinker, an alarmist, this makes my heart melt. Because without this kind of laboratories, the future looks like hell; but I promised not to play the alarmist. Ecological crucibles of cultures are—at this time in the history of mankind—'enterprises', not business but adventures that could be vital to neighbourhoods, suburbs and cities in general. As Parckfarm is a residual hybrid space, used as a commons with several groups involved, trying out temporary uses in an informal, bottom-up way, it might be considered a spatial *interface*.

Whoever is looking for practical alternatives to the repressive neoliberal urge for continuous austerity policies—to make the profit of the few grow—should come here. The other way exists. Here and now. And the other way is for everyone, for everyone who is committed to the neighbourhood. It involves issues such as ecology, food sovereignty, and environmental justice—a better model than the dangerous madness of the growth-economy at this moment in history. Progress can only be called transition these days. Parckfarm is a small, not-so-small, concrete, very concrete utopia. Without much ideology or big words. I believe this is what anthropologist Rik Pinxten calls 'small revolutions'. Let's just do it and keep on doing it. Today Parckfarm, tomorrow the world.

Note

* These three blogs from 2014 give an idea of my first reflections on urban activism. They should one day lead to a collective book with comrade in arms Gideon Boie, a colleague with whom

I then started teaching the by now locally legendary course 'Architecture and Activism', at the Brussels Sint-Lucas Campus of the Department of Architecture of the Leuven University. But as snapshots they contain enough seeds to situate urban activism in the struggle for the urban commons.

The Potato War and the Slow Science Manifesto: On the 'GMO Event' in Flanders

The Potato War of Wetteren

On 29 May 2011, in the East Flemish municipality of Wetteren two manifestations came together at a test field for genetically modified potatoes of Ghent University, the VIB—the Flemish Institute for Biotechnology—and the multinational BASF. On the one hand 'Save our science': scientists mostly from Ghent, whether or not connected to the VIB, and their sympathizers, who saw the freedom of research threatened by 'fanatics' and 'irrational reflexes'. On the other hand, the 'Field Liberation Movement' (FLM): ecological activists, organic farmers, citizens, NGO people and activist-scientists who oppose GMOs, and *les Faucheurs Volontaires (the voluntary Reapers),* a European network of which many French people are part because anti-GMO activism took root much earlier and much deeper there. This movement originated as part of the Alter-Globalization Movement, particularly under the impulse of farmer-activist politician José Bové.[1] The confrontation was already announced in the press as 'the potato war'.[2]

The FLM succeeded in breaking through the fences and doing a 'potato exchange' or 'field liberation' as a 'direct action'. A few people were injured, both activists and police officers. There was an immediate outcry in the media and at the universities, and even in the highest echelons of Flemish politics. The words 'violence', 'sabotage of scientific research' and 'destruction of property' were the key words. When one views the video footage,[3] it looks more like a game of cat and mouse with the police officers, but apparently a few people were injured in the course of that game. In retrospect it would become apparent that, according to the researchers themselves, only 15 percent of the harvest had been destroyed: that means that 85 percent had remained intact. A fact that defenders of the action took advantage of to state that this was indeed a symbolic destruction.

Barbara Van Dyck, doctor of bio-engineering, who was involved in the organization of the action and defended the 'potato exchange' in the media, was immediately fired by the KU Leuven (Catholic University of Leuven), where she worked as a researcher.[4] Almost on the same day, a support committee for Barbara Van Dyck was set up.[5] A petition was immediately launched and widely signed. Of course, there were also polemics in the slipstream of the events. Over the years, opinion pieces were written back and forth. My polemics with Prof Marc van Montagu and with Prof Johan Braeckman, which we will look at later, should be seen in that context.[6] And finally, a 'Slow Science Manifesto' was written, which was presented at a colloquium at the VUB (Free University of Brussels) after a joint editing session of a few months, and has since been signed by 740 academics.[7]

The '11 from Wetteren', the 11 persons from the entourage of the FLM who were effectively prosecuted, including Barbara Van Dyck, were on trial for voluntary damage to private property and for 'gang formation' (*bendevorming*) or 'organized crime', no less. A hundred people showed their solidarity as 'voluntary accused'— including philosopher of science Isabelle Stengers, MEP Bart Staes (who really stuck his neck out in this case while Groen!, his party, quickly distanced itself), Michel Genet, then director of Greenpeace, and... the author of this text—but these were never accepted by the judge. Each hearing was an occasion for demonstrations. Greenpeace was also strongly involved in this, all the more so because shortly before it was also plagued with persecution by Electrabel for 'organized crime'.[8] The judge convicted the '11 of Wetteren' of destruction of property and blows and injuries, but not of organized crime.

As a columnist for the daily newspaper *De Standaard*, professor of ecclesiastical law and TV personality Rik Torfs thought the dismissal of Barbara van Dyck was a bad idea and when, after his short career as a politician at the CD&V (Christian Democratic and Flemish), he ran for rector, he promised to reinstate her. A few months after he took office in August 2013, before Christmas, Barbara van Dyck was back at her department. Professor Frank Moulaert, Van Dyck's immediate superior, was a combative *go-between* all that time. This concludes my rough sketch of the events and the discourses that unfolded around them.

What Isabelle Stengers, already in 2008,[9] called the 'GMO event' ignited in Flanders, so to speak, the 'Potato War'. The 'GMO event' is, in short, the public debate and civil protest against the alliance of scientists and multinationals around genetically modified crops or GMOs. The extent to which the potato war affected public opinion can be gauged not only from the general fuss in the newspapers, but also from the many panel discussions devoted to this case. As far back as Wetteren itself, on the occasion of the first anniversary, there was a panel discussion about the potato war, in which it became clear that the local population was strongly alarmed.[10]

The aim of this text cannot be, of course, to write the full history of the potato war in particular and of the GMO controversy in general (this could be a subject for a PhD). Here I would like to limit myself to a close reading of the judgment of the Ghent Court of Appeal in this case, of a number of polemics between academics in the press, especially those in which I myself was involved, and of the Slow Science Manifesto resulting from the controversy and instigated by the action committee of Barbara Van Dyck. This Slow Science Manifesto, which explicitly defends the independence of the university, paints a clear picture of what 'academic freedom' could or should mean today. Inevitably all this is undertaken from my perspective, as an active participant in the debates, in that sense it is also a kind of 'action research', which ipso facto starts from one's own participation in actions.

The Decision of the Court of Appeal

It is worth dwelling on the decision of the Ghent Court of Appeal in this case, because it paints a picture of the arguments of the defendants and shows how the Court 'juridifies' a political action and thereby also criminalizes it. The decision of the Court of Appeal in Ghent of 23 December 2014 in the case 'Hogeschool Gent and others vs. D.S. and others' first describes the facts in detail from a legal point of view.[11] Subsequently, the arguments of the defence are disproved one by one. The notion that this is about freedom of expression is rejected: 'The charges that are the subject of the present criminal action against the accused ... only relate to offences that were committed by the accused in question during the action and that are qualified as offences under criminal law, namely the malicious destruction of field fruits (charges D), the destruction of national barriers (charges E), acts of rebellion and the deliberate infliction of blows, committed against police officers (charges F and G)'.[12]

One can understand that the court chooses this strategy as criminal acts are criminal acts, even if they happen in an explicitly political context. The action, says the Court, was not hampered but rather facilitated by the police—there was a march with banners and so on—so there is no question of restricting freedom of expression. And vandalism and especially beatings and injuring police officers are a step too far. The latter is problematic, the officers' injuries are accidents since at no time was any of the activists deliberately using violence, as can be seen from the video images on YouTube. But for the court, the wounded prove that it was a violent action. '... it [is] blatantly contrary to the truth that the defendants pleaded it was a "non-violent action", since violence was indeed used—witness, incidentally, the fact that there were casualties both on the side of the activists and on the side of the police.' This is a *non sequitur*: if someone is injured at a football match, it does not follow that a football match is not a non-violent activity. It is abundantly clear that the activists opted for non-violent action, and had no interest in violence either, but that of course, as in a football match, or a game of cat and mouse, injuries may be inflicted on both sides.

Civil disobedience is not accepted as a qualification either.

Again, the judge takes an illogical shortcut. The good intentions of the activists are not accepted. From the outset, the judge assumes that these are proven criminal offences, so there can be no question of civil disobedience, i.e., breaking the law with political intent, because these are proven criminal offences. That is an exemplary *petitio principii* or circular reasoning. The judge decides, as was to be expected and foreseen, that these are criminal offences and not civil disobedience. Also, the state of emergency and the illegality of the field trial are dismissed—even if the field trial was not entirely in order, that is no reason for direct action. In any case, the crimes committed by the defendants cannot be justified on the grounds that they 'wish to denounce this unlawfulness and its damage to the environment on the basis of concern to safeguard the interests of the environment and public health', nor on the grounds that 'they were thus compelled, by means of an act of civil disobedience, to make the unlawfulness known to the general public while at the same time stopping its harmful effects on the environment'.

Those were indeed the stakes, however, and precisely because of the 'direct action', it also succeeded in a certain sense. The public has been alarmed and BASF has withdrawn from the GMO potato business. From this point of view, the action was an unmitigated success. Also interesting is the decision that summarizes the defendants' motives: 'The legal assets that the defendants intended to protect, and which they said were in great danger, concern more specifically: the protection against GMOs planted on a trial field that they consider to be improperly licensed; the protection of the environment (paying attention to the loss of biodiversity, increased use of pesticides and herbicides, unpredictable consequences of GMOs, etc.), public health and the economic interests of small and organic farmers; independent scientific research'.

Although the court correctly lists the reasons for the action, it has always, also in the first instance, refused to hear scientists and politicians put the case in a broader context, because this was precisely what they did not want. It had to be a criminal act and not a political ecological act, an act to make ecology political, which according to Stengers and Latour is the stakes of what they call 'political ecology', or even 'cosmopolitics' (we will come back to this).

As to the necessity of the action, the Court of Appeal rejects the defendants' entire line of argument. What the defendants had to do, the Court does not say, 'after all, it is not for the Court to judge the "usefulness of the action"'. Now, this usefulness can no longer be disputed, as said BASF has withdrawn from the GMO-potato business and the entire public opinion looks on with suspicion as soon as the word GMO is mentioned. However, the judge also dismisses this argument, which justifies the action in retrospect (*post factum*), because it has changed the entire climate of the debate and therefore did act as an alarm call. In other words, the judge remains deaf to the arguments of the defence. Because, from the outset, he only wants to see the criminal facts and ignores the political context and the political intentions, so that the case only concerns the destruction of crops, while he himself indicates that this was not really the real stake of the action. But all's well that ends well: the qualification of organized crime is rejected by the Court of Appeal. So, in the end the Court of Appeal follows the argument of the defence that there was no criminal intent, without of course admitting this in so many words.[13]

Perhaps the judgment of the Ghent judge was perceived by the FLM and the sympathizers as a legal defeat, but in fact it was a moral victory. In the end, the deliberate criminalization of ecological activism in Belgium had not succeeded. One may suspect that the ecological movement is not sufficiently aware of this, as always with movements of this kind—blind to their victories, as David Graeber indicates in a witty and instructive essay on the alter-globalization movement.[14] For if the question is: who won the potato war? Then, in our opinion, the answer should be: the coalition of activists and academics, politicians, and farmers. Here in Belgium and Europe, the multinationals have buried their hopes for the large-scale deployment of a GMO-based agro-industry. At least for the time being.

Save our Science? A Series of Polemics Between Academics

The core of the GMO case
Let us now have a look at the public debate surrounding the potato war. In this part of my 'action research' I will reflect as a theorist upon the discourse of the (academic) activist, by taking the polemics I was involved in as a case study.

Strangely enough, what is not addressed in the entire judicial dossier, at least not visibly and hardly in any of the arguments, is the core of the GMO case: the privatization of seeds. In a first piece on GMOs, in *tempore non suspecto*, on 28 April 2009, that is three years before the potato war, the polemicist we will now follow in more detail, on the occasion of 'International Seeds Day' (on 26 April 2009), writes a fierce piece against the privatization of seeds, under the crude title 'Stay clear of our seed!'[15]

He takes Germany, which rejected Monsanto's patent on corn, as an exemplary model and compares it to Iraq, where U.S. diplomat Paul Bremer abolished the law on the freedom of organic raw materials and forced farmers to buy seeds from Monsanto. He emphatically rejects this because seed is and should be a common good: 'The privatization of seeds is a crime not only against farmers, but a crime against humanity and the planet'.[16]

A few days after the potato war (31 May 2011) he repeats this thought under the title 'The core of the GMO cause'.[17] He puts the potato war in Wetteren in a very broad, even planetary framework: 'The twenty-first century will be dominated by a struggle for the ecological balance of the planet (just today the International Energy Agency warns that we will not succeed in limiting CO_2 emissions and that the temperature on Earth will probably rise by more than two degrees by 2100, maybe even by four degrees). On the contrary, we should consider many more things as commons. Not only air, which we haven't privatized yet, although emission rights are in that logic, and water, which we are privatizing, but the whole environment. The entire ecosystem is common good. One could say: the highest good.'

Activism is not violence

The dismissal of Barbara Van Dyck, which happened immediately after the action at Wetteren and was separate from the lawsuit against the activists, became a symbolic dossier that contributed to an awareness of the existence and dangers of GMOs, but also of the neo-liberalization of the university. On top of that, it put the theme of knowledge and education as a common good on the map. In spite of the fact that Barbara Van Dyck refused being presented as the face of the whole affair, so as not to betray the essentially collective nature of the action, everyone will have to admit that in the context of the university in general and academic freedom in particular, one cannot ignore her specific case, her dismissal. This was clearly also the opinion of our polemicist who immediately wrote a barrage of articles.

The first piece, under the programmatic title 'Activism is not violence (and defending activism most certainly not)', as the title rather clearly announces, opined that activism is not violence. The author is angry about the criminalization of activism and argues that such academic activism of defending activism—for that was why Van Dyck was fired—is rather an important contribution to the debate: 'Activism is more than just free speech, in the sense of speaking and writing, it is more than discourse. An action is a political act. Without that act, nothing moves. It is not with an opinion piece that we are going to change the world'.[18]

Particularly the qualification of organized crime in the accusations against Greenpeace and the 11 of Wetteren is unacceptable to our writer. '"Gang formation" is explicitly intended by the legislator for criminal and clandestine organizations. Greenpeace is not a criminal and clandestine organization, ergo whoever, like Electrabel, files a complaint against that organization for organized crime, should himself be punished for abuse of the law (and if possible, also punished by the consumer). The same applies to the Field Liberation Movement. They are idealists who do not have the slightest criminal intent and had announced their action openly months in advance. Anyone who wants to label this as a '"gang formation" or "organized crime" is abusing the law. Which is, of course and unfortunately, typical of the climate of criminalization of activism that has prevailed in Belgium since 9/11 too.'[19]

At least this time, our opinion maker has spoken in correct legal terms, as the legal text is crystal-clear: 'An organization whose actual purpose is exclusively political, professional, humane, philosophical or religious, or that pursues exclusively any other legitimate purpose, cannot as such be regarded as a criminal organization'.[20] It may be strange that the judge did not explicitly refer to this passage in the Law.

On this nail our polemicist will keep hammering, and he will repeat this emphatically in an open letter to Rik Torfs, the then brand-new rector.[21] His conclusion is that such activism, especially the academic activism of the dismissed Barbara Van Dyck, is a contribution to the social debate and thus to democracy. 'This is what activism does, more than dozens of opinion pieces and civilized debates: making the debate inevitable. Now the debate is inevitable. And it the debate is on: about GMOs, about cisgenic potatoes, about beehives, about the consequences for the environment, about the principle of prudence, about the independence of science, about the expropriation of the common good and the privatization of profits, about academic freedom and free speech, about violence, and about … the right to activism.'[22] A second piece was pure entertainment, an amusing intermezzo, against the background of the K (which stands for Catholic) of KU Leuven: 'A Small Theology of Activism'.[23]

The politically most important piece from that first phase was, of course, the petition pleading for the cancellation of Van Dyck's resignation, which was signed by more than 2000 academics from Belgium and abroad and was published in *De Standaard* on 10 June 2011. The writers, the action committee Barbara Van Dyck, consider the measure disproportionate and 'a true mockery of labour law and the principles of academic freedom and freedom of expression'.[24] The petition recalls 'international charters, such as the 1997 UNESCO recommendation: "All teaching staff of higher education institutions should enjoy freedom of thought and conscience. … They should not be prevented from exercising their rights as citizens, including the right to contribute to social change by freely expressing their thoughts. … They should not be penalized for exercising these rights".' Moreover, according to them, the freedom of expression of the person in question is definitely being stifled and criminalized: 'Moreover, the university authorities are violating a basic democratic right functioning as the cornerstone of our society, i.e., the freedom of expression. By dismissing a staff member for expressing sympathy with an action, KU Leuven is entering a new climate of criminalization of activism, and even of criminalization of sympathy for activism.' They feel that the action is being stigmatized: 'Mixing the action against the test field into an act of violence (against potatoes?) distracts attention from the necessary social debate.' They conclude with an appeal to undo the dismissal.[25]

Science as Salvation and Devil's Pact (De Cauter vs. Van Montagu).
One of the protagonists in the GMO story in Flanders is Professor Marc Van Montagu, who pioneered work on genetic modification and was awarded the World Food Prize 2013, by a consortium linked to Monsanto. In an interview by Joël De Ceuleer in *De Standaard*, under the title 'Resisting GMOs is criminal', he expresses himself very disparagingly about the resistance to GMOs. 'I don't want to make fun of them, but I compare the opponents of GMOs with Jehovah's Witnesses: they also believe they know the truth, and they feel better because they think they are doing something useful.'[26] And further: 'I always assumed that rationality would prevail. Now I know it doesn't work that way, that there are two ways of thinking, what psychologist Daniel Kahneman calls fast and slow thinking. There is the fast, emotional, and intuitive way of reacting. And there is the slow, rational, intellectual way of thinking. But the latter requires an effort, and most people are a little lazy.' Finally, he considered the resistance as an expression of ignorance. 'I can't blame her. Mrs. Van Dyck is a sociologist, so you can't blame her for not having enough knowledge.'[27]

Then our polemicist on duty takes up his pen and writes an open letter entitled: 'Science as Salvation and the Devil's Pact', in which he immediately reverses the roles. It is Van Montagu who has a religious faith: '... But who is the zealot here? The belief of salvation which, in the background of your interview, always sounded as the ultimate legitimation, as if GMOs would solve food problems, has already been refuted a hundred times. In the answer to your interview by bioengineer Wouter Vanhove *(De Standaard*, 1 July), but also by Olivier De Schutter, the UN Special Rapporteur on the right to food.' Subsequently, our activist academic argues that in today's concrete reality GMO research cannot be dissociated from exploitation by multinationals. He first quotes Van Montagu: '"People find it disturbing that large multinationals concern themselves with food. But multinationals are equally concerned with cars and computers. And monopolies are also formed in other sectors. I am not defending that, but it has nothing to do with GMOs." You will have to explain this. GMOs are only developed for patents and that patenting is all about privatization and profit, that is the only motive. Denying this is called moral schizophrenia: there are GMOs and there is monopoly, but no, these things have nothing to do with each other. You, like so many scientists, live in denial of the social complicity of your research, here with the ruthless capitalist appropriation of seeds and the exploitation of farmers worldwide.'[28] This platonic conception of Science, which would only accidentally be used by multinationals but is of itself deeply and completely independent, is a very stubborn and widespread notion among scientists (as we shall see, Stengers and Latour have tirelessly emphasized this in their writings). What also disturbs the writer is the inaccurate information: 'Then you condone: "And by the way, GMOs only represent a small percentage of the turnover of companies like Monsanto. ..." You know as well as I do that Roundup is one of the most widely used herbicides worldwide ... Wikipedia says: "The entire Roundup production line (including GMOs) accounts for about half of Monsanto's annual revenues." Who is the ignoramus here?'

Next, our activist academic states that Van Montagu is ill-informed when he dismisses those who resist as non-scientists and therefore ignorant and gives his colleague a lesson in the sociology of science: 'You are also ill-informed about your opponents. Barbara Van Dyck is not a sociologist, whom you "can't blame for not having enough knowledge", but a doctor in bioengineering. There goes your whole house of cards about the intellectual laziness and criminal ignorance of all those who oppose GMOs. This mistake is typical of what one might call scientific arrogance: It must be excluded that anyone who knows what it is about can be against GMOs. Well, that kind of belief is religious and fanatical. Science fundamentalism—that would be a good term for this kind of idolatry of science as salvation. You should also know that Isabelle Stengers, the famous philosopher of science (by training a chemist) is another one committing this "'criminal resistance' to GMOs" ... Science, my dear colleague—and you can read that in her books—is not a "monoculture" of the one truth, but a social practice full of controversies.'

Finally, he also reverses the accusation—not so much the resistance against GMOs is criminal but the defence of agro-giants. 'As long as you do not distance yourself from the practices of multinationals such as Monsanto and co, you are passively complicit in these practices. Or at least victim of a devil's pact. So, think twice before you call resistance against GMOs criminal.'[29]

Professor Van Montagu doesn't answer at first, but then with the commotion surrounding the visit of Robert Frailey, Monsanto's number two, on the occasion of the celebration of the 20th anniversary of the VIB, the Flemish Institute of Biotechnology,[30] he does answer when the open letter is relaunched via the news site *De Wereld Morgen* six months later.[31] The tone is very different this time.[32] It is a nuanced and respectful, almost friendly speech about the possibilities of separating biotechnology from the multinationals and even integrating it into an agro-ecological agricultural model. The conclusion sounds hopeful: 'My hope is that all technologies will be used in an integrated agricultural model. The agricultural challenges are enormous, but if we use the best conventional, agro-ecological and biotechnological insights, we can continue to supply the world with plant products in a sustainable way.'[33]

Old Irrational fears and Ignorance (De Cauter vs. Braeckman)
In an interview with *De Standaard* two years later, the Ghent philosopher of science Johan Braeckman and several colleagues, through scientific research, or so they claimed, once again come to the conclusion that resistance to GMOs is in our genes. It is an atavistic fear of technology that appears in mythical stories of the Golem, and especially Frankenstein. It is a kind of vital reflex that starts from a false image of what nature is and what is natural.[34] To this, our polemicist responds bitterly that the so-called scientific consensus on GMOs is a blatant lie; that they coyly conceal the fact that scientists who stand up against multinationals are silenced; and that for champions of science this is a strange and rather unforgivable omission.[35]

To cut a long story short, the recurring argument about fear and ignorance and regressive, atavistic reflexes shows not only that a number of people who have come to the side of 'Save our science' not only disdain public opinion and political debate, and thus perhaps democracy,[36] but also have a totally naive image of what science is today. Or at least they use with conviction an image of Science that is outdated or untruthful because it is a platonic idea, which Isabelle Stengers has unmasked in many books for decades, followed and supported (and above all surpassed in terms of impact) by Bruno Latour: Science (always with a capital letter and in the singular) is a rhetorical fiction and an authority argument. The sciences are a fundamental plurality of social practices that are essentially based on controversies between different opinions, hypotheses, paradigms, and disciplines. The sciences are heavily 'embedded' practices dealing with power, politics, money, interests, and so on. This relatively simple truth, which until then had been a well-kept secret in the circles of scientists or science ideologues (philosophers I wouldn't call them), has penetrated the wide circle of public opinion as an awareness because of the GMO event.[37] In this sense it is true that we learned a lot from the GMO controversy—something which Stengers always emphasizes in her books. Public opinion is better armed against 'Science' as an argument of authority, as a sacred cow that is above the interests of society and must be saved from the irrational reflexes of the always ignorant population.

The Slow Science Manifesto

Although the Belgian 'Slow Science Manifesto'[38] has *prima facie*— to speak with the judge of the Ghent Court of Appeal—nothing to do with the potato war and at no time explicitly refers to it, one has to know it is a direct consequence thereof. Isabelle Stengers also makes that link.[39] Because the text is not very well-known, I take the liberty to quote it extensively. From the start, the Manifesto situates itself as part of a movement.[40] Now, it's quite difficult to map out this so-called slow science movement; it's more like a few cores, a few texts (like the 2010 Berlin Manifesto mentioned above), a few incidents, which are symptomatic of a widely shared dissatisfaction, or at least anxiety, in the academic world about the 'neoliberalization' of the university and the predominance of the 'management ideology'. About the name itself, the Manifesto says: 'Slow science is obviously not idle science. Neither is it science as done "in the past", in some Golden Age when research and the researchers' independence were presumably respected.' Under the heading 'Science is not a business' the authors' collective writes: 'Universities have been subjected to totally new conditions: a business model currently redirects work and working conditions towards competitive and utilitarian outputs. Research is to a considerable extent streamlined through externally defined programmes of R&D, privatized research resources and results (patents; spin offs), and—mainly quantitative—criteria of scientific "excellence". Workloads have become excessive and labour contracts precarious. Curricula were "flexibilized" and "modularzed" to enable the commodification of courses meeting individual needs.

This business model of academia, based on principles of intellectual and economic meritocracy, needs critical appraisal and resistance. The increased privatization of education and research needs to come to an end. The university should not take part in the perverse neoliberal logic of the socialisation of costs and the privatization of gains. State (and therefore tax payers) subsidized research should not be at the service of spinoffs of all sorts. Overwork and (self) exploitation of young, precarious academics should not be the norm. Contributing to the glory of corporations is not the aim of academic work. The university is neither the R&D branch of business corporations nor the endorser of a (politically supported) knowledge economy.'[41]

This analysis is harsh and negative, but under the heading 'Science at the service of society as a whole', they unfold a rather radical programme, in any case a strong, positive vision: 'Society faces global change and systemic challenges. Universities have specific responsibilities not only because the knowledge it produces will play an indisputable part in the answers to these challenges, but also because of its position as an intergenerational institution. The students of today and tomorrow are part of the generation that will have to actually confront what we now can hardly imagine. We deem it urgent that universities address this new responsibility and we strongly feel that this daunting task is made impossible by the one-sided relationship of academia with the knowledge society through the privileged channels of the knowledge economy, biased by private interests and fast science.'

This is no less than a new model of knowledge: 'Slow Science favours the establishment of research agendas based on the priorities of actual global challenges. … Slow science also needs embedding in what should become a true knowledge society: a society where different kinds of knowledge, be it academic or locally embedded, are recognized as crucial components for reliable co-productive modes of knowledge production.'

Here one clearly feels the hand of Isabelle Stengers and that of Eric Corijn, who want to bring science in the very broad sense, the academic world, into vital contact with civil society. So 'the separation between those who "know better" and those who have to adapt' has to be made. The core of the whole programme is there-fore education and research as a common good, as commons: 'Education is a human right and science should be common for all. By choosing the term "slow", we connect with other "slow" move-ments resisting the privatization of common concerns and the resulting bad quality of the answer to these concerns. Privatized science means fast science, that is superficial science, and in that respect often bad science. Science, like language, is not a private affair and it should not be privatized. The 'commoning' of science, as opposed to privatization, is one of the main goals of our move-ment. Sharing knowledge and increased transparency of knowl-edge production are keywords.'

This programme will then be concretized with practical recommendations, but it would take us too far to get into that.[42] The Manifesto was presented on 30 March 2012 during a collo-quium at the VUB (Free University Brussels)[43] and it was signed online in a short time by some 700 academics.[44] It was, so to speak, an overnight success, and it certainly had a certain effect, but there was clearly no plan, no strategy. It is perhaps regrettable that the Belgian group behind the Slow Science Manifesto quickly pro-ceeded to the order of the day (and other urgencies), and that there was no follow-up to the colloquium where the Manifesto was pre-sented. This can be explained by the typical short cycle of an action committee, but also by the fact that other parallel initiatives, such as the 'atelier de chercheurs pour une désexcellence des universités' and the 'Actiegroep Hoger Onderwijs' (Higher Education Action Group), kept the matter on the agenda.[45] In the meantime a second-generation group 'slow science Belgium' has emerged.[46]

Nevertheless, the Slow Science Manifesto has been a significant contribution to the debate, indeed to a movement that has made itself felt just about everywhere in the world. Resistance to the neoliberalization of the university also grew internationally.[47] The recent student occupation of the Maagdenhuis[48] in the Netherlands is a clear example of how this *slow-science movement* (without always calling itself that) regularly rises up and tries to stop the neoliberalization of higher education. There are also signs that it is beginning to dawn *within* the boards of the universities themselves. In any case, the Slow Science Manifesto paints a clear picture of what 'academic freedom' could or should mean today.[49]

The GMO Controversy as an Event

The potato war was an emblematic event. Two worldviews collided, so to speak: on the one hand the tidy but naive positivism that embraces and defends the multinationals, represented by the ad hoc group 'Save our science', against the playful radicalism of the Field Liberation Movement. Stengers describes the GMO event as follows: 'If the GMO issue was an event, it's because it was a school of learning that raised questions that made both scientific experts and state officials stutter, that sometimes even made politicians think, as if a world of problems they had never posed became visible to them.'[50]

What is important here are not so much the victories or defeats but the process—the new alliances and the transdisciplinary mutual learning process that comes with it. Stengers regards the GMO case as an event in the philosophical sense of the word because there was a before and an after, because it set many things in motion, because it triggered something that is irreversible, because people and groups who had never been in contact before now thought and acted together: farmers, academics, NGOs, activists, politicians, and so on. This mutual learning from each other, not by reading, but by doing, by experiencing something, is for her a school in 'the art of paying attention' (*l'art de faire attention*): 'The time of struggle and the time of creation must learn to work together without confusion, through feedback, continuation and mutual learning of the art of paying attention, otherwise there is a risk of mutual poisoning and the field is set free for the coming barbarism.'[51] This art of paying attention is a variant of the precautionary principle that underlies virtually all protests against GMOs: Because we do not yet know enough about the ecological impact of GMOs (and their associated herbicides), it is premature to apply them in the open field. It was an event because in one specific moment many problems and their connections were embodied and made concrete in an almost paradigmatic way.

Let me conclude, without claiming completeness, by listing the elements that came to light in the potato war: 1) direct action or civil disobedience as an effective alarm signal for putting a social problem on the map and opening a public debate,[52] immediately linked to it; 2) the criminalization of academic activism and thus a sharpening of the old theme of academic freedom; 3) the privatization of the common good; 4) the complicity between university scientists and multinationals;[53] 5) the privatization of knowledge; 6) the neoliberalization of the university and the domination of management ideology (fast science); 7) the power of collective reflection, the Slow Science Manifesto; 8) the impact of transdisciplinary action (academics, politicians, NGOs, organic farmers, citizens), which Isabelle Stengers sums up in the formula, as a mantra in her work, 'learning to think and act together';[54] 9) and *last but not least, of* course, the awareness of the ecological dangers of GMOs (biodiversity, the use of herbicides, such as Roundup, which is now known to be carcinogenic).

The GMO event is a paradigmatic case of what Latour and Stengers call 'political ecology': 'Political ecology presupposes bringing the sciences into politics, but that does not mean ... a reduction of sciences to politics or a 'politicization' that would contaminate their "neutrality".'[55] Neutrality is explicitly mentioned here in quotation marks. According to Stengers, the so-called neutrality of the Sciences and Scientists has been definitively unmasked by the GMO event. No one who has followed the GMO debate still believes in this neutrality, and the polemics have made it clear how naive and cynical the Ghent professors have defended their case. In fact, it was the people of the slow science group who stood up for academic freedom rather than those who called to 'Save our science'. If there is one thing the GMO controversy has taught us, it is this: Academic freedom has been fiercely threatened by the privatization of knowledge by multinationals and by the overly intimate bond between academics and corporations.

At this moment in history, Isabelle Stengers considers this 'fast science' as dangerous, because 'the intrusion of Gaia', as she calls it, climate change and the ecological catastrophes that will accompany it, oblige us to slow down and learn to practice the art of paying attention.[56] That is what she calls cosmopolitics. In *Une autre science est possible. Manifeste pour un ralentissement des sciences (Another Science is Possible. Manifesto for a Slowing Down of Sciences)*, the book that emerged from her reflections on the occasion of the Slow Science Manifesto, she argues (with an expression borrowed from Whitehead) for a 'civilizing of the sciences', and hence for a slowing down of sciences. According to her, the classical scientists of 'fast science' are fundamentally irresponsible, because they are blind to the consequences of a development that has come along with it, but which has proved unsustainable (ecologically speaking). A responsible science therefore presupposes a slowing down.[57]

She writes at the end: 'The cosmopolitical slowing down demands that we think, on our own strength, from our own political, scientific sources and our imagination, that the sense of urgency is part of the test imposed on us, on us who are so ill-equipped, perhaps worse than ever, to learn to deal with Gaia.'[58] This is the horizon in which to place this academic activism. The potato war, as a catalyst and focal point of the 'GMO event' in Flanders, has set beacons of resistance in all sorts of areas: in the discussions on academic freedom and the criminalization of activism, on the future of universities and especially in the relationship between science and society. It has made the alliance between science and multinationals, and especially ecological precaution, a public, political, even cosmopolitical matter.

Notes

1   This French affiliation is even mentioned in the judgment of the Court of Appeal: 'The opponents of the field trial apparently found their inspiration in similar actions in France by the so-called Faucheurs Volontaires.' http://www.elfri.be/rechtspraak/vrije-meningsuiting-en-vernieling

2   Lieven Sioen, 'Aardappeloorlog in Wetteren' ('Potato War in Wetteren'), De Standaard, 28 May 2011 (that's one day before the event), online: http://www.standaard.be/cnt/023aoqdd.

3   See YouTube: 'Aardappelveld Wetteren' https://www.youtube.com/watch?v=W4hOjBGjrjM. See also: https://www.youtube.com/watch?v=d6WOVgKmKZU

4   'KU Leuven ontslaat GGO veldactiviste' (KU Leuven dismisses GMO potato field activist), De Standaard, 3 June 2011, http://www.standaard.be/cnt/dmf20110603_114. Van Dyck was associated with the Planning Research Group, part of the Department of Architecture, to which I also happen to be associated as a philosopher. Rector at the time was Marc Waer.

5   Members of the action committee were Prof Eric Corijn, Dr Mathias Lievens, Dr Anneleen Kenis, Prof Frank Moulaert, Prof Chris Kesteloot, Prof Em. Albert Martens, Prof Isabelle Stengers, Seb, a French-speaking faucheur-activist, myself, and a few others, including of course the person involved (and her partner).

6   Of course there were also other episodes, such as the arrival of Robert Frailey, Monsanto's number 2, on the occasion of the 25th anniversary of the VIB (Flemish Institute for Biotechnology), which led to a petition and protest (a protest party on 12 November 2013). In the end, Frailey didn't come. See also 'Protest party against GMOs in general and against Monsanto in particular', De Wereld Morgen, 6 November 2013, http://community.dewereldmorgen.be/blogs/lievendecauter/2013/11/06/protestfeest-tegen-ggos-in-het-algemeen-en-monsanto-in-het-bijzonder.

7   Slow science manifesto, see: http://www.petities24.com/slow_science_manifesto

8   A first complaint was about the dumping of coal in front of Electrabel's headquarters: http://electrabel-klachten-plaintes. skynetblogs.be/archive/2007/08/20/de-klacht-van-electrabel-tegen-greenpeace.html and http://www.hln.be/hln/nl/957/Binnenland/article/ detail/418742/2008/09/16/Greenpeace-niet-vervolgd-voor-bendevorming.dhtml but also http://www.standaard.be/ cnt/7v36b22k. And then there is a second complaint for actions against nuclear power plants, a procedural battle that lasted for seven years: http://www.greenpeace.org/belgium/nl/pers/-Electrabel-veegt-best-voor-eigen-deur-/.

9   Isabelle Stengers, *Au temps des catastrophes, Résister à la barbarie qui vient*, Paris: La découverte poche, 2009, p. 29, passim. (Online available in English: http:// openhumanitiespress.org/books/download/Stengers_2015_ In-Catastrophic-Times.pdf)

10 Wesley Poelman, 'Panel discussion potato war', *Het Nieuwsblad*, 3 June 2012: http://www.nieuwsblad.be/cnt/ blwpo_20120604_002.

11 Judgment of the Court of Appeal in Ghent Court of Appeal of 23 December 2014 in the case "Hogeschool Gent and others v. D.S. and others". Available online at: http://www.elfri.be/ rechtspraak/vrije-meningsuiting-en-vernieling

12 Ibid.

13 Ibid.

14 David Graeber, 'The shock of victory', in *Revolutions in Reverse, Essays on Politics, Violence, Art, and Imagination*, London, New York: Minor compositions, s. d., pp. 11-30.

15 Lieven De Cauter, 'Blijf van ons zaad af!' ('Stay clear of our seed', Indymedia, 28 April 2009, see: http://www.indymedia.be/ index.html%3Fq=node%252F32849.html.

16 Ibid.

17 Lieven De Cauter, 'De kern van de GGO zaak: de aarde is niet te koop' ('The core of the GMO business: the earth is not for sale'), *De Wereld Morgen*, 31 May 2011: see http://www. dewereldmorgen.be/artikels/2011/05/31/de-kern-van-de-ggo-zaak-de-aarde-niet-te-koop.

18 Lieven De Cauter, 'Activism is geen geweld (en activisme verdedigen al helemaal niet)' ('Activism is not violence and defending activism even less so), *De Wereld Morgen*, 6 June 2011: http://www.dewereldmorgen.be/artikels/2011/06/06/ activisme-geen-geweld-en-activisme-verdedigen-al-helemaal-niet.

19 Ibid.

20 The Belgian law on organized crime, to be found at: http://www. ejustice.just.fgov.be/cgi_loi/change_lg.pl?language=nl&la=N&c n=1867060801&table_name=wet.

21   Lieven De Cauter, 'Geweldloos protest zal niet genoeg zijn'
     ('Peaceful protest will not be enough'), *De Wereld Morgen*, 12
     June 2013: http://www.dewereldmorgen.be/artikels/2013/06/12/
     vreedzaam-protest-zal-helaas-niet-genoeg-zijn.
22   Op. cit.: http://www.dewereldmorgen.be/artikels/2011/06/06/
     activisme-geen-geweld-en-activisme-verdedigen-al-helemaal-
     niet
23   Lieven De Cauter, 'Kleine theologie van het activisme: een
     standbeeld voor Barbara Van Dyck' (Small theology of activism:
     a statue for Barbara Van Dyck)', *De Wereld Morgen*, 20 June
     2011: http://www.dewereldmorgen.be/artikels/2011/06/20/
     kleine-theologie-van-het-activisme-een-standbeeld-voor-
     barbara-van-dyck. (The K of KU Leuven of course stands for
     Catholic).
24   'Neen aan het ontslag van Barbara Van Dyck' ('No to the
     dismissal of Barbara Van Dyck'), *De Standaard*, 10 June 2011,
     http://www.standaard.be/cnt/gs3b5ojj.
25   Ibid.
26   Joel De Ceuleer, 'Verzet tegen GGO's is misdadig' (Resistance to
     GMOs is criminal), *De Standaard*, 28 June 2013, http://www.
     standaard.be/cnt/dmf20130628_00640580.
27   Ibid.
28   Lieven De Cauter, 'Wetenschap als heilsleer en duivelspact:
     open brief aan Marc Van Montagu' ('Science as salvation and
     devil's pact. Open letter to Marc van Montagu'), *De Standaard*,
     4 July 2013: http://www.standaard.be/cnt/
     dmf20130704_00647370.
29   Ibid.
30   A petition against the visit of Robert Frailey is launched and
     signed by some 2900 people, see: https://www.change.org/p/
     keep-monsanto-out-of-our-universities, see also: http://www.
     dewereldmorgen.be/blogs/lievendecauter/2013/10/17/petitie-
     tegen-feestje-voor-monsanto,
     and a protest manifestation is set up at De Kouter in Ghent.
     http://community.dewereldmorgen.be/blogs/
     lievendecauter/2013/11/06/protestfeest-tegen-ggos-in-het-
     algemeen-en-monsanto-in-het-bijzonder
31   Lieven De Cauter, 'Open letter to Marc Van Montagu. Science
     as devil's pact and salvation doctrine', 6 November 2013, http://
     www.dewereldmorgen.be/blogs/lievendecauter/2013/11/06/
     open-brief-aan-marc-van-montagu-wetenschap-als-heilsleer-
     en-duivelsp.
32   Marc Van Montagu, 'Verwar GGO's niet met big business'
     ('Don't confuse GMOs with big business'), *The standard*, 11
     November 2013
     http://www.standaard.be/cnt/dmf20131111_00833186?utm_
     source=feedburner&utm_medium=feed&utm_

campaign=Feed%3A+dso-news-wetenschap
And republished on the website of the VIB, http://flandersbio.
be/news/marc-van-montagu-verwar-ggo-technologie-niet-met-
big-business/ The publication on the website of the VIB should
probably also be seen as a charm offensive in view of the party
and the protest action of the following day.

33   http://www.standaard.be/cnt/dmf20131111_00833186?utm_
source=feedburner&utm_medium= feed&utm
campaign=Feed%3A+dso-news-wetenschap

34   Pieter Vandoren, 'We zijn van nature tegen GGO's' ('We are all
by nature against GMOs'), *De Standaard*, 13 May 2015: http://
www.standaard.be/cnt/dmf20150512_01678997.

35   Lieven De Cauter, 'Wie is de nuttige idioot hier? ('Who's the
useful idiot here?'), *De Wereld Morgen*, 14 May 2015, http://
www.dewereldmorgen.be/artikel/2015/05/14/wie-is-hier-de-
nuttige-idioot.

36   Rancière makes an incredible point when he defines democracy
as the participation in politics of those who are not authorized
to do so. (Jacques Rancière, *La haine de la démocratie*, Paris: La
fabrique, 2005.)

37   Both in *Politique de La Nature* and in *Face à Gaya*, Bruno
Latour puts much more emphasis on the role that climate
controversy has played in this awareness. Both the climate
controversy and the GMO event are relevant cases. Bruno
Latour, *Politique de la Nature*, Paris: La Découverte, 2004
(1999), and Bruno Latour *Face à Gaya*, *huit conférences sur le
nouveau régime climatique*, Paris: La Découverte, 2015.

38   Not to be confused with the earlier but much less radical and
very concise Berlin 'Slow Science Manifesto' of the so-called
Slow Science Academy. The slow science academy, 'The Slow
science manifesto', Berlin, 2010: http://slow-science.org/

39   'As some of you may know, one of the consequences of Barbara
Van Dyck's resignation is an initiative of researchers who want
to defend and promote *slow science*, i.e. resist the fast,
competitive, benchmarked research that, seemingly inevitably,
is becoming the norm' (Isabelle Stengers, 'Een andere
wetenschap is mogelijk. Pleidooi voor een slow science', *De
Wereld Morgen*, 27 March 2013 http://www.dewereldmorgen.be/
artikels/2012/03/27/een-andere-wetenschap-mogelijk-een-
pleidooi-voor-slow-science; see also : *Une autre science est
possible. Manifesto pour un ralentissement des sciences*, Paris:
La Découverte, 2013, p. 86)

40   Slow science Manifesto: http://www.petities24.com/slow_
science_manifesto (because only the original English text is
available on the internet, I take the liberty to quote extensively
from the Dutch translation)

41   It is a tricky choice to mention names, because one can forget

names as well. But for the historical-scientific documentation of this constellation, here's an attempt: on a few notes by Prof Geography Kris Kesteloot (KU Leuven), I wrote a very first outline for a manifesto in August 2012, which was then taken up by Prof Eric Corijn, social geographer (VUB), Dr Barbara Van Dyck, bio-engineer, Prof Kris Kesteloot, Prof Eric Swyngedouw, social geographer (Manchester university), and Prof Isabelle Stengers, philosopher of science (ULB). In addition, Dr Mathias Lievens, philosopher (KU Leuven), Dr Kathleen Kenis, social geographer (KU Leuven), and perhaps also Prof Frank Moulaert (KULeuven) contributed.

42 See: http://www.petities24.com/slow_science_manifesto
43 On the occasion of this colloquium, Oikos published an earlier lecture on slow science by Isabelle Stengers on http://www. dewereldmorgen.be/artikels/2012/03/27/een-andere-wetenschap-mogelijk-een-pleidooi-voor-slow-science (as a prepublication of the translation that was to appear on paper in Oikos).
44 Now, during the final editing of this book, the count is at 760 signatories, so the petition is still signed sparingly.
45 See http://lac.ulb.ac.be/LAC/home.html, See also la charte de la désexcellence: http://lac.ulb.ac.be/LAC/charte.htmlv. Or in Flanders: http://www.demorgen.be/binnenland/vlaamse-academici-in-opstand-tegen-publicatiedruk-bb4c28c0/ and in the Netherlands there was the already legendary occupation of the Maagdenhuis. See for example: http://www.elsevier.nl/ nederland/article/2015/03/de-bezetting-van-het-maagdenhuis-gewoon-geen-mening-over-1732143W/ or http://www. volkskrant.nl/binnenland/wat-heeft-de-bezetting-van-het-maagdenhuis-opgeleverd~a4244680/
46 See https://slowscience.be/
47 Although one cannot deny that only very few traces are to be found on the internet. The Wikipedia article in question excels in brevity, and provides hardly any references, except to the extremely concise Berlin slow science manifesto (see above).
48 This occupation from February to April 2015 of the administrative headquarters of the university of Amsterdam is part of a tradition of protest since the sixties. For a reflection upon its results see (in Dutch only): https://www.parool.nl/ nieuws/wat-is-de-opbrengst-van-de-bezetting-van-het-maagde nhuis~b1e121a6/?referrer=https%3A%2F%2Fwww.google. com%2F
49 Unfortunately, if one skims the internet, the public forum of our time, the slow science movement, turns out to be a storm in a teacup. One of the few 'hits' on google when typing 'slow science movement' is an ironic blog of the same year 2011, written shortly after the potato war and before our manifesto

existed, The "slow science movement must be crushed" by a certain John Horgan (after making a list of the existing links, for him the reason that the movement must be suppressed, is that, as a science journalist, he would have no more work): https://blogs.scientificamerican.com/cross-check/the-slow-science-movement-must-be-crushed/. But the honesty compels us to conclude that there is no reference on the internet to 'our' slow science manifesto. Fortunately, there are the oeuvres of Stengers and Latour to give us hope. So: there is still work to be done. Or was the rumour, the 'idea' of *slow science* enough? The many related protests (which we mentioned above) point in that direction.

50 Isabelle Stengers, *Au temps des catastrophes. Resister à la barbarie qui vient,* Paris: La découverte poche, 2009, p. 29 (The English translation is available online: *Isabelle Stengers, In catastrophic times. How to resist the coming barbarism, 2015: http://openhumanitiespress.org/books/download/Stengers_2015_In-Catastrophic-Times.pdf*)

51 Isabelle Stengers, op. cit., p. 94.

52 Isabelle Stengers also stresses that those who invoke violence as the red line of the debate forget that social problems and issues are only put on the agenda through civil disobedience (Stengers, *Une autre science est possible. Manifesto pour un ralentissement des sciences*, Paris: La Découverte, 2013, p. 88). The history of social movements, such as the 8-hour working week or the suffragettes (who did not shy away from vandalism and even arson) proves that she has a point.

53 Take a look at the work of Stengers, for example the passage from her *Une autre Science est possible* about Liebig as the inventor of *fast science* that massively supplied *fast* chemists to industry. (pp. 97-104)

54 Isabelle Stengers, *Au temps de catastrophes*, p. 138, passim.

55 Isabelle Stengers, *Une autre science est possible*, p. 132.

56 In addition to the book mentioned in the previous footnote, also see *Au temps de catastrophes*. From our conversation in Kaaitheater it appeared that *L'intrusion de Gaia* was the original title she had in mind. See: http://www.dewereldmorgen.be/blog/lievendecauter/2016/02/28/over-kantelmomenten-en-de-intrusie-van-gaia.

57 Isabelle Stengers, *Une autre science est possible*, pp. 105-111.

58 Ibid., p. 141.

Key Features of Activism Today (Speech for a Night Conference on Resistance*)

0

*We have to learn to look at the history of protest movements as
waves.* Those who claim that the new generation is no longer out on
the streets have a short memory. They forget one of the most
important constellations for a reflection on activism today: the year
2011, the Year of the Protester, according to *Time Magazine*. Think
of 'the Indignados' and 'Occupy Wall Street', ... fuelled, strangely
enough, by the Arab Spring, and the events in Tahrir Square in
Egypt. I remember it well: 'Everywhere Tahrir Square!' was my
slogan that entire year. This was a second wave of the anti-
capitalist protests that started in Seattle in 1997 and culminated
in a broad different-globalization movement with the famous
clashes in Genoa and elsewhere. It also gave rise to the World
Social Forum, which had its heyday in Porto Alegre (the WSF still
exists, but has lost much of its importance), which in its turn was a
follow-up to the protests of May 68... So, there is indeed protest,
here in the lowlands too. The protests against TTIP and CETA, the
trade agreements with America and Canada, respectively, must
also be seen as successors to the various alter-globalization
protests. As Negri and Hardt demonstrate in their *Empire* trilogy,
the various protests come in waves. It is part of the image of the
world that the mainstream media present to us that makes us
think that the protest is much more a thing of the past. (Of course,
while editing this text for this book, we have already seen new
cycles of protests, the Climate Strikers in 2019, and Black Lives
Matter, a second wave still ongoing...)

So, we have to learn to look at the history of protest movements as waves. And this gives perspective, it teaches us that there
is continuity in spite of the apparent defeats or failures. More
importantly, we must also learn to see victories. In order to better
understand our strengths and weaknesses, and also to see differences with past protests, I will try to list a number of key
features, trajectories, forms and methods of today's activism
(mostly drawing from actions I was involved in or that were near or
dear to me):

1

*The rediscovery of the commons is one of the most promising events
of our time.* It is time not so much for resistance but for transition,
'practices of commoning', with which we can tackle, if not resolve,

the unbelievable challenges we face—climate change, superdiversity, migration. We must learn to see the world from the point of view of the commons: both the local and the global, both the private—a city garden or a local electricity network on solar panels—and the universal, such as the oceans and the sky but also language, 'nature' just as well as the 'digital commons'. The rediscovery of the commons is the utopia we need. Self-organization and concern for the common good against the privatization of everything and against the withdrawal of the state. Open source, Peer2Peer, repair cafés, urban gardening, and so on. The resurgence of the commons also happens in waves, according to historian Tine De Moor. There was a wave at the beginning of the sixteenth century, associated with the name Thomas More, and also a wave in the nineteenth—the mutualism of the labour movement, so now we would be experiencing a third wave. It is important to see that. The rediscovery of the commons is always a response to a wave of enclosures. At the beginning of the sixteenth century it was the fencing off of sheep pastures, now it is the privatization of everything, of knowledge, of seeds, of public services, of all the public and the common good, under the hegemony of neoliberalism. The defence of the common good, both the biosphere and cultural common good and the making of commons, is one of the most important issues of our time (I've said and written this many times, but we have to keep repeating it).

2

Self-organizing, worldwide civil protests and movements are a (relative) novelty. They are part of digital globalization. It is not necessary to believe in the revolutionary power of the crowd, the almost mystical 'multitude' of Negri and Hardt, to see that the internet, or more broadly the network society, has led to the emergence of new forms of organization of social movements. Self-organization in horizontal networks is indeed a novelty in the history of activism, I would think. The trade unions, the suffragettes, did of course also try to create networks, but these were mainly 'circles' based on proximity—the factory or the circle of acquaintances of women—and mostly hierarchical. How big this difference is, would require a separate treatment. It would require quite a bit of media theory, historiography, or sociology of social movements. Is this horizontal global self-organization a qualitative leap? Maybe so. We can communicate worldwide, there is global activism for the first time. The largest demonstration of all times, the one against the illegal invasion of Iraq, on 15 February 2003— it should be made a public holiday—brought 30 million people to the streets worldwide. It was the biggest manifestation ever in London, Tokyo, Rome and also big in Brussels, Paris, Madrid, and so on—which could only be organized via the internet and the new social media (at that time mostly just email, I believe, but that too would require further research). The speed with which for example the women's marches against Trump, the 'Pussyhat March' against sexism and for women's rights (on 21 January 2017, a few days before this lecture), are organized worldwide was completely unthinkable before the internet and social media. In three months, it just went viral (see Wikipedia under 'Pussyhat' for the entire story). Viral action networks are the future.

3

The new citizen movements are democracy in action. Civil movements are a form of broad 'radical democracy', à la Mouffe and Laclau. Rancière says that democracy is the form of government of those who should not rule, those not 'entitled' to rule. So, it is also always incomplete, the inclusion is never total. After women, the minorities must now also be involved in democracy. Democracy is an eternal upstream struggle and must always be enforced from below. Politics is only that threshold moment, what we call party politics is just 'police', according to Rancière. Social movements and activists play an important role here. Take, for example, the Oosterweel case: stRaten Generaal and Ademloos, two action groups, armed with extensive knowledge, defeated the government and its plans for the gigantic Lange Wapper bridge in Antwerp. They successfully challenged the Oosterweel route in a court case before the Council of State—a stalemate that perhaps will lead to dialogue and a better solution—and closed the ring road further away from the city. Recently, after years of conflict, they have found a workable compromise and the activists are now actively involved in the process of realizing the plans.

4

This brings us to *the importance of cities: urban activism in all its forms is one of the exciting phenomena of our time.* From squatting to guerrilla knitting, from temporary occupation to protests of all kinds, from festive interventions in difficult places to urban gardening—cities are new focal points for collective, social, and political identity and citizenship and therefore they have taken on a new meaning for activists. Urban movements are local, but there are also networks of cities: Mayors against Climate change… It would lead us too far to go into all this, so I would like to refer to the work of Eric Corijn and Benjamin Barber, but one can also think of the work of Henk Oosterling and his project 'Rotterdam Vakmanstad', in which an ecological education must teach children and young people to become not only professionals but also world citizens. It all needs a separate treatment, and I have written about it elsewhere, and plan to make and entire book about it, but I hope my point is obvious: urban activism is important today.

5

Most new civil movements are non-violent civil disobedience, and it works. Civil disobedience is indeed a form of resistance (and not just commitment), which is still very valid today. It works because it creates a fact, which is more than a hundred opinion pieces do. I often give the so-called 'Potato War' as an example as it is at the same time an instance of 'direct action'. Barbara Van Dyck was fired from Leuven University at the beginning of June 2011 for defending the symbolic destruction of a GMO test field with genetically modified potatoes in Wetteren (on 28 May 2011). Together with eleven of her comrades of the Field Liberation Movement, she was also on trial for no less than 'bendevorming' ('gang formation', or organized crime, which is an extremely severe qualification). She has been reinstated by a new rector at the University of Leuven. The 11 were convicted of violence and destruction of property but not of organized crime. The result of this, for now and evermore, is that many things are now on the map simultaneously: the conflict of interest between universities and multinationals and the privatization of knowledge, the neoliberalization of the university (which resulted in the Slow Science Manifesto), and last but not least, the public awareness of the dangers of GMOs. The lesson is clear to me: civil disobedience and direct action pay off!

6

A boycott is a valid form of non-violent political action, a non-violent means of pressure. The best-known example today is the BDS movement (Boycott, Divestment & Sanctions) against the occupation policy, the systematic human rights violations, and war crimes and apartheid system of Israel. I focus on BACBI, The Belgian Academic and Cultural Boycott of Israel (as I was one of its founders). The first campaign took place in May 2015 when the Ghent arts centre Campo wanted to participate in the Israel Festival in Jerusalem with a piece by theatre maker Miet Warlop. Following the publication of an open letter and responses from several public figures, Warlop and Campo decided to withdraw from the Israel Festival. The second campaign was in May 2016, in an open letter to the rector of Ghent University, fifty professors were protesting against UGent's cooperation with Technion, the Israel Institute of Technology, and with Israel Aerospace Industries. Technion more than any other university is intertwined with Israel's military-industrial complex. It is at the forefront of innovative military cutting-edge technology. Israel Aerospace Industries, owned by the government and one of Israel's biggest arms companies, has a close partnership with Technion. It produces tailor-made weapons for the army. This includes the production of military drones. The action led to a Charter of Human Rights in Research to avoid such collaborations in the future. A third BACBI campaign is opposed to the 'Law Train' research project, a cooperation of the Federal Justice Service and the KU Leuven with the Israeli police and the Israeli Bar Ilan university. This research project concerns interrogation techniques of persons under arrest, has a total value of more than five million euros and is funded through the Horizon 2020 fund of the European Union. In addition to Belgium, Spain and Portugal are also involved. Portugal has since withdrawn. In September 2016, some thirty academics from the University of Leuven wrote an open letter to their rector Rik Torfs. BACBI supported this action but did not take the lead (as it was not based on the argument of Boycott, but on human rights). After two years of action, with a group of professors and local activists of Leuven, the new rector, Luc Sels, decided not to prolong the collaboration. It is important to note that BDS is a global movement that acts locally but wants to have an effect in the Middle East. This is a good example of an important wisdom for activists: 'Think global, act local'.

7

The defence of freedom of expression is and remains a most urgent task. Particularly vis-à-vis the state of exception called the 'war on terror'. Since 9/11, activism has been systematically criminalized. Opinion pieces and polemics in the press play a very important role in these cases, often the subject of lawsuits. During the potato war there were dozens of opinion pieces and polemics (in which the undersigned was involved) and, very recently, the resignation of Abou Jahjah. Dyab Abou Jahjah, who after his perils with the publisher De Bezige Bij—some authors of the publisher did not want a book by him to be published, for he was casted as anti-Israel and therefore anti-Semitic, and so on—was recently fired as a columnist at *De Standaard* because he called an attack on Israeli soldiers with a truck an act of resistance. 'By any means necessary. #FreePalestine', he had tweeted and then 'violence against soldiers of an illegal occupation is resistance under international law'. His 'By any means necessary' was considered a call to violence, but it was in fact a quote from international law. The 'bandwidth of free speech' is very narrow when it comes to Israel. The room is guaranteed to split in twain like a swirling Red Sea if we would go into this. But whether one agrees with him or not, his right to freedom of expression must be defended. Even when it comes to Israel. In France, calling for a boycott is already punishable as anti-Semitism. And that in the land of Voltaire—unimaginable. Same for Germany. (In the meantime, in early 2020, the European Court for Human Rights has overruled this: calling for a boycott forms an integral part of non-violent freedom of expression). To conclude with some other spicy examples: I signed a letter to defend the right to privacy of extreme-right politicians who had a love affair, and got a letter of gratitude, even if they knew fully well I was a left-leaning public intellectual (and *they* always say: 'rather dead than red'). Worse: I co-signed a letter with my old-time comrade in arms professor Jean Bricmont, a radical 'chomskyian', defending the right of the former very conservative Archbishop of Belgium, *Monseigneur* Léonard, to write that homosexuality was a disease. Yes. *The right of freedom of expression is the right to a wrong opinion.* For if only the right opinions are acceptable, you live under an authoritarian regime, or a dictatorship of political correctness. So, defending freedom of expression is also an eternal task, the core business of the public intellectual, certainly in these times of anti-terror measures in which the rule of law defends itself by abolishing the rule of law, or at least restricting it; and in times of right-wing populism that wants to silence critical voices; and in times of postcolonial, antiracist, antisexist political correctness. Yes.

8

The 'professionalization' of activism or, better, the interdisciplinary approach, seems to me to be a very important development in the contemporary methodology of activism and social movements. It is about truly transdisciplinary coalitions of very different groups and individuals, which yields many learning processes and knowledge exchanges (here too, the internet, the network society is bearing fruit, I believe). One can think once more of the potato war, where professors, human scientists, bio-engineers, organic farmers, worried citizens, NGOs such as Greenpeace, and politicians (of the ecological party [Groen!]) found each other, supported and reinforced each other and learned from each other. The Belgian philosopher of science Isabelle Stengers, who was involved in both the potato war and the Slow Science Manifesto, speaks in her writings almost enchantingly of 'learning to think and act together', 'practicing together the art of paying attention'. The beforementioned Oosterweel-case supplies an even more splendid example of such professionalization and transdisciplinary coalitions. Urban activists who bring a gigantic building project with a huge machinery of state, city, and large capital behind it, to a halt through petitions, referenda, manifestations, elaborated alternative routes, plans, studies, complaints to the Council of State, and so on. That means that there are marketeers, architects, urbanists, citizens, lawyers, working together and reinforcing each other. The 'Ringland' movement, pleading for a covering of the ring road, was the crowning of it.

The outcome, the ultimate effect of civil protests, of activism is always uncertain and victories can turn out to be pyrrhic or temporary ones, but often there is more influence in the long term than you might think. Often invisibly, in the riverbed of (local) history a stone has been moved. The awareness—yes also the theoretical impact of those temporalities, the slow impact of often short-lived actions—may be part of the 'professionalization' of the civil movements. We also need to learn—and that is a task for committed academics or activist academics—to see victories, and indirect influences, to see the indirect impact of events, such as the potato war, such as the other-globalization movement, such as the Indignados, that worked through in Podemos and SYRIZA and in a certain sense also in our local movement 'Hart boven Hard' [Heart over Hard].

9

Small local actions and large social movements should ideally enter into coalitions. We must also take small activist projects seriously. I often give Parckfarm as an example: A Brussels public park in an old railway trench, a post-industrial piece of romantic urban landscape, with allotment gardens for the neighbourhood, a chicken coop, a beehive, a dry toilet, a large communal table full of edible herbs, and the conservatory, as a stopping place for all kinds of groups engaged in neighbourhood (and youth) activities and organic food and short supply chains. Parckfarm, a kind of commons under the auspices of the BIM, the Brussels Institute for the Environment, but run by local residents and volunteers, where all kinds of beautiful things happen, which are good for the neighbourhood and good for the environment, and the one via the other, and vice versa, that is beautiful... It will not save the world, but it is still a very concrete step taken here and now, hence I have christened it rather optimistically a 'concrete utopia'. The lesson I learned was this—a concrete utopia can bring people together and connect micro- and macro-politics, superdiversity and ecology, the two major challenges of the twenty-first century. This kind of micropolitics works 'globally'. Think global, act local, remains the message. One could also call it a 'glocal' utopia.

A second lesson from Parckfarm, for me personally, is the task of intellectuals to give publicity to these fragile initiatives, supporting them discursively by reflecting on them as fellow travellers. I think this is also an important contribution (although it may be a lame excuse for my lack of green fingers and aversion to all things practical), albeit at the risk of promoting gentrification with that publicity and attention (see my reflections on urban activism elsewhere). But Parckfarm is sowing its seeds in all sorts of ways in the city. Pool is Cool is a kind of continuation—a movable swimming pool in the summer to bring all the people together via children from disadvantaged neighbourhoods and to give under-used places some aura... We should learn to see this kind of dispersion, this kind of temporal impact and yes, indeed, we have to investigate it. I have been doing this for years with students, nowadays, in the architecture department, and Master theses and PhD dissertations are being written about urban activism and urban social movements.

We must continue to work on a coalition of the small, often apolitical commitments and initiatives and the big picture, the real political activism of the big social movements. 'Klein Verzet'—as journalist Tine Hens called it, meaning not only small resistance, but also low gear ratio and small entertainment—in the cracks of capitalism and in major movements such as the Climate Marches may turn the tide. Chantal Mouffe calls this kind of coalition 'l'équivalence des luttes', the equivalence of the struggles: Heart over Hard, for example, tries to combine the protests of the cultural and healthcare worlds and the library system and of the trade unions across society, a wonderful movement that is unseen in the low countries and which brings together practically all actors of civil society, the 'midfield' (as we call it) against the austerity policies and harsh rightist populist politics. A unique coalition that is still widening (even if, at the time of editing this text, the wave seems gone).

All this is very well, I hear you think, but what to do about Wilders and other populists across Europe and beyond? What to do about the wave of anti-globalization and anti-migration, mostly outright racist sentiments of right-wing populism, which has both America and Europe in its grip? I do not know. I do know. The recent Pussyhat Marches point the way—the intersectionality, the equivalence of women's rights, 'black lives matter', all kinds of issues came together in a broad movement. We must keep trying. The worldwide manifestation of women, one day after the inaugu-ration of Trump, has made an impression. Who knows, Trump may unite the forces of those who strive for justice, human rights, and therefore for women's rights and minorities, and those who are committed to saving the planet, and many others. We must continue to expand coalitions and equivalences as in the concept of climate justice—linking justice and ecology and human rights. Who knows, the Pussyhat project might become a global movement of self-organizing citizens under the banner of the commons. Who knows?

It is also interesting how rapidly this wave has disappeared; this lecture of 2017 has aged... or is it that our memory of social movements is short? This deserves an entire paragraph, as combined with the long temporalities it is a paradox.

But then again, even this remark has aged. Now, in summer 2020, while I do the final editing, the wave of Black Lives Matter is up like never before and in its wake the statues of King Leopold II are being vandalized here in Belgium, and statues of colonial figures all over the World are under attack; even Columbus himself has been toppled...

10

'Structural Activism' or 'activist lobbying' may well be a necessity. If I draw the conclusions from the previous paragraphs and put together the key feature of professionalization and coalitions, I arrive at this almost bewildering observation. Activism is important, but has a modest and often slow impact, certainly on global problems, anyway. Politics in the narrow sense remains extremely important; reformism of structures will have to take place through politics, through parties, states, and negotiations. Transition or catastrophe? That will ultimately be settled politically. Structural intervention in capitalism, for example by obliging it to switch to a zero-emission economy, is urgent. We cannot first abolish capitalism (if there would be consensus, *quod non*) and then save the planet. We can only hope that there is enough political will to force capitalism through civil activism that becomes real politics, 'realpolitik'. The NGOs who participated in the debates at the climate conference in Paris have understood this correctly and are practising what I would dare to call structural activism.

From a purely political point of view, perhaps only the line that runs from Bernie Sanders via Jeremy Corbyn to Podemos and SYRIZA contains the vague political contours of a real political alternative (Oops, that hope has in the meantime vanished in thin air too), but structural activism is, for the time being, a much more certain option. Sitting down with banks to convince them to withdraw from investments in fossil fuels for instance. That is what we need, anyway. That is a consequence of the transdisciplinary, the professionalization of activism and the formation of coalitions and the search for equivalences, in the hope of actually getting something done structurally. The decisions of the Paris climate conference are, in that sense, with all doubts and uncertainties, a bright spot. Some call this structural activism 'resistance from within'. Maybe that is also, and above all, the kind of resistance we need today.

Or is all this reformist hope bogus, and is only revolutionary uprising an option, as Extinction Rebellion has it? Reformist ecological politics and activism have failed, they claim, and the past forty years are there to prove them right. So, mass civil disobedience now!?

Conclusion. The purpose of all activism remains clear today: the defence of the commons, both local and global, both particular and universal, both natural and digital, and the defence of the rights of commoners, the Fundamental Rights, Human Rights, Social and Environmental Justice. In every activist action, in every 'practice of commoning' there is a utopian spark. The world system as it currently functions, and, even more so, does not function, is unsustainable, both ecologically and socially. We have to do something anyway. Doing nothing is not an option. 'Rebel Against Extinction We Must'. My battle cry therefore remains: 'pessimism in theory, optimism in practice'.

Note

*   'Nachtconferentie: de mens in opstand' ('Night conference: Man in Revolt'), Amsterdam City theatre, January 26, 2017. A brief report here (in Dutch) https://www.groene.nl/artikel/de-mens-in-opstand

Extinction Rebellion: Civil Disobedience for an Ecological State of Emergency

Given the fact that nothing substantial has been done by our governments about climate change and that after 30 years we have to admit that climate activism has largely failed, Extinction Rebellion claims that the only option now is to force our governments, by mass civil disobedience, to declare an ecological state of emergency. Once the governments are forced to give in, citizens panels should draw up a radical action plan for transition to a circular economy and a close-to-zero carbon society. It is the only way to avoid mass extinction of both human and nonhuman lifeforms on the planet.[1]

One cannot understand Extinction Rebellion without referring to the notion and tradition of nonviolent civil disobedience: Henri David Thoreau, Rosa Parks, Martin Luther King, Mahatma Gandhi... For if you do not take that tradition into consideration, the actions of Extinction Rebellion may seem examples of 'the end justifies the means', of disrespect for law and lawfulness.[2] While it's almost the other way around: This global action group wants to wake people up to improve the laws. This is at the heart of civil disobedience: Adjusting politics, breaking unjust laws, waking up society by the radical but non-violent breaking of the law. It suffices to read the pamphlet *On the Duty of Civil Disobedience* by Henri Thoreau.[3] This is the opposite of Machiavellianism.

To make this a bit more concrete, we refer to the 'Royal Rebellion', an action of XR Belgium at the Royal Palace in Brussels on Saturday 12 October 2019. Some two hundred people tried to occupy the big space in front of the Royal Palace in Brussels for as long as possible. It started with discussion panels, but after a day, as they were blocking public transport, the police moved in heavy-handedly and arrested around a hundred people. The police violence was such that it was reported in the press and an investigation was started.[4]

Some people think this sort of action is pseudo-activity, therapeutic behaviour, but they do not understand how bad it is for people who have really informed themselves to let the coming ecological collapse happen without rebelling. Such a person is Olivier De Schutter, professor at UCL, former UN Special Rapporteur on the right to food. He was there at the Royal Palace and was unnecessarily treated to a dose of pepper spray by the police. The photos were circulating on Twitter.[5] These kinds of individuals know that we are heading for unprecedented catastrophes if we go to three degrees global warming, which the IPPC[6] predicts if we continue to do business as usual. From three degrees upwards, other processes, such as the melting of the permafrost, are triggered and push us towards a global temperature increase of five degrees. Then it is game over for humanity, the mammals, and the biosphere as we know it. Perhaps the lichens and cockroaches will survive, who knows. This possibility is increasingly thematized by climate scientists, and this hypothesis is called: 'Hothouse Earth'—the earth as an oven.[7]

But even without that extreme possibility we are in serious trouble as we are experiencing the sixth mass extinction ever on Earth. And this is not abstract or exotic ('the eyes of the panda') but very concrete and incredibly close. Insect populations in most countries of Western Europe have declined by 75 percent since 2000, as a study in Germany conducted by the Radboud University Nijmegen has revealed.[8] So, that Great Extinction is now, not in some distant future. And it threatens our food supply, because without pollinators there are no fruits. It's all connected. Our planetary ecosystem is not a machine but a complex organism. The ecocide committed by capitalism in its pursuit of profit is irresponsible if not downright criminal, the most ruthless form of 'the end justifies the means': Everything has to give way to profit and all the overexploitation that comes with it is collateral damage. By the way, this looting is becoming more and more extreme with fracking, tar sands oil, and deep-sea oil.

Those who, on scientific grounds, know what catastrophes we are heading for, perhaps a total collapse of both our ecosystem and our social systems, cannot just idly stand by and watch. Extinction Rebellion starts from that knowledge as an established given. A protester who was participating in the Royal Rebellion, said it clearly: 'We are just concerned citizens. So are many young parents, afraid for their children's future. I don't know what impact our actions can have. But I had to do something. I couldn't sit at home any longer as a powerless onlooker.' It is indeed a symbolic action, it would be a total mistake to take the action of those concerned citizens literally, because civil disobedience is essentially symbolic. Of course, the people of Extinction Rebellion know full well that the King of Belgium has no political power according to the Constitution. This is an open letter via the symbolic embodiment of the nation, the King, to the entire Belgian population and its politicians: 'Wake up before it is too late!' That is the true scope of this action, and all the actions of XR worldwide.

But the climate negationists, who say 'climate change is fake news', and in their wake the climate quietists, who say 'it's not so bad', have still not understood: 'Our house is on fire.' Demanding the declaration of the ecological state of emergency, through actions of civil disobedience, is at this moment in history scientifically justified. It is certainly no coincidence that about 400 scientists support the actions of Extinction Rebellion in a petition—we *are* in an ecological emergency.[9]

The actions of Extinction Rebellion have nothing to do with disdain for democracy or the constitution, on the contrary. The ecological and social collapse will wipe out the constitution and the state of law and this is exactly what Extinction Rebellion wants to prevent with its actions of the last chance, by pleading for radical political and therefore legislative action. This ecological emergency they are calling for is not dictatorship, or 'eco-despotism', but a contingency plan.

Notes

1   A sort of stark manifesto of the movement and its methods, criticized and not official, but worth reading is Roger Hallam's *Common Sense for the 21ˢᵗ Century*: https://www.rogerhallam. com/wp-content/uploads/2019/08/Common-Sense-for-the-21st-Century_by-Roger-Hallam-Download-version.pdf

2   As did Mia Doornaert, (in)famous columnist for our local quality newspaper *De Standaard*: https://www.standaard.be/ cnt/dmf20191016_04667199. This article was originally written as an answer to her, but I substantially rewrote it to focus on Extinction Rebellion and not on the polemic with her.

3   See: https://www.ibiblio.org/ebooks/Thoreau/Civil%20 Disobedience.pdf

4   See press links on XR website: https://www.extinctionrebellion. be/en/royal-rebellion

5   See: https://twitter.com/XR_Belgium/ status/1183416358626832389

6   The Intergovernmental Panel on Climate Change, A UN body, got the Noble Prize for Peace in 2006 (together with Al Gore). It is worth to check them out: https://www.ipcc.ch/

7   See: https://www.greenpeace.org/international/story/18394/rex-weyler-hothouse-earth/; and the original scientific article: https://www.pnas.org/content/pnas/ early/2018/07/31/1810141115.full.pdf ; I also discuss this hypothesis in 'End of the Anthropocene' in this book.

8   See: https://www.ru.nl/english/news-agenda/news/vm/ iwwr/2017/three-quarters-total-insect-population-lost/

9   See: https://www.reuters.com/article/us-climate-change-scientists/scientists-endorse-mass-civil-disobedience-to-force-climate-action-idUSKBN1WS01K

V Zoöpolitics and the Age of Pandemics

The Corona Pandemonium (Blogs on the Covid-19 Crisis)

Corona Limbo
(*De Wereld Morgen*, April 27, 2020)

We are in a strange kind of in-between, an interstitial situation. '*We're in limbo*,' somebody said to open the holiday class. We had decided to support the many international students who were stranded here in Belgium in their isolation during the 'lockdown' by continuing the classes during the Easter holidays, albeit without a programme and without obligation, just to keep in touch. The uniqueness of these lessons immediately shows how strange this period is: 'holiday lessons', a kind of contradiction in terms. When I checked my lesson notes afterwards, I was immediately grabbed by the first word: LIMBO.

We're in limbo. We're in purgatory. Yep. But limbo is something other than purgatory, I would think. Yes. Checked it. Limbo is the eternal place of natural bliss for unbaptized children. It was abolished by the Vatican in 2007. Better late than never. Purgatory was the waiting room for heaven, meant for all those people who were not good enough for heaven and not bad enough for hell. Not yet abolished, but in transition to be quietly dismantled after eternal renovations. Hell and heaven are not very popular destinations anymore, except among fundamentalists.

Although all these theological places now seem outlandish, these are hellish times all the same. Some of us do find themselves in hell, or experience hellish situations: in the Covid-19 units of our hospitals and now especially in severely ravaged rest homes for the elderly. Strange how rest homes and cruise ships can turn into real infernos at times like these.

While others, like my girlfriend and I for instance, create an almost guilty little paradise, with lots of reading and writing, some teaching, walks through the city and bike rides to the woods of Brussels, seeing interesting or great movies, enjoying good food with good wines, and *last but not least*, good… sleep. (The quarrels I place between brackets for the sake of the argument).

But purgatory, limbo, hell or guilty paradise, anthropology is a better discipline to tackle the corona crisis than theology. Anthropology of the Covid-19 crisis! Actually, that is what many of our conversations were about during the holiday lessons. There is a need for an ethnographic study, with (depth) psychology and (surface) sociology as auxiliary sciences. In order to eventually move on to philosophical anthropology: What does all this teach us about humankind?

The first lesson is immediately obvious: The image of man presented by neoliberalism is shattered. The ambitious, individualistic, competitive, self-assured, and obviously selfish individual, in short 'the entrepreneur' is: a) not an ideal image; b) not a good description of what humans are; and especially c) not the one who will save the world—as Ayn Rand and all her self-declared and unconscious followers believed.

However, an ethnography, or old-fashioned phenomenology, a more or less philosophical description of this our corona limbo is indeed... not an easy matter. Everyone wants to to their hand at it though, you can tell by the flow of publications on corona. There are some very good pieces, no doubt about it. Still, it is hard to come to grips with it. Me too, I feel like writing a new piece about it almost every day. That proves it is a quandary. I can't come to terms with it, so to speak. Sounds dangerously theological again. All right, then. *It bugs me. It bugs us.* On closer inspection, the expression hits the nail on the head: viruses are bugs, and a lot of bugs are viruses. If something doesn't work, French speakers say: *'C'est buggé'* (believe it or not). That is this suspension: *'Notre monde est buggé, quoi!* Thinking this suspension, this in-between, this limbo and describing what it does to us, that is the task.

We must call the beast by its name. The pandemic, a medical disaster, brings about an objective state of emergency, a need for urgent measures, as with any natural disaster. This leads to a legal state of emergency, or state of *exception*: the suspension of fundamental rights, such as now first and foremost the right to move freely. Quite fundamental. This suspension, this temporary suspension of fundamental rights, destabilizes normal life and leads to other suspensions of fundamental rights, such as the right to work and the right to assemble.

It is a temporary suspension of our freedom, and that restriction of freedom in turn leads to the suspension of our sense of existence. We are destabilized in our being, in the very essence of our being: our daily routine, our everydayness. That is the existential essence, so to speak, of this lockdown, this quarantine, this 'confinement'. Nothing is what it used to be and the return to normal remains highly uncertain. What, when and how, everything hangs in the balance. The return to normality is uncertain and even risky. And it will not be real normality anyway, certainly not in the first year.

The lockdown is not only a suspension of political normality, but also a cessation of normal economic activity. The result is a gigantic contraction of the economy, an unprecedented economic crisis that hangs over the world like a thundercloud and sharply increasing the inequalities in our already very dualized world.

So, we are not only stuck in the present, but the future is murky too, dark, and even threatening. Our 'protention'—to really use a word from philosophical phenomenology—has been put out of action. According to Edmund Husserl, man does not only perceive and experience the present and also not only the past ('retention'), but is also focused on the future ('protention'). Certainly in our world of projects and 'targets', of strategic planning, of projection, we have all become projectiles of future-orientation. This obsessive future orientation is now blocked. All our plans are now hanging in thin air or are simply shattered. Our lives are on hold.

Our professional and social life has become virtual, but we quickly discovered the limits of digital sociability. It is not convivial but permeated with alienation. Estrangement is our share. And just when we think we can go back to normal, the second wave will be awaiting us.

We are in a twilight zone, *entre chien et loup*, neither fish nor fowl. This is a bad 'holiday'. Time is open, vacant, in the sense of empty. We are without regular work, locked up, and therefore on anything but a holiday. Caught between a rock and a hard place, between heaven and hell. Ignorant as unbaptized children, we must dare to stutter, we must dare to admit that we have no grip on this strange, unreal phenomenon. After Descartes' methodical doubt, let us methodically stutter over corona. If necessary, in a kind of *double Dutch*, a *Corona-limbo-Lingala*.

Of course, it's no trifle, this Great Confinement, perhaps the biggest lockdown in world history. Never before have such draconic measures reigned over just about the entire planet. No wonder we're all a bit shell-shocked. We just don't know anymore. We are in uncharted territory, in limbo.

The Nightmare of Foucault: From Corona Plague to Cyber-panopticon
(*De Wereld Morgen*, May 5, 2020)

Discipline is one of the key words of this historical moment. This is not surprising, but it is symptomatic of the exceptional situation we find ourselves in. Or, to put it another way: It is highly surprising. Discipline had, until recently, somewhat disappeared from our attention and from our daily lives, like the punch clock in most companies: silently removed. The word discipline itself had begun to sound a bit corny.

Some would undoubtedly attribute this to the wretched legacy of 1968, which quashed authority and hierarchy, and thus discipline. The informal society, you know. Discipline belonged to a number of old institutions, such as the prison, the correction house, the madhouse, the village school, the army, and of course the factory. Fordism, or the conveyor belt, was the pinnacle of discipline: Workers drilled by machines, making standardized movements like automatons. Think of Chaplin's *Modern Times*. In the 'post-Fordist', information-technology-based knowledge economy of the horizontal network society, that type of discipline has disappeared from the centre of social life or has been hidden from view because of relocation to the sweatshops of the South. The 'entrepreneurial self' is, by nature or out of necessity, a flexible workaholic, a neo-liberal Stakhanovite—no longer in work suits but in jeans and T-shirts: Capitalism itself has become 'informal'.

In his classic book *Surveiller et Punir* (*Discipline and Punish*), the French philosopher Michel Foucault begins a famous chapter of this genealogy of discipline with the disposition of drastic measures in a city hit by the plague, referring to the military archives of Vincennes. These measures, which for years were considered extreme, primitive, exotic, and improbable—in the present day and age unthinkable and impracticable—are now back in force: the division of space and the closure of houses, curfews, quarantine for contaminated person, constant daily, strict controls and meticulous bureaucratic registration. For Foucault, the plague functions as the origin of the idea of discipline. So, it is worth taking a moment to think about it today.

He writes: 'The plague as a form, at once real and imaginary, of disorder has as its medical and political correlative discipline.' This typical Foucauldian sentence now sounds rather ominous. I tend to translate it in reverse for the occasion and read Foucault against the grain: 'The medical and political discipline has, as its counterpart, the plague as both a real and imaginary form of disorder'. For, even though the return of discipline is the subject of this text, disorder threatens. Yes, it does. From the second wave that terrifies hospital staff, to the horror stories that reach us from Ecuador and Brazil, past the negative price of oil (unimaginable, mind-blowing, right?), with *en passant* images of heavily armed scum protesting against the lockdown in America, to solid articles and authoritative reports that talk about a possible world crisis without precedent, about 'biblical famines' (headline in our local quality newspaper *De Standaard*) and who knows even the collapse of the global economic financial system. Not to mention the ongoing demographic and especially ecological catastrophe. The locust plagues are also on the scene. And none of this is 'imaginary', but unfortunately all too real.

You start to get dizzy when you try to think of the interference of all those factors combined. It may well be that what we are now experiencing is a phenomenon that the Americans call 'the perfect storm' with a rather frivolous but apt expression: the simultaneous gathering and intertwinement of many calamitous omissions, mismanagement, and outright disasters. Disastrous omissions and mismanagement, such as the deliberate neglect of the health care sector and the reduction of social security. Outright disasters: a 'minor flu' that brings the world to a standstill. An unsightly little lifeform, a virus, might unleash a chain reaction of catastrophes that could lead to *The Big One,* the great landslide, the collapse of the social order, of the world as it was. If the dominoes start to fall and continue to do so, maybe that will be it. The perfect storm, delightful *lapidary* expression. Irresistibly sardonic.

After the quoted sentence Foucault continues with a phrase that now, if possible, sounds even more ominous: 'Behind the disciplinary mechanisms can be read the haunting memory of "contagions", of the plague, of rebellions, crimes, vagabondage, desertions, people who appear and disappear, live and die in disorder.' This phantom that Foucault describes as rather imaginary, could well become reality, a real nightmare—in many places it already is. So, give us today our daily dose of discipline and above all self-discipline. We learn more about the connection between discipline (from above) and self-discipline (from within) as we read on.

[handwritten margin note: self discipline must come naturally]

The second model of discipline is, in the same core chapter, the panopticon, the well-known 'dispositive' or 'apparatus' with the central tower and the cells around it, invented by the utilitarian philosopher Bentham to counter corporal punishment and cruelty and to enforce self-discipline through visibility. It was intended not only for prisons but also for schools or hospitals. In practice, however, it was only used for prisons. To date, many prisons have been directly or indirectly inspired by the panopticon, the so-called panopticon prisons indeed. For Foucault, this model of disciplining through visibility was a paradigm that went much further and wanted to discipline the whole of society through visual (self-) control. All this is well known. Foucault for beginners. And also ubiquitous: the security cameras everywhere are now as banal as muzak in shopping centres, another form of crowd control.

But… It could be that these two dispositions of discipline, these two contrasting paradigms of the 'disciplinary society', of which Foucault wanted to write the monumental genealogy, are now brought to a new synthesis. The corona pandemic could give rise to a kind of cyber-panopticon if we focus on digital control to contain the pandemic. With the Chinese 'social credit' system as a deeply creepy example. A real nightmare—which, like the perfect storm, is also a kind of sinister oxymoron. Big Brother *meets* the big helmsman—a nightmare, I tell you. The alliance of artificial intelligence, *big data* and the military-technological complex of the security and surveillance industry will have golden days. I am afraid so.

That is the essence of the discussion about the famous tracking apps in this corona crisis. For the time being, this panoptic cyberpunk nightmare seems to have been averted, at least in Belgium. But it will return many more times, as nightmares do. Because as a society we always have to choose between, or weigh up, security and freedom, discipline and anarchy, fear and courage (care, responsibility, solidarity). And of course, it must be said: between public health and economy. In any case, we are already groping, with a lot of trial and error—still without enough mouth masks and massive tests—in the search for a synthesis between plague measures and cybertechno-cholera, so to speak. For the *deconfinement* threatens to become a *discomfiture* and the end of the lockdown a deadlock. This will be the case until there is a vaccine. And that is not for tomorrow. So, the challenge for the near future is responsible disciplinary measures and a moderate analogue and perhaps also digital tracing, a delicate exercise. It remains a choice between the plague and cholera.

Biopolitics and the Open Society
(*De Wereld Morgen*, April 5, 2020)

It is not surprising that the term 'biopolitics' suddenly pops up in the mainstream media (in our case *De Standaard* of 27 March and 30 March). Foucault defined biopolitics as a new sovereignty: the old sovereignty was the power to kill subjects. The new sovereignty of the emerging modern states was the control over and care for life. He used the examples of the rise of social medicine and early urbanism, and indeed the radical measures against the plague, which he had first interpreted in terms of discipline. So today, talking about biopolitics is absolutely to the point.

At this time of pandemic, however, this term, very predictably, rekindled a decades old polemic between—and now, before you know it, every description is an offense, because that's how it goes in polemics—right-wing or otherwise liberal fans of science or 'positivists' (or worse 'science fundamentalists') and left-wing 'postmodern' relativists (in *De Standaard*: Steven Blancke, Patrick Loobuyck and Maarten Boudry versus Bert De Munck). Some have been saying since Carl Popper that we should trust in an open society and the logic of scientific research, while others, following in Foucault's footsteps, say that we should always fear the power factor hiding under (bio)politics and science.

Both positions very quickly become ideological rather than philosophical and both have their blind spots: the fans of science are often blind to the power the multinationals have over science and the limitations of science, while the followers of Foucault often tend to see a dark sovereign (bio)power behind democracy, because they don't take it seriously, a constellation in which science becomes an instrument of power.

Isabelle Stengers, a Belgian philosopher who has largely remained a prophet without honour in her own country, and her self-proclaimed apprentice (and sorcerer) Bruno Latour, may be able to help break the deadlock and the rather blatant ideological trench warfare—or rather the firing at cardboard caricatures of the enemy at a fairground shooting gallery. Science as such does not exit, there are only sciences in plural. Scientific controversy and links with vested interests, such as those of states and multinationals, are inevitable. So, the Platonic conception of the *believers* in Science is untenable. But certainly Latour is a fervent defender of the sciences, and he refers to the climate: in the fight against the climate, we will badly need all sciences, as the IPPC proves abundantly.

We must, of course, pay attention to the attempts to close down the open society through the corona crisis. The Hungarian president Orbán is the embodiment of this, but the Big Brother tendencies to not only lock us up but also to follow us by mobile phone are writings on the wall that a cyber-totalitarian post-corona state is perfectly possible. China is doing it without any reserve, and without using corona as an excuse, for that matter. So, a Foucauldian gaze at the panoptic apparatuses may be helpful.

The good news is that a useful term has been introduced into the public debate: biopolitics. Anyone who reads Foucault attentively will notice that he is trying to conceptualize a new modern sovereignty that works on the basis of two 'modern' concepts: population and public health, in opposition to the old sovereignty of the king, who sits in judgement over the death of his subjects but is not at all interested in their lives. Pity the readers who read only postmodern relativism in this. In doing so, the king corrects and enriches his own theory of discipline: discipline, on the one hand, aimed at the control of the individual based on institutions (such as the clinic and the prison), biopolitics, on the other hand, is based on the state, aimed at care (or insurance, '*assurance*' is the word he uses) for the life of the population as a whole. One could say that Foucault, in his genealogy of biopolitics, exposes the roots of the welfare state. The rise of urbanism and social medicine are, as mentioned above, his main case studies. Indeed, after the cholera epidemics of the mid-19th century, Brussels decided, based on the scientific observation that the epidemic originated from contaminated water, to cover the river Senne and build the central avenues, following the example of Paris.

If we read Foucault correctly and do not inflate biopolitics into a kind of dark conspiracy of the state to install martial law (in the footsteps of Agamben), then there is no reason to make a caricature of him, or the term, and dismiss his thinking with the all too easy term 'postmodern'. He can help us to be alert, but we should indeed not underestimate the *checks and balances* of democracy, the open social discussion. At the same time, Trump, Bolsonaro, and Orbán, and so many populists with them, prove that democracy is constantly under threat, and in times of crisis we need to be even more alert. Being alert without paranoia is the challenge these days. But the conundrum remains, well expressed in an old witty wisdom: 'Just because you're paranoid, doesn't mean you're not being followed.'

The Return of Biopolitics? The Corona Pandemic and the Neoliberal Dismantling of the Welfare State
(*Apache*, April 14, 2020)

Foucault called the state's concern for the life of the population 'biopolitics'. Now, during this pandemic, it becomes clear how fatal the neoliberal dismantling of biopolitics has been. The dismantling of the welfare state under the guise of inevitable austerity, under the influence of the neoliberalism that has conquered the world since Thatcher and Reagan, and has even been embraced by the socialists, in the form of 'the third way', was in fact a dismantling of the concern for the life, health, and well-being of the population. Reduction of hospital beds and cutbacks in scientific research into viruses considered not profitable are now proving to be acts of guilty neglect. All this for what was not a clean-up of public finances, but an upward redistribution to the super-rich, shareholders, and multinationals.

With the rise of the modern states and later the welfare state in and by biopolitics, the good life became the protected life (*bios*). The right to health became a human right, but of course this human right could only be realized in the welfare states, and so it was not a truly effective universal human right. The welfare state had a downside, the neo-colonial extractivism of the global South, and it left capitalism and its logic of growth, extractivism, consumerism, planned obsolescence, and so on, essentially untouched.

The dismantling or rather the conscious ending of biopolitics led to a different kind of politics related to life. One could call it the rise of 'zoöpolitics': the reduction to mere life (*zoè*) of the individual through the exclusion from the protected life (*bios*) of the citizen. This applies not only to so-called illegal migrants, the homeless, refugees in camps, slum dwellers—experts hardly dare think of what Corona could do there—but also to the entire world's precariat.

Capitalist zoöpolitics is the precarization, the reduction to mere life of the individual: without health insurance, unemployment benefits or pension, the citizen is at the mercy of a survival strategy of the working poor, with double jobs in order to make ends meet… An almost disenfranchised citizen, who only as a consumer can buy such social protection from profit-based private companies, if (s)he can afford it,. This partly explains the misery that now prevails in New York and elsewhere in the US: besides the medical disaster, the pandemic is also a social bloodbath. The neoliberal obsession with the flexibilization of labour was a way to endlessly fragment and atomize what used to be called the industrial proletariat. There are no more workers to unite. This is one of the great victories of post-industrial capitalism, or cognitive capitalism and the so-called new disruptive platform economy (Uber/ Facebook /Deliveroo /Amazon, and what have you). One could call it the new zoöpolitical phase of capitalism.

Biopolitics, the protection of the life of the population by the state, has, however, made an unexpected comeback because of the current pandemic, at least here in Europe, where even the most rabid neoliberal policies have failed to fully implement this dismantling of the welfare state and social security. Just like the state is making a full come-back despite all the neoliberal attempts to make it 'lean' and subject it to the so-called free market (i.e., the interests of quasi-monopolistic big business). Democracy was not only threatened by populism but also by lobbyists. After the exceptional measures and executive powers to fight corona, it is high time to strengthen democracy.

What Foucault called 'thanatopolitics', the old sovereignty that is not interested in the lives of its subjects but rules by the power to deprive them of life, is of course still present in the many wars all over the world, but also in the European push-back politics that de facto is costing the lives of thousands of people who want to cross the Mediterranean Sea every year. 'Necropolitics' is the name that Achille Mbembe gives to the ruthless (neo)colonial policies, which sow death and destruction.

It is more than an irony of history that New York, one of the world capitals of capital, the city of Wall Street, has become the second epicentre of this corona pandemic, and Europe the first (after Wuhan, where things were under control relatively quickly). It is as if colonial necropolitics are ravaging the mother countries of colonialism and neo-colonialism, as if history strikes back. In any case, neoliberal zoöpolitics turns into necropolitics. The many deaths in Europe and certainly in New York are—and most commentators and specialists agree—a consequence of a ruthless neglect of care in general and of medical care, prevention, and precaution in particular. It is not only the reduction in the number of beds but also the curtailing of scientific research and planned pandemic response, which in essence cannot be profitable.

More than ever, it is clear that we need to return to a kind of sensible biopolitics, or 'affirmative biopolitics' (Roberto Esposito), the care for the life of the population by the state, with the welfare state as the best real existing model. This is only possible if neoliberal, zoöpolitical, and necropolitical capitalism is cast aside, and the conspiracy against the welfare state disbanded. What we need is a new social contract, in which the economy becomes subordinate to society. What this pandemic makes clear as never before is that we live in an upside-down world. Care personnel is ten times more important than all CEOs combined. It is time we put an end to this upside-down world.

It is also high time for a cosmopolitics, a politics that is both cosmopolitan and cosmic. Cosmopolitan, meaning at the same time international, multiracial, multicultural, and indeed planetary, as the bitter lesson is that viruses know no borders. And at the same time cosmic: ecological, in tune with the web of life and the fragility of the biosphere. At this point in history, biopolitics must be extended to all living beings, to the biosphere as a whole. Cosmopolitics is a post-anthropocentric, posthumanist biopolitics.

Of course, a return to business as usual will most likely be the option of the powers that be, of both the states, the banks, and the big companies, but at the same time they will try to maintain and exploit the control of the population (through big data, apps and the like). Chances are real, that we will, in a mix of populism (Trump, Orbán and all the rest of them) and the Chinese model, end up living under an authoritarian form of neoliberalism: totalitarian capitalism. That is the choice humanity faces after this pandemic: totalitarian capitalism or a democratic, socio-ecological biopolitics.

The Postcorona Manifesto
(*De Wereld Morgen*, April 2, 2020)

For several days, right from the beginning of the lockdown in fact (that was Friday, March 13 in Belgium), I have been dreaming of a postcorona manifesto in which the best minds of our generation would plead for the necessity of radical change. In my vision it was nothing less than a 'Charter for The Future'.

Neo-liberalism was the first to be cast aside, this pernicious ideology with its upward redistribution towards the wealthiest and their tax paradises. Away with market fundamentalism. In reality the market is regulated, heavily subsidized, and the quasi-monopolies of a handful of mega multinationals rule the world economy. Neo-liberalism needs to be overhauled because by cutting back the welfare state it is an accessory to this crisis. Many pages have been written about this, but not always explicitly naming the culprit. Now we know how important the healthcare sector really is and how indispensable social security. The best minds provided, in my dream, the ammunition to silence all those think tanks (From Mont Pelerin to our local Itinera) and expose them, once and for all, as lackeys of the most rabid capitalism. So, point one in positive terms: recovery of the welfare state! Redistribution and reciprocity are the anthropological basis of every community. The economy at the service of society and not vice versa. The corona crisis is a historical occasion to overcome that upside-down world. Not the end of the world.

It brought me to the second point: We must avoid climate catastrophe and repair the biosphere. Not easy. We're all in the same boat—that is something this crisis has taught us. The planet is indeed one and indivisible, like humanity, which is all the way, from north to south and from east to west, threatened by the pandemic. We need to take better care of the biosphere, Mother Earth, as much as possible, posthumanism... Also because this pandemic is actually, according to specialists, an ecological problem, namely due to 'zoonosis' or 'zoonotic overspill', a virus jumping from animals to humans due to a too great promiscuity between humans and wild animals.

Three. Strengthening solidarity, resilience and solidarity, end of hate populism. I got tears in my eyes when I saw the images on television of the social housing block here around the corner. The whole block made a festive noise to support the healthcare sector. Yes, those from 'hell hole' Molenbeek (as Trump called it after the attacks on Brussels), exuberantly showing their respect to all people in the frontline of the crisis. In this way, our multicultural fellow humans prove that they do feel part of our society. That is a life lesson for all of our society: solidarity, respect!

Four. Strengthening and restoring democracy. In my dream, not only Uncle Orbán really had to be put in the corner when this crisis is over. He really is overdoing it, he is now a real dictator, within a permanent state of emergency. But it is also a warning to all. Sophie Wilmès (our prime minister) is growing, unwillingly, into our very own female Churchill. But let this not become a habit, those full powers for the executive. The 'creeping coup' must be stopped everywhere and democracy must be restored, and above all, enriched. And here too we can learn from this crisis. Citizens and civil society took the lead, universities decided to close their buildings and switch to online learning when politicians hesitated and were still sending out irresponsible messages.

Point five was a very difficult one. World inequality is literally life-threatening, this pandemic makes that painfully clear once again. We are *not* all in the same boat. The residents of slums and refugee camps, but also the homeless of the world, risk becoming the worst and most unjust victims. Furthermore, a future global order should undo this structural injustice of neocolonial extractivism for the North and informal economy for the locals. This new global order should go hand in hand with structural change within our own societies, how we teach, the terminologies we use. We cannot bring down the master, using the master's language. 'Giving a voice to the voiceless', 'helping the South', 'send aid to Africa', are but a few of the almost gimmicky statements used in the public domain as an inherited language of dominance and self-righteousness.*

With those five points I was already over the moon in my dream. I saw, unfortunately too vague, five other points—fair taxation, reform of education, scientific research for the benefit of humanity and not for profit, even a new spirituality, why not…— but I left them for the best minds of our generation, or the next for that matter. Otherwise, it would be too long again for an opinion piece, I thought, almost awake from my dream. And thousands of personalities from all over the world signed this post-corona manifesto, millions of citizens endorsed it. It was adopted in the UN General Assembly…

Unbelievable? I know. Well, it was just a dream. But the need for radical change? Our societies must wake up. We need to wake up from the nightmare of growth, profit, neoliberal rogue capitalism which leads to climate disasters and catastrophic inequality. In that sense, this pandemic is a historical opportunity, and of course I am not the first or only one to say it. But 'they', the powers that be, will do everything they can to switch back to the order of the day as soon as possible, or worse: business as usual but with the maintenance of all kinds of authoritarian surveillance and digital Big Brother control meanwhile established. In that sense, all sorts of instances of civil society should now join forces for a post-corona manifesto. A Charter for the Future.

Note

*   Thanks to Khalda El Jack, for decolonizing my point 5.

The Rise of Zoöpolitics (Introduction to a Conference on 'Architecture and War'*)

Synopsis

If we take to hart Agamben's distinction between *zoè*, the reduction to bare life, and *bios*, the cladding of life with culture and rights, we could and maybe should introduce a new concept in addition to biopolitics: *zoöpolitics*. Foucault's idea of biopolitics is directed at the care for and control over the life of the population, as some of his main examples, such as the urban reorganization of Nantes or the rise of social medicine testify. It is the new power leading to the welfare state, as opposed to the old sovereignty, which was based on the power to take life and which Foucault calls thanatopolitics. The reduction to bare life (one of the main themes of Agamben's *Homo Sacer*-cycle) is another form of power and sovereignty that should not, in our opinion, be called biopolitics for it is the opposite in almost all regards: it is not assuring, or catering by 'governance' but reducing and excluding; it is not directed at the population but at the individual.

What we're experiencing now is the end of biopolitics, the demise of the welfare state based on redistribution, and the rise of zoöpolitics. Indeed, the refugee is excluded from the *bios* and from welfare biopolitics and is reduced to bare life in the most radical way: he or she is just a mere body. This form of radical exclusion from the *polis* and the *bios*, can lead to a return of thanatopolitics, the thousands of dead refugees who drowned in the Mediterranean are the tragic and cynical testimony of this.

After outlining this distinction between thanatopolitics, biopolitics and zoöpolitics, and their dialectics, this paper will focus on urbanism and war, where they can be seen at work in a raw form. Urbanism as a discipline is a paradigm, if not *the* paradigm of biopolitics. The thanatopolitics that warfare constitutes is returning today in urban warfare, it is subsumed under the neologism 'urbicide'. The urbanism of zoöpolitics is the main focus of this paper. The architecture of military occupation in Israel will be taken as an example of the urbanism that might await us. As our nation states increasingly want to exclude the 'surplus humanity' (Zygmunt Bauman) of refugees and the poor, by reducing them to bare life, and the ecological disasters sharpen the dualization of society in haves and have-nots, the rise of zoöpolitics and an architecture of confinement, control, and exclusion, seems inevitable.

Introducing Zoöpolitics

Biopolitics is the opposite of thanatopolitics. The old sovereign, of the ancient regime, takes life; the new sovereignty, the governance of the modern state, gives life. That is the well-known, lapidary formula which Foucault repeats in the fundamental passages where he introduces the term biopolitics.[1] In opposition to biopolitics as politics of life, he called the politics of death thanatopolitics. Many of his examples make it very clear what biopolitics is: the rise of medical care, hygiene and public health, and the sanitation of cities is the kernel of the new sovereignty that gives life, that caters, regulates, and *assures* life, the words Foucault uses,[2] as opposed to the old sovereignty, which takes life.

Of course, what Foucault sketched as a historical shift from the ancient regime to the early modern state, is in fact a dialectics (as he was also well aware of, but he did not use the word): both biopolitics and thanatopolitics are at work in our society. It is too obvious for words—warfare is and remains the manifestation of the sovereignty that takes life. In fact, we have seen a very overt return of thanatopolitics as the permanent war on terror, terrorism, but more specifically the old top-down sovereignty of taking life took on two forms recently: the massive 'shock and awe' of the Iraq invasion, and the much more insidious almost surgical drone warfare. Both have something of divine violence: omnipresent, invisible lethal force striking from above.

Biopolitics is, as Foucault stresses, directed at a new entity: the population. Whereas discipline—Foucault's first cycle of research—is directed towards the individual, biopolitics is directed towards the population as such, in its entirety, and it 'caters for' or 'assures' life. This has important consequences. It means that fingerprints, airport checks, iris scans, the entire security routines we have to undergo under the state of emergency due to the war on terror, is not to be captured, as the great Italian philosopher Giorgio Agamben does, under the term of biopolitics. It might be called biometrics, but it is not biopolitical in the strict sense of the word.

However inspiring and paradigmatic the work of Agamben in general and the *Homo Sacer*-cycle in particular is, his use of the term biopower constitutes a serious shift away from Foucault, precisely because in Agamben the sovereign is always the old, Schmittian sovereign who decides on the exception, declares the state of exception. In a sense, Agamben dismisses the entire history of the modern state, with its division of powers, checks, and balances, and above all, dismisses the welfare state with its gigantic machinery of 'catering for' and 'assuring' life, as if non-existent.

Hence the proposal to add a logical third concept:[3] besides thanato- and biopolitics, zoöpolitics.[4] That is completely in line with Agamben's very own and rather influential, if not crucial distinction between *bios* and *zoè*, cultured life (clad with language, culture, rights) and bare life (animal life, natural life, the body minus language, culture, rights). Biometric security technology checks us on the level of our bare life, and in doing so, in a sense reduces us to bare life. This reduction, which is omnipresent in politics of security and control, we could call zoöpolitics.

By introducing this new term of zoöpolitics, I try to show that biopolitics in the sense of Agamben is not biopolitics in the Foucauldian sense, for it is not directed towards the catering and assuring of life but towards the control of suspected of rejected subjects and not directed at a population, but towards the individual.

For those who like dialectical schemes: if thanatopolitics is the thesis—the right of sovereignty to take life—and biopolitics is the antithesis—sovereignty that gives life—then zoöpolitics could be seen as a sort of synthesis; it doesn't take or give life, but controls it by the reduction of the human life form (*bios*) to mere body (*zoè*). It can also often be an instable synthesis, the point where biopolitics can and sooner or later will turn into thanatopolitics.

The most famous catch phrase of the entire *Homo Sacer*-cycle, should probably be rewritten: The camp is not the biopolitical but the zoöpolitical (and-at-times-thanatopolitical) paradigm of the planet. The concentration camp is the place where biopolitics turns into zoöpolitics, the extermination camp is the place where zoöpolitics shifts into thanatopolitics. Of course, any concentration camp can always be turned into a thanatopolitical apparatus. The same can be said of refugee camps, unfortunately, which should be apparatuses to protect and save lives, and therefore are in essence biopolitical devices. There is a continuum of these three politics, and yet they are very different, and should be seen as (dialectical) poles.

Now we can start to look at our topic: urbanism and war. These three terms, biopolitics, thanatopolitics and zoöpolitics, will enable us to highlight three ideal-typical politics towards the city: urbanism, urbicide and security, control, with its strongest paradigmatic version—colonial occupation.

Urbanism as Biopolitics

Urbanism is a paradigm of biopolitics, if not *the* paradigm. That is what Foucault meant and many of his examples are linked to it. The rise of medical care, hygiene and public health and the sanitation of cities was the kernel of the new sovereignty that gives life, that caters and assures life of this new entity called the population, as opposed to the old sovereignty that takes life. In

Sécurité, territoire, population he explicitly takes the early urbanism of the late eighteenth century, with the case of Nantes as an example, and aptly perceives that it is not sovereignty, discipline, order, or symmetry that is at stake (which is done in cities like Richelieu), but circulation in the largest sense: circulation of goods, circulation of air, circulation of people.

The sanitation of the city, the healthcare and care for the well-being of the population through sewer systems, infrastructure, and architecture is the essential drive of urbanism. I do believe that it is important to stress this: urbanism, urban design is one of the most paradigmatic forms of biopolitics, of care for the population, of the democratization of well-being, the rise of the welfare state, of progress, of modernity in general. That is an important lesson we can learn from Foucault's genealogy of 'governance' and biopolitics in his courses at the Collège de France.

Urbicide as Thanatopolitics

If urbanism, as essentially the sanitation and organization of the city, is the basic paradigm of biopolitics, what would then be the 'urbanism' of thanatopolitics? Urbicide in all its various degrees and forms could well be the one term that encapsulates it.[5] Indeed, urbicide supplies the exact opposite of urbanism as a paradigmatic form of biopolitics as the assuring the life of the population, because it constitutes radical thanatopolitics directed towards the city. It is somehow the urban counterpart to ethnic cleansing.

Urbicide is a recent term, derived from genocide, and means literally 'the killing of a city'. Although it was introduced to a wider audience by Marshall Berman to describe the transformation planned by Robert Moses in New York,[6] it is an age-old phenomenon. It is an antediluvian, mythical form of power. The primordial model of sovereignty, God, destroyed several cities: Sodom and Gomorra were wiped from the Earth, and Nineveh only escaped his wrath to teach the prophet Yonah a lesson... This divine *tabula rasa*, this erasure can be conceived of as the archetype for later sovereign erasure, the archetype of total war on the city.

In a similar vein, the epic of epics, Homer's *Iliad*, is the story of urbicide: the destruction of Troy. This sort of total destruction was not only happening in a mythological past but also in real history. A legendary but very real urbicide was the destruction of Carthage by its archenemy Rome. It was not only razed to the ground, but even the soil was poisoned with salt so it would be infertile for ages to come. Note that in these examples urbicide is also politicide: the erasure of a political community, of an identity, of a culture. So, destroying the urban fabric is often a way, if not the best way, to destroy the identity of a people, to wipe out the enemy, not only physically but meta-physically, so to speak: not only psychologically, but sociologically, even anthropologically, by wiping out the culture itself.

Given this fact of politics as the fight over life and death of collective entities, according to the definition of *The Concept of the Political* by Carl Schmitt, the city has always been a stronghold, a military defence base, as all classical authors from Thucydides to Mumford and McLuhan testify. The medieval fortress city was built to protect its population, the bourgeois within the *bourg*, the *Bürger* within the *Burcht*. But this has to be seen in a dialectical way. The castle in the city was not only a safe haven in case of an enemy siege, it was also the dungeon or prison for criminals and enemies of the king and was a stronghold against popular uprisings of the citizens. This ambiguity is crucial to all sovereignty. Sieges and sacking were part of subjugation. Charles V subjugated Ghent and had the population walk about with ropes around their necks as if they were to be hanged, in an ultimate form of symbolic humiliation of the stubborn and proud population of the city where he himself was born. This strange political ritual gave the inhabitants of Ghent their popular nickname, the 'stroopkes' in Dutch, literally—'the nooses'. But the *sacco di Roma,* the plunder of Rome, is a more famous incident of ruthless subjugation, by the armies of this same Charles V.

Yet there was a period that warfare did not affect cities so much. Even if the famous Vauban fortifications testify to the city as stronghold, especially along the borders of France warfare was often a matter of armies confronting each other in the open. Waterloo is almost a household name for this sort of deadly war tournament in the middle of nowhere, far from the city. Historians could study this possible correlation between Napoleon's urbanism—I think particularly of Antwerp—and his attempt to spare cities from siege. Tolstoy's epic novel *War and Peace* attests to this warfare in the open, the movement of armies confronting each other outside and sometimes far away from the big cities. The plane and hills near Austerlitz are not exactly a central major city.

It is in fact only in the twentieth century that the city again becomes heart and target of warfare, with the total destruction of Ypres as classical example from the First World War and the bombings of London, Berlin or Dresden and Hiroshima as the painful paradigmatic examples of the Second. Due to urbanization, MOUT—Military Operations in Urban Terrain—have come to the fore in recent decades as a very important branch of military affairs. As in ancient times, the city is again the target, albeit often not necessarily in an urbicidal logic, but more in a logic of control, subjugation, colonization. Especially the transformation from linear, symmetrical warfare of state against state, armies against armies, to non-linear, asymmetrical warfare, states, or coalitions of states, against terrorist or insurgent networks, has contributed to this 'urbanization of war'.

Zoöpolitical Urban Security Regimes

This brings us to our third angle. What is the urbanism of zoöpolitics? It is our hunch that this is the most basic form of urban politics today, even if it has many faces. It is a combination of the smart city, the security routines and cameras everywhere, and of course, the closed detention centres and (concentration) camps for 'illegal migrants' and refugees, that are so topical today. If urbanism is biopolitical and urbicide is thanatopolitical, then militarized control and occupation could be called zoöpolitical.

We take Israel's 'architecture of occupation', as Eyal Weizman has called and described it in *Hollow Land,* as a model here. Our point is that this occupation is increasingly providing the model of our securitized urban spaces. The devices of these control-like checkpoints or biometrical security routines are based on zoöpolitical screening and on isolating the individual as body, as bare life, often reducing individuals to their frail animality (*zoè*) and stripping them of their citizenship or cultural being, their being human (*bios*). One can highlight the essential process of this apparatus of occupation by stressing its zoöpolitical character. It is precisely because of the reduction to *zoè* that it can be so oppressive: a way of humiliating the colonized.

In this repressive urbanism of occupation, zoöpolitics and thanatopolitics form poles in a continuum, like in the camp.[7] The refugee camp can at any time transform, like an army camp can easily be turned into an extra-legal prison like Guantanamo, and even turn from a detention centre into an outright ghetto under siege. Dheisheh Camp in Bethlehem was totally locked during the second intifada, as it was one of the epicentres of the Palestinian uprising. Of course, this logic of incursion and lockdown can be extended to all occupied territories: the sieges of Ramallah, Nablus, and Jenin during the second intifada are eminent cases of these shifts. This shift is also visible on a larger scale.

By retreating from Gaza, Israel clearly shifted from the zoöpolitics of occupation to the thanatopolitics of outright siege and destruction—calling Gaza a ghetto is not, alas, a metaphor. Operation Cast Lead and Operation Protective Edge were 'shock-and-awe' attacks with the aim to massively destroy infrastructure and massively kill people. Israel's retreat and subsequent ruthless bombing are emblematic of the shift from zoöpolitics to thanato-politics.

We live in times of ethnic cleansing, not only in Israel, but all over the Middle East. In Africa, at least in the region of the big lakes, it is the disintegration of failed states into lawlessness, indeed at times into the state of nature, into overt civil war, ethnic cleansing and alas, outright genocide, like in Rwanda. In Latin America and elsewhere in Africa and Asia it is the economic cleansing by new enclosures and land grabs by the agro- and biofuel industry of the multinationals... These massive and ongoing, if not very well reported events—crimes against humanity that seem to largely escape the mainstream press—are not to be captured under the term of biopolitics. On the contrary, it is zoöpolitics and thanatopolitics, but not biopolitics as the giving, and catering for, and assuring life of the population as such.

In order to understand the dialectics of war and cities in a philosophical frame we should also learn from Deleuze and Guattari's 'nomadology' in *Milles Plateaux*: the war machine of the nomads operating in 'smooth space' and the sedentary state operating in 'striated space'. Of course, the state 'captured' and learned from the nomadic war machine—in a sense the army is in essence a nomadic war machine. In any case, the opposition of *espace lisse* and *espace strié* is most useful to understand urban warfare. The city—especially older cities with their dense urban tissues—represents a blocked space, a space full of resistance, as opposed to the smooth space without hindrances of the open field. Here it is inevitable to see haussmannization also as a response to the urban barricade battles: on the large, straight boulevards it was easy for the army to move around the city and almost impossible to build barricades. In that vein, mostly to subjugate an uprising, the colonizer or occupier will destroy part of the urban fabric and make easy entrances for the troops. This way of drastic 'haussmannization' was famously introduced in what is now Israel by the British colonizer, cutting a big anchor-shaped form in the urban fabric of Jaffa, with Operation Anchor in 1936.

The 'walking through walls' is a more recent way to invade the dense city fabric of old cities and camps. This 'walking through walls', to refer to Eyal Weizman's *Hollow Land* once more, of the Israeli army in Jenin and Nablus has become almost iconic. By penetrating via 'wormholes' cut through interiors, the Israeli army inverted the logic of space: the built fabric as smooth space for the war machine of the Israeli, the street as striated space for the Palestinian resistance. Inspired by Deleuze, the Israeli army inverted the street (smooth space) and the built fabric (striated space) by cutting and moving through walls, moving like worms through the flesh of the cities, moving invisibly through private space, surprising and encircling the resistance from within, so to speak, and forcing the resistance fighters onto the streets.

In a more general frame, Israel has put an apparatus in place that creates smooth space for the colonizers, an archipelago of well-connected cities and settlements for the Israeli, and a set of disconnected enclaves for the Palestinians. The same distance that Israeli colonists can drive in minutes, takes the occupied Palestinians hours, if not an entire day. The matrix of areas (A, B and C), the wall, and the checkpoints make a set of isolated enclaves of the territories, that can be sealed off at any moment. That is the essence of Israeli apartheid. Alessandro Petti pointed out in his book *Arcipelaghi e enclave. Architettura dell'ordinamento spaziale contemporaneo* that this double geography of Israel might be paradigmatic for our future spatial order. In *Hollow Land* Eyal Weizman has mapped all the three-dimensional strategies used to put this matrix into place.

In this matrix of control the population is reduced to bare life. The revolving doors at the checkpoints encapsulate this reduction to being just a body. The recent habit of arresting children at night is a way of traumatizing, not only the children themselves, but the entire community, turning them into helpless traumatized people, at the mercy of the occupier. The zoöpolitical logic of control can be reverted to thanatopolitics and urbicidal warfare, as soon as it serves the overall political agenda—as said, the 'decolonization' of Gaza was the prelude to its total ghettoization (starvation included) and the 'shock-and-awe' military attacks on it.

This zoöpolitical phase of 'disurbanism', with its thanato-political extremes, is becoming generalized. The opposition of striated space and smooth space also points to one of the big paradoxes of our time, the paradox of globalization: free traffic of commodities and insiders, the haves, in the space of flows and the return of hard borders to stop the outsiders, the have-nots. Neither the contemporary state nor the so-called super-states, or contemporary capitalism, are able to come to grips with this dilemma. Hence the return of hard borders in an attempt to turn the smooth space of globalization, the 'space of flows' of Castells, into the immobilizing hindrance of striated space. In any case, dealing with migration will become more and more militarized.

To understand this condition as one of the results of globalization the late Zygmunt Bauman might help us. The second chapter on 'humanity on the move' in his book *Liquid Times* is a chilling account of the fact that modernity and globalization have produced a tremendous amount of 'human waste' (meaning wasted humans): a surplus humanity. But whilst in modern times they could be disposed of in faraway territories (America, Australia), there are no blank spaces left on the map to send them to or let them migrate to. The combination of population growth, neoliberal capitalism with its by now universally accepted dualization and increasing inequality, and war politics, has produced all sorts of people without place, perspective, or means of survival: illegal migrants, unemployed youth, also often of migrant background. We find this 'human waste' in ghettos, in no man's lands, in failed states, as refugees of wars, of civil wars, as ecological refugees, and of course also as economic refugees, impoverished people seeking a better future. Like so many emigrants who moved to America from the poorest regions of Europe, such as Ireland and Sicily, did before them to escape hunger, as evoked in *Angela's Ashes,* the moving novel by Frank McCourt. We have a short collective memory.

The most concrete, if not obscene form of this human waste are the thousands of people who drown in the Mediterranean while trying to make it to Europe. According to UNHCR in 2015 there were 3771 deaths, in 2016 some 4000. As a UNHCR official said, 'From one death for every 269 arrivals last year, in 2016 the likelihood of dying has spiralled to one in 88.'[8] In 2019 the count is some 1200.[9] But over the last five years (2014-2019), according to UN sources, 18.000 persons drowned.[10] This sort of unbearable calculus gives an idea of zoöpolitics as a counterpart to thanato-politics. Another concrete image of 'surplus humanity' are the 20 million people chronically facing starvation (since 2017) in Nigeria, South Sudan, Somalia, and Yemen. It is in the news for a day or two and then disappears. So, to make a long and sad story short, this 'surplus humanity' has to be controlled and processed in a zoöpolitical way, at best. Think of the Moria camp on Lesbos. This new sort of society I have called 'the capsular civilization'.

Israel is the extreme, the ultimate paradigm, the *model state* (or *state-model*) so to speak, of this security urbanism, this multi-dimensional spatial colonization and apartheid. Moreover, Israel is often involved in supplying know-how and the devices to make this apparatus or matrix of military subjugation work all around the world: from the pacification of Bagdad after the invasion of Iraq, the infrastructure and technology of controlling borders against illegal migrants, to the security routines at airports. It supplies the model *and* the business-model of 'disaster capitalism', as Naomi Klein has aptly termed it. All this infrastructure of control is made of what one could call infra-architecture.

The Rise of Infra-architecture

In line with Baudrillard's concept of the hyperreal, of hyperreality, we coined (in a text called 'Meditations on Razor Wire', written with Michiel Dehaene) the concept of the infra-real, of infra-reality. It is that part of the real world that is invisible in the simulations and simulacra that surround us, phenomena that are unrepre-sentable, or repressed—the slums, the war zones, the land grabs and enclosures, the ongoing colonization, the overcrowded, flooding low lands in Bangladesh and elsewhere, the poverty, the famine, and so on.[11] The walls and fences we build are meant to keep hyperreality and infra-reality apart. Of course this hyperreality was very much the ideal world of the spectacle, the inside of the matrix Baudrillard was talking about, but now the bubble of simulation and hyper-normality is bursting. One could say that exactly nowadays the split between hyperreality and infra-reality is breaking down. Even more reasons to build fences and retreat in

→ news contradicts this invisibility

our virtual world of screens and camera surveillance and other security routines. The reality of war is always infra-real. It is not representable, despite all the war films, because it is *unspeakable* forever and a day. It is the dark side of landscape, of architecture, of urbanism, of politics, of anthropology, of the *polis*, of the human species in general.

We made a link between hyperreality and the hyper-architecture of iconic buildings, the so-called star architecture (subsequently shortened to 'starchitecture'), and between infra-reality and what we then logically called 'infra-architecture': we thought of slums, camps, detention centres, fences, checkpoints. At first, this binary opposition seems dualistic, but it should be conceived of as dialectical poles of architecture. It is a continuum, but it has its extremes. Military architecture is one such extreme. It is mere infrastructure. The zero degree of all architecture.

Infra-architecture is the architecture of bare life, the architecture of zoöpolitics. All military architecture is infra-architecture, and all military intervention reduces the existing built fabric to infra-architecture. This suggests, on an ethical note, that the architect, a profession devoted to biopolitics, like that of the urbanist, has no business building these devices or collabo-rating in the making of these apparatuses. I would dare to suggest that in most architecture that will deal with migration and security in the twenty-first century, we will see zoöpolitics at work on a large scale and we will be confronted with a lot of infra-architecture.

The End of Biopolitics (Conclusion)

The rise of neoliberalism, which Foucault treated in his *Naissance de la biopolitique*, might in fact be the beginning of the end of biopolitics. The catering for life of the new sovereignty that culminated in the welfare state (as a redistribution system) shifted towards privatization, deregulation and 'flexibilization', and to 'responsibilization': you are responsible to cater for and assure your own life. The end of biopolitics is very concrete, in a sense. Under neoliberalism, 'care' becomes your own problem. That is one way to understand the whole idea of 'responsabilization' of the citizen, as individual, as consumer. In a sense, we see the rise of a new disciplinary society: the internalization of the rules of universal competition and the omnipresence of management jargon and ideology via all sorts of institutions. It is at the same time a society of control, as Deleuze called it: the externalization of (para)military apparatus of security. With terrorism, the state of exception has become the rule—almost five years after the terrorist attacks of 2016 the army is still patrolling the streets, airports and railway stations of Belgium—so Agamben was right. 'The militarization of urban space', Mike Davis was warning us against in his *City of Quartz*, has come true, in a more literal sense than even he could have thought. The craze of SUV vehicles that now have become the standard form of car, testifies to this militarization. These SUVs are not only irresponsible, as they cause more fatalities in traffic accidents, but also irresponsible in ecological terms as they are heavier and pollute more.

With the demise and wilful destruction of the welfare state, the biopolitical sovereignty comes to an end, like urbanism in a sense has come to an end. State-organized public health care, and social security, public education and accessible art and culture are also under threat or being abolished by subsequent waves of austerity policies. The rise of the security industry and the disintegration of social security are two faces of the same coin. The demise of the welfare state is correlated to the rise of 'armed government'—the term proposed by Bart De Wever, the most powerful politician in Belgium, who in the same breath proposed to inscribe the state of exception into the constitution. This new form of governance cannot be simply captured in Foucault's very localized, historical transition from the old sovereignty of the ancient regime to the biopolitics of the modern state, culminating in the welfare state. The zoöpolitical control will increase as information technology and cyberspace is enclosing us.

For Foucault, biopolitics is directed towards the population and the population is limited to the territory, that is the biopolitical inscription of the new-born (*natus*) into the nation state. In the age of deterritorializations and reterritorializations, the age of migration and mobility, biopolitics is literally losing ground. The ecological crisis is aggravating all this. Migration frays the biopolitics of the welfare state in Europe to the breaking point, so walls and camps, mobile border controls and security routines become a matrix of surveillance that has to defend this biopolitical inside space from the dangerous outsiders. They make an apparatus of zoöpolitics, of the retention and detention of bodies that are refused the status of citizen (*bios*) and instead are reduced to bare life (*zoè*). This zoöpolitical control of 'illegal migrants' is always on the verge of shifting to thanatopolitics.

According to Alliez and Lazzarato, in their devastating book *Guerres et Capital*, war is the essence of capitalism. It feeds a multicity of wars: civil wars, race wars, economic wars, colonial wars, wars against women, like the witch hunts, dispossessions, and so on. In any case, urban warfare and urbicide are on the rise, from Sarajevo to Fallujah and Gaza. In the words of Lebbeus Woods: 'Sarajevo was only the beginning of a new trend resulting from globalization, a proliferation of regional, often insurgent-driven wars that have resulted in the piece-by-piece destruction of cities and the killing of their inhabitants.' The war on terror as asymmetrical and nonlinear warfare has only enhanced this urbanization of warfare and this militarization of urban space. The conclusion could we be that we live in *the end of biopolitics*, we witness *the rise of zoöpolitics* and, alas, also an unseen proliferation, if not *metastasis of thanatopolitics*.

Notes

*   Architecture and Wars, ETH Zürich 2-3 June, 2017, curated by Samia Henni. This lecture remained unpublished, and will become part of a book on the Spatialization of Power in a more finished version (with more referencing and all that), but, given the corona crisis, I think it is relevant, and in a sense urgent to publish it now, even in its lecture version, as it is a background to several of my articles on the corona crisis that are in a way postscripts to this text.

1   These passages are in a sense few and rather short. At the end of *La volonté de savoir,* where Foucault introduces the term for the first time and in *Il faut défendre la société,* where he opposes it to discipline. The term is scarce in *La naissance de la biopolitique,* which, as the title of this course suggests, should have been entirely devoted to biopolitics, but then got stuck so to speak in a genealogy of neoliberalism, and in Sécurité, territoire, population', where in an attempt to pinpoint the technologies of biopolitics he first focuses on 'appareils de securités' (apparatuses of security) to then rather abruptly turn to governance (*gouvernementalité*), which indeed is a logical switch, for the modern state is not only about (repressive) security, but about controlling and organizing economy and society, and the lives of the population in a well-functioning, self-regulating way.

2   Foucault, *'Il faut défendre la société, Cours au Collège de France (1975-1976),* Seuil/Gallimard, Paris, p. 223

3   For a lengthier argument on biopolitics and the introduction of the term zoöpolitics, see my text 'The negation of the state of nature' in *Entropic Empire, On the City of Man in the Age of Disaster,* Rotterdam: nai010publishers, 2012.

4   I propose to write it with the unusual diaeresis in order to avoid the zoo, zoöpolitics is not the politics of the zoo, even if the human zoo of colonial exhibitions would make one of the paradigmatic, original, and in any case allegorical examples of reduction to bare life, and there, zoo-politics would coincide with zoöpolitics. A Dutch sociologist, Willem Schinkel, has by the way proposed something similar, but he called it 'zoëpolitics'.

5   For a quick overview of the origin and uses of the term I refer to the excellent Wikipedia article on the concept https://en.

wikipedia.org/wiki/Urbicide. But the work of Stephen Graham, who introduced me to the term, really deserves to be mentioned here. Check him out for further reading.

6   The modernist *tabula rasa* also comes to mind, Le Corbusier's Plan Voisin in Paris for instance, or the urbicidal 'Manhattan plan', which destroyed the Brussels North Quarter.

7   The original and literal meaning of a concentration camp is: a confined place where you isolate or concentrate certain groups, forced labourers, or internal 'enemies' of all sorts—besides Jews and Roma-people, also gays and communists, let's not forget that. Its origin is often forgotten: the colonial camps where forced labourers were concentrated.

8   http://www.unhcr.org/afr/news/latest/2016/10/580f3e684/mediterranean-death-toll-soars-2016-deadliest-year.html

9   https://missingmigrants.iom.int/region/mediterranean)

10   https://www.voanews.com/europe/un-migrant-refugee-death-toll-mediterranean-tops-1000-6th-year

11   'Meditations on Razor Wire. A plea for Para-architecture', was written for the exhibition *Visionary power* of the Rotterdam Architecture Biennial 2007, and published in the catalogue. A version of it was reprinted in my book *Entropic Empire* nai010 publishers, Rotterdam, 2012.

Postcorona City: City of Capsules. Notes on Urbanity in the Age of Pandemics

The '(post)corona' city is, and will be for the foreseeable future, a city of capsules. My old book *The Capsular Civilization* (2004) seems indeed to have gained a new topicality with the Covid-19 crisis.[1] All sorts of forms of 'encapsulation' or 'capsularization' as I called it, are at the core of almost all corona measures. Not only the lockdown and confinement have subjected us to a capsular logic, but the exit strategies too are doomed to follow all kinds of measures that are all based on this logic: the mask, the bubble, the online teleworking, the drive-in city, not to mention the partition of all spaces, from terraces to shops and museums. Add to that the cyber panopticon of tracing apps and neoliberal dualization of society and you have a grim picture.

The capsular logic of the postcorona city starts with the now popular concept of the 'bubble', a singular social cell. That is the first capsule. Since time immemorial, at least since the Pest of the fourteenth century, the spatial 'economy' of the plague is based on the *oikos* (household): the dissolution of the city into its tiniest cell or building stone, in line with Aristotle's definition of the *polis*: a autarkic political entity, a congregate or aggregation of villages formed by households.[2] This *oikos,* as the nucleus of society, should now be as closed as possible. The challenge of 'deconfinement', of exit from the lockdown, is to limit contact between these bubbles. Initially, on 10 May 2020, the directive here in Belgium was to merge no more than two bubbles. This cautious loosening of the absolute capsular logic of closure was obviously intended to avoid getting too readily into a network of bubbles that could quickly enable the virus to start spreading again, causing the much dreaded second wave. Elementary epidemiology, yet a braintwister for every family. The question of exiting the lockdown could, in terms of Sloterdijk's *opus magnum* on *Spheres*, be formulated in this way: how will the bubbles start to 'foam' again?

But the bubble is, like Sloterdijk's spheres, rather abstract, or social and it is the spatial logic we want to focus on here. All spaces are to be treated in the logic of partitioning and this capsular logic. All sorts of lines, obstacles, and screens are put in place to separate people and the omnipresent masks are the micro-tools of this insularity and insulation, the age-old logic of quarantine, of separating bodies. Isolation and insulation are key concepts today. The city is partitioned to create insularity, it becomes an archipelago of tiny closed-off islands. Beside the infamous mask, the famous and fundamental 'social distancing' is the capsular logic at its minimum: our bodies should be closed off from contact with any alien body.

This logic of partitioning, confinement, distancing, closure, masking, is at odds with the urban, with 'urbanity' itself. If we go back to the definition of what is urban, we feel how fundamentally anti-urban this logic of closure and confinement is. Louis Wirth, in his classic essay 'Urbanism as a Way of Life' from 1938, defined a city as follows: 'A city may be defined as a relatively large, dense, and permanent settlement of socially heterogeneous individuals.'[3] All these elements of this definition are now problematic: large masses of heterogeneous individuals constitute an epidemiological nightmare. The word 'heterogeneous individuals' opens up a perspective onto the class, racial, racist, ethnic layers and tensions that are particular to this pandemic city.[4] But even more strikingly, of course, in Wirth's definition are the words 'relatively large, dense, and permanent'. Density is now a deadly force. The proximity of multiple bodies being in close contact over long periods of time, which defines the urban experience, turned into a life-threatening risk, the Achilles heel of entire societies. The city is indeed an assemblage of various spaces of proximity of increasing densities: parks, squares, streets, cinemas, theatres, bars, cafés, restaurants, not to mention dance halls and nightclubs, where proximity culminates in the anonymous electrification of a moving, touching, sweaty multitude of bodies. Those were the days...

Every space, every public space, but especially all interior spaces must now be turned into an archipelago of isolated mini spaces. In open spaces and shopping centres this can be more or less easily implemented, but it is more difficult to imagine this for the abovementioned spaces of close encounters (of any kind). There is a whole new micro-architecture of partitioning appearing, even new typologies: the capsular terrace, for instance. A restaurant in Amsterdam with tiny greenhouses for two to three persons on a waterfront was on the news and appears to be already booked for two months in advance.[5]

There is possibly also a grander scale anti-urban logic at work. Some specialists already see an intensification of the trend of young families in Flanders leaving the cities. The countryside, the suburbs, now seem heaven: the detached house with garden as safe haven against the pandemic.[6] This Decameron logic, people retreating to the country house whilst the Pest hits the city, is age-old and may now determine the trends for the coming years, if not decades, once again. In a similar vein one can fear the massive return of the car as the main means of transportation. Public transport is riddled with dangerous proximity. The car is a perfect solution now: it is a capsule, almost as perfectly capsular as a space capsule.[7] You can go from your house to any destination without even touching the ground or anything. The drive-in cinema seemed a nostalgic dream of America in the fifties, but it might now return as a formula for safe mass events: besides drive-in movies we can have drive-in festivals, drive-in theatres, concerts, and so on. Of course, the online shopping and home delivery is part and parcel of this new capsular, car-based setup. It has boomed immensely since the Covid-19 crisis, making Jeff Bezos of Amazon even more obscenely rich than he already was.

And then there is the digital world, which is virtually totally hygienic, because it is a network based on separated virtual capsules—personal computers, laptops, smartphones. It is an undeniable fact that the internet and information technology have proved a saving grace in this time of the new plague. But there is more to come. Smart cities have been a promise for a while now. The Covid-19 pandemic will give a new boost to this city based on information technology, big data, and artificial intelligence.

Entire institutions such as universities moved into virtual mode. Most of their activities such as classes, exams, and academic research are continued online. Equally, culture is trying hard to move online, but so far has encountered more difficulties in doing so than universities, as the event, the encounter, the live experience is quintessential to a concert, theatre piece, or exhibition.

The same goes for social relations, as the telephones and webcam chat platforms such as Skype, Zoom, MS Teams and so on are the tools par excellence to keep in touch with friends and family. The virtual communication platforms were the preeminent meeting places during the lockdown, but we quickly discovered their limitations. A webcam chat is not a real encounter, at least not for most people. The capsular logic has spread throughout our daily lives, and as we are completely locked in the private sphere, the home, just about all our communication takes place online. One of the 'laws' of encapsulation from my book on the Capsular Civilization, namely, 'no network without capsules', could be reversed: 'no capsule without network'. People from different bubbles who walk together were, in my experience, rather the exception. When people met acquaintances by chance during their daily 'airings' (the bicycle ride, the daily walk), one rather noticed an unfamiliarity, an awkwardness, a new detachment, an inner distance. We don't know yet how to deal with social distancing and so we tend to say goodbye quickly and continue on our way. We will have to invent an entire new 'urbanity'—without kissing, hugging, handshakes, and pats on the shoulder. Quite a challenge for the social, affective, sensuous, and sensual animals that we are.

But the dark side of the smart city, of population control via all sorts of apps is a very real and present danger too. Tracing apps are the talk of the town and will remain so for the foreseeable future. It is a huge public debate. For now, European governments seem reluctant to infringe much on individual privacy, but sooner or later some combination of old-fashioned plague measures like confinement and lockdown and what I have called 'the cyber panopticon'—camera's, heat registration, tracing apps, data mining, and so on—will be implemented. The smart city as an archipelago of real and virtual capsules under totalitarian capitalism, remains indeed a not so improbable script for the future.

Opposed to this possibility, or near certainty, of this online, drive-in, dualized, encapsulated city of control and security is the spaced-out eco-city, the walkable city, the city of of cycles and circular economy, of local production, the city of proximity. There are hopeful signs that cities all over the world are pushing this option via 'tactical urbanism'—temporary measures to test a more permanent urban transformation, away from the car-based city. So, the first images we can draw of the postcorona city are in a stark black and white, to make things clear. But given our dualized world, a capsular smart city under a digital control via all sorts of tracing apps, under a form of totalitarian techno-capitalism, is and remains the most probable option. It will depend on the art of the *polis*, politics, to determine the outcome. Civil activism and awareness will be crucial in this process. It is exactly the need for social distancing that brings cities all over the world to take back space from the car and turn streets and squares and roundabouts into pedestrian spaces. Let's hope this alternative wins the day.[8]

The precondition is that citizens and politicians realize that the eco-social, pedestrian, green city is the only good option, and the way to turn this crisis into a chance. And that a vocal critical mass is prepared to support these alternative measures, and even to act up to defend these policies. Think of the *Gillets jaunes* leading to the citizens panel on climate change in France now forcing President Macron to keep his promise to implement their quite radical 155-point plan, one of which is making destruction of nature a crime,[9] or think of Extinction Rebellion, pleading for an ecological state of emergency and citizens panels everywhere.

But turning this crisis into a real urban 'transition' will not be easy. As the capsular logic and the business-as-usual, car-based, drive-in, deeply suburbanized city is a much easier alternative, not only because it is perfectly compatible with capitalist consumerism, but also because it appeals to deeply entrenched habits and ideals: the suburban dwelling in a detached house with garden as the universal middle-class dream and the car as the transportation capsule of ultimate individual freedom. The existence of the city as we knew it, of 'urbanity' as a way of life, is at stake.

Notes

1   Lieven de Cauter, *The Capsular Civilization. On the City in the Age of Fear*, nai010 publishers, Rotterdam, 2004.

2   Aristotle, *The Politics*. Here this famous passage: 'The family is the association established by nature for the supply of men's everyday wants, (…) But when several families are united, and

the association aims at something more than the supply of daily needs, the first society to be formed is the village. (…) When several villages are united in a single complete community, large enough to be nearly or quite self-sufficing, the state comes into existence, originating in the bare needs of life, and continuing in existence for the sake of a good life. And therefore, if the earlier forms of society are natural, so is the state, for it is the end of them, and the nature of a thing is its end. For what each thing is when fully developed, we call its nature, whether we are speaking of a man, a horse, or a family. Besides, the final cause and end of a thing is the best, and to be self-sufficing is the end and the best. Hence it is evident that the state is a creation of nature, and that man is by nature a political animal.' http://classics.mit.edu/Aristotle/politics.1.one.html

3   Louis Wirth, 'Urbanism as a way of life', (*The American Journal of Sociology*, vol. 44, no. 1 (July, 1938), pp. 1-24. See: http://www.yorku.ca/lfoster/2006-07/sosi3830/lectures/LouisWirth_Urbanismasawayoflife.htm

4   https://www.curbed.com/platform/amp/2020/5/20/21263319/coronavirus-future-city-urban-covid-19?utm_campaign=curbed&utm_content=entry&utm_medium=social&utm_source=twitter&__twitter_impression=true&fbclid=IwAR31bqrLYQfXm-IQgoditvz7ri08VbJiliEKJz4_NQvtQNnpNyPn6TxD6Ek

5   https://www.insider.com/amsterdam-restaurant-mini-green-houses-cubicles-social-distance-2020-5

6   https://www.standaard.be/cnt/dmf20200508_04951870

7   Kisho Kurokawa referred to the car and the mobile home as models, beside the space capsule, in his 'Capsule Declaration' (1969). See on this my book *The Capsular Civilization*, pp. 65-68.

8   Here some manifestos and opinion pieces instigated/written by my colleague and comrade in arms architect/philosopher Gideon Boie: 'De stad hertekenen, nu kan het' (*De Standaard*, 15 April 2020): https://www.standaard.be/cnt/dmf20200414_04922610 ; 'Naar de exit zonder auto' *(De Standaard*, 12 May 2020) https://www.standaard.be/cnt/dmf20200511_04954752; 'Une nouvelle feuille de route pour une nouvelle mobilité' (*Le Soir*, 12 May 2020) https://plus.lesoir.be/300076/article/ 2020-05-12/une-nouvelle-feuille-de-route-pour-une-nouvelle-mobilite?; 'Open letter to Belgium's security council and expert group on the need for a spatial recovery plan' (*The Bulletin*, 12 May 2020): https://www.thebulletin.be/full-open-letter-security-council-and-expert-group-need-spatial-recovery-plan?

9   https://www.france24.com/en/20200621-french-climate-council-urges-macron-to-hold-referendum-on-making-destruction-of-nature-a-crime; See also: https://www.standaard.be/cnt/dmf20200622_04998315

Coda

A Cyberpunk Futurology of the Present (Epilogue to my 'Millennium Trilogy')

Here my millennium trilogy comes to an end. It began in 2004 with *The Capsular Civilization - On the City in the Age of Fear*. Then came *Entropic Empire - On the City of Man in the Age of Disaster* in 2012, and now, in 2020, it ends with the book you have just read or opened on the last page to find out how it ends.

It all started with a tiny newspaper article I read about the completion of the fence in Ceuta and Melilla to keep 'illegal African migrants' out of Fortress Europe. That was the shock that set this entire endeavour in motion: thinking about the ugly sides of our world at the turn of the new millennium. Reading the future in the present was the task I set myself. Hence the tendency to paint stark contrasts—it was an exercise in the art of overstatement. It became a science fiction Noir theory for the new ominous twenty-first century, a cyberpunk philosophy for our time.

It's impossible to summarize this mosaic of our age, but it was about the post-industrial city as theme park, about fortressing and gating and the deep capsular logic in our society, about the coming ecological disasters as 'permanent catastrophe' or 'Mad Max phase of Globalization', about the post-nine-eleven era as a planetary state of exception, about the American neocons, about entropy and chaos in our world order, the possibility of implosion, a relapse into lawlessness, the state of nature; and of course, about all the things discussed in this book, beginning with the end of the Anthropocene.

However dark in colour, reading this trilogy as a prophecy of doom would be a mistake, given the emphasis in part three on the commons and activism, as a sort of theoretical looking back on some twenty years of my own activism. But the first two volumes also contain texts on utopia and commitment, on the other-globalization movement or the Arab Spring. Likewise, heterotopia was a concept recurring in the three volumes. Over the years it became more and more a space of alterity and hope.

My motto remains, forever and a day:

PESSIMISM IN THEORY

OPTIMISM IN PRACTICE

'Rage and Rebel Against Extinction We Must'

Acknowledge-ments

First of all, I wish to thank quite a few generations of students who, between 2013 and the present, have seen different versions of the texts in this book come into being. Our discussions have inspired me.

Then I certainly have to mention my colleague and comrade in arms, Gideon Boie, with whom I have been co-teaching two courses (at the Department of Architecture of KU Leuven, campus Sint-Lucas Ghent and Brussels) for the last six years, 'Ethics and Critique' and his very own invention, 'Architecture and Activism' (which is a festive Friday afternoon, with reading sessions, student presentations, public talks, the so-called 'sofa talks', aperitif and dinner—until corona spoiled it all). Teaching with him is a joy. And many of the themes in this book, particularly on the commons and urban activism, find their origin in our collaboration.

I also wish to thank Rudi Laermans, a long-term intellectual companion, for being my critical sparring partner over the years. Although he did not contribute to this book directly, he is somehow always there with his lucid feedback on the several stages of the composition of this book. Karel Vanhaesebrouck, a barely shorter-term intellectual companion, and enthusiast co-inventor/editor of several books, I should thank for his comments on parts of the book. Annette Kuhk for her contributions and critical advice on some texts on the commons and some exciting collaborations on others. Miek Monsieur for helping correct or translate some of the texts, while we were amusing ourselves working on another, much lighter book (part III of the 'book of Amazement').

And I wish to thank with all my heart Eneida Berisha, an architecture student from Albania, who, stuck in Belgium over the summer holidays due to the corona pandemic, was a saving grace by helping me with correcting and final editing. Her feedback was precious, her stamina impressive. It was a pleasure to work with her. Leo Reijnen, the final editor for the publisher, needs to be mentioned too, as his incredible precision and superior sense of the English language were a godsend.

(After) Last but not least, I should mention my new partner Joëlle Evita who tolerated me during the long working days of the final editing and surrounded me with a thousand and one tender attentions.

Origin of the Texts

Ending the Anthropocene

Reflect #12

'Boarding the Anthropocene' was originally written as an opening text in September 2018 as overture to my courses of that academic year and published on my blog for students. 'Lessons in Urgency' on *De Wereld Morgen*, a critical leftist news website: https://www. dewereldmorgen.be/artikel/2018/09/24/postscript-to-the-anthropocene/

'A Small Anatomy of Political Melancholy' was written in the frame of a project by colleagues Dominiek Hoens and Klaas Tindemans on politics and melancholy, and published in September 2016 in *Crisis & Critique*, Volume 2, Issue 3, (special issue co-edited by Dominiek Hoens), also available online: http://crisiscritique.org/special09/cauter.pdf

'End of the Anthropocene' was written for my students and published online in January 2020: https://www.dewereldmorgen. be/community/end-of-the-anthropocene/

'Common Places...', my first text on the commons was written as a long comment on a brainstorm session with RITCS-student Benjamin Deboosere and a friend on Tempelhofer Feld in Berlin, where they did a project and it led me to formulate my very first musings on the commons as theme. It was published as 'Common Places: Preliminary Notes on the (Spatial) Commons' in October 2013 on *De Wereld Morgen*, https://www.dewereldmorgen.be/community/common-places-preliminary-notes-on-the-spatial-commons/ It was subsequently published in Pascal Gielen (ed.) *Interrupting the City*, Valiz, 2016.

'Utopia Rediscovered' was written in the framework of the festivities at KU Leuven on the occasion of the 500[Th] anniversary of the publication of More's *Utopia* and published in a festive academic book for that occasion as 'Utopia Rediscovered: A Redefinition of Utopianism in the Light of the Enclosures of the Commons', in: Veerle Achten, Dirk Bouckaert and Erik Schokkaert (eds.), *A Truly Golden Handbook': The Scholarly Quest for Utopia*, Leuven: Leuven University Press, 2016, pp. 534-545.

'Dis-closures of the Commons (Proposal for a New Term)' was written to fill a gap in the discourse and was published on my blog for students 'Lessons in Urgency' in January 2020: https://www. dewereldmorgen.be/community/dis-closures-of-the-commons-proposal-for-a-new-concept/

'Political Postscript to the Rediscovery of the Commons' is the last part of a text which was originally written for a collective lexicon book (but subsequently considerably reworked): 'Common(s)' in: Joost de Bloois, Stijn De Cauwer and Anneleen Maschelein (eds.), *50 Keywords of Contemporary Cultural Theory*, Pelckmans Pro; Kalmthout, 2017; pp. 70-75.

'Beyond identity' was written in 2013 for a debate organized by a right-wing think-tank (see footnote to the title of that text) and published first in Dutch, then in English on my blog for my students: https://www.dewereldmorgen.be/community/beyond-identity-overwriting-identity-overriding-identity-politics/

'Other Spaces for the Anthropocene. Heterotopia and the Disclosure of the (Un)common' was written for an collective academic book (that is why it is somewhat laborious): Simon Ferdinand, Irina Souch and Daan Wesselamn (eds), *Heterotopia and Globalisation in the 21st Century*, Routledge, London, 2020, pp. 19-33.

'Toothpaste and Taboo' was an exuberant letter to the 'Cinemaximiliaan family' (see former text for the description of this initiative), here in a considerably shortened and rewritten version, but published in full on my blog in August 2018: https://www.dewereldmorgen.be/community/toothpaste-and-taboo-first-letter-to-the-newcomers-of-cinemaximiliaan/

'Mary Poppins and the Climate Strikers' was the result of reading Rancière in class and attempting to explain his theory in a playful, but relevant way. It was published in our local quality newspaper *De Standaard*, May 9, 2019.

'Theses on Art and Activism' was written for the opening symposium of the arts festival Steirischer Herbst, Graz, October 2013, where it caused a real quarrel, subsequently published several times (as some curators present liked it), also on my blog (in December 2023: http://www.dewereldmorgen.be/blogs/lievendecauter/2013/12/12/theses-art-and-activism-in-age-globalisation. Here a considerable rewrite.

The 'Blogs on Urban activism' were written for immediate use, inspired by my collaboration with Gideon Boie, published in 2014, subsequently translated and published for didactic use on our blog 'Lessons in Urgency': https://www.dewereldmorgen.be/community/from-hotel-central-to-

picnic-the-streets-small-panorama-of-urban-activism-in-brussels/
https://www.dewereldmorgen.be/community/reclaim-the-steps-a-
message-to-the-population-about-the-depoliticization-of-
downtown-brussels/
https://www.dewereldmorgen.be/community/parckfarm-as-
concrete-utopia/

'The Potato War' was written for a book on academic freedom to
finally reflect in an academic way on at least one of the actions I
was involved in, 'De Aardappeloorlog en zijn gevolgen: over de
GGO-gebeurtenis en het 'Slow Science Manifesto' in: Klaas van
Berkel en Carmen van Bruggen (eds) *Academische vrijheid,
Geschiedenis en actualiteit,* Boom, Amsterdam, 2020, pp. 49-169. It
was first published in Dutch in *Oikos* in a shorter version (*Oikos*,
81, 3/2017: available online: https://www.oikos.be/tijdschrift/
archief/jaargang-2017/oikos-83-3-2017/1124-83-03-de-cauter-de-
aardappeloorlog/file). I translated this shorter version for this
book.

'Key Features of Activism Today' was written for a night on
resistance in the Stadsschouwburg [city theatre] of Amsterdam in
January 2017, and published on that occasion on my blog in Dutch
and then translated for international use on my blog 'Lessons in
Urgency' : https://www.dewereldmorgen.be/community/key-
features-of-activism-today-keynote-speech-for-a-night-conference-
on-resistance/

'Extinction Rebellion: Civil Disobedience for an Ecological State of
Emergency' is a rewrite of an article I published in reply to my pet-
hate columnist Mia Doornaert writing in *De Standaard,*
'Extinction Rebellion en de Grondwet. Een antwoord aan Mia
Doornaert': https://www.dewereldmorgen.be/artikel/2019/10/19/
extinction-rebbelion-en-de-grondwet-een-antwoord-aan-mia-
doornaert/.

'The Corona Pandemonium: Notes on the Covid-19 Crisis' is a
series of blogs mostly published on my blog on *De Wereld Morgen* in
Dutch and one on the news website *Apache,* some texts were
translated:
https://www.dewereldmorgen.be/community/the-postcorona-
manifesto/
https://www.dewereldmorgen.be/community/the-return-of-
biopolitics-the-corona-pandemic-and-the-neoliberal-dismantling-
of-the-welfare-state/
Dutch: https://www.dewereldmorgen.be/artikel/2020/04/02/het-
postcoronamanifest/
https://www.dewereldmorgen.be/artikel/2020/04/05/biopolitiek-en-

de-open-samenleving/
https://www.apache.be/gastbijdragen/2020/04/14/corona-en-de-
neoliberale-ontmanteling-van-de-verzorgingsstaat/
https://www.dewereldmorgen.be/community/coronalimbo/
https://www.dewereldmorgen.be/artikel/2020/05/05/het-
spookbeeld-van-foucault-van-coronapest-tot-cyberpanoptikum/
(Interestingly, when I had to give them a logical instead of a merely
chronological order, I almost inversed the latter: as if I first started
to think what could come after and then slowly began to dig into
the crisis itself).

'The Rise of Zoöpolitics' was an opening lecture to a colloquium on
Architecture and Wars at ETH Zürich in June 2017, curated by
Samia Henni, and left unpublished until the Covid-19 crisis:
https://www.dewereldmorgen.be/community/the-rise-of-zoopolitics-
introduction-to-a-conference-on-architecture-and-wars-eth-
zurich-2-3-06-2017/

'Postcorona City: City of Capsules' was written on a double
invitation by a magazine (*Samenleving en Politiek* [*Society and
Politics*] where it appeared in a Dutch translation - https://www.
sampol.be/2020/07/postcorona-city-stad-van-capsules) and the
Desired Spaces initiative of VAI/CIVA (https://www.desiredspaces.
be/contributions-projekten-projects/postcorona-city-city-of-
capsules), but it was initially promised for a book on *The Common
City*, to be edited by Thijs Lijster and Pascal Gielen, where it will
become a longer, more academic text.

'A Cyberpunk Futurology of the Present' (Epilogue to my
"Millennium Trilogy")' was, like the 'Concise Overview', expressly
written for this book, of course. (After a book full of overstatements,
the author finally manages to state the obvious. Bravo. But then
again—first axiom of *the* forthcoming, age-old *Book of Openings*:
'Only exaggeration is truthful'.)

Credits

This publication was made possible with financial support from The Royal Institute for Theatre (RITCS), The Department of Architecture KU Leuven, Campus Sint-Lukas Brussels

Cover illustration: 'Thames Estuary', by Carl De Keyzer, Magnum, from the project 'Moments Before the Flood'. The Maunsell Forts are fortified towers built in the Thames and Mersey estuaries during WWII to help defend the United Kingdom and named after their designer Guy Maunsell. In the mid-1960s, various forts were re-occupied by pirate radios. There have also been proposals to convert them into luxurious hotels. For the time being they remain powerful ruins, midway between steampunk and cyberpunk.
Translation: the author with Miek Monsieur and Odette Dijt.
Copy editing: Leo Reijnen
Design: Joseph Plateau
Publisher: Eelco van Welie, nai010 publishers

© 2021 Lieven De Cauter and nai010 publishers, Rotterdam

nai010 publishers is an internationally orientated publisher specialized in developing, producing and distributing books in the fields of architecture, urbanism, art and design.
www.nai010.com

Available in North, South and Central America through Artbook | D.A.P., 155 Sixth Avenue 2nd Floor, New York, NY 10013-1507, tel +1 212 627 1999, fax +1 212 627 9484, dap@dapinc.com
Available in the United Kingdom and Ireland through Art Data, 12 Bell Industrial Estate, 50 Cunnington Street, London W4 5HB, tel +44 208 747 1061, fax +44 208 742 2319, orders@artdata.co.uk

Printed and bound in The Netherlands
ISBN 978-94-6208-611-1
NUR 740; BISAC POL003000, POL033000

Keywords: activism, Anthropocene, biopolitics, commons, corona crisis, eco-feminism, ecology, heterotopia, political philosophy, urban theory, zoöpolitics